Replication Research in Education

Providing an overview of key issues in theory and practice, *Replication Research in Education* is designed to identify and discuss the benefits and challenges facing replication studies in education. Both clear and practical, this groundbreaking volume covers how to introduce, develop, conduct, report, and discuss these studies, and the issues they raise for policy and practice.

Bridging theory and practice, this book considers what replication research should look like, how it should be conducted, and how to judge when it has been successful. It enables researchers to plan and conduct studies successfully, from their earliest stages through to completion. This key text:

- brings together in a single volume, existing issues, claims and counterclaims, discourses, and practices of replication;
- introduces, covers, and extends this field of research, indicating its possibilities and limits;
- expands and adds to existing discussions and practices;
- will enable researchers to design, conduct, evaluate, and critique studies.

The comprehensive and exhaustive coverage of issues and practices within *Replication Research in Education* make it a 'must read' for all novice and experienced educational researchers who are considering, conducting, and reviewing replication studies in education.

Keith Morrison is Professor of Education and Vice-Rector at the University of Saint Joseph, Macao, China.

Replication Research in Education
A Guide to Designing, Conducting, and Analysing Studies

Keith Morrison

LONDON AND NEW YORK

First published 2022
by Routledge
2 Park Square, Milton Park, Abingdon, Oxon OX14 4RN

and by Routledge
605 Third Avenue, New York, NY 10158

Routledge is an imprint of the Taylor & Francis Group, an informa business

© 2022 Keith Morrison

The right of Keith Morrison to be identified as author of this work has been asserted by him in accordance with sections 77 and 78 of the Copyright, Designs and Patents Act 1988.

All rights reserved. No part of this book may be reprinted or reproduced or utilised in any form or by any electronic, mechanical, or other means, now known or hereafter invented, including photocopying and recording, or in any information storage or retrieval system, without permission in writing from the publishers.

Trademark notice: Product or corporate names may be trademarks or registered trademarks, and are used only for identification and explanation without intent to infringe.

British Library Cataloguing-in-Publication Data
A catalogue record for this book is available from the British Library

Library of Congress Cataloging-in-Publication Data
Names: Morrison, Keith (Keith R. B.) author.
Title: Replication research in education : a guide to designing, conducting and analysing studies / Keith Morrison.
Description: New York : Routledge, 2022. | Includes bibliographical references and index.
Identifiers: LCCN 2021030007 (print) | LCCN 2021030008 (ebook) | ISBN 9781032068688 (Hardback) | ISBN 9781032068695 (Paperback) | ISBN 9781003204237 (eBook)
Subjects: LCSH: Education—Research. | Replication (Experimental design)
Classification: LCC LB1028 .M6455 2022 (print) | LCC LB1028 (ebook) | DDC 370.72—dc23/eng/20211022
LC record available at https://lccn.loc.gov/2021030007
LC ebook record available at https://lccn.loc.gov/2021030008

ISBN: 978-1-032-06868-8 (hbk)
ISBN: 978-1-032-06869-5 (pbk)
ISBN: 978-1-003-20423-7 (ebk)

DOI: 10.4324/9781003204237

Typeset in Goudy
by Apex CoVantage, LLC

For irreplicable Fun Hei

Contents

List of figures viii
List of tables ix
About the author x
Acknowledgements xi

   Introduction 1

1 Why we need replication studies 3

2 Types of replication studies and the challenge of sameness 18

3 Conceptual replications in education 36

4 Quantitative and qualitative replications in education 59

5 Planning a replication study in education 68

6 Data analysis and interpretation in a replication in education 90

7 Reporting a replication study in education 125

8 Training for replication research 143

9 Conclusions and the future of replication studies in education 156

References 164
Index 174

Figures

2.1	The continuum of replication studies	19
6.1	Confidence intervals for a mathematics test	99
6.2	Confidence intervals in a history test	102
6.3	Confidence intervals for standardised scores on a history test	103
6.4	Comparing confidence intervals and standard errors	104
6.5	Precision and accuracy in measurement	104
8.1	Deciding the original study for replication	145

Tables

1.1	Key reasons for having replication in educational research	9
1.2	Reasons for replicating an original study	13
1.3	Assessing the desirability of replication studies	14
2.1	Concerns in considering sameness in a replication study in education	25
2.2	What should remain constant and what the replication study might change	28
2.3	Comparing the replication study with the original study	30
3.1	Making changes in a replication study	38
4.1	Judging the replication of qualitative studies	66
5.1	Finding and selecting an original study for replication	69
5.2	Criteria for evaluating an original study with a view to replication	70
5.3	Practical questions in deciding whether a replication is possible	72
5.4	Deciding 'success' in a replication study	79
5.5	Components of the research design in a replication study	81
6.1	Assumptions of statistical tests	95
6.2	Questions in comparing the original study and the replication study	111
6.3	Agreement and disagreement between original and replication study	121
7.1	Comparing the findings of the original study and the replication study	134
7.2	A template for writing up the replication study	137

About the author

Keith Morrison worked formerly at the University of Durham, UK and, since 2000, has worked in Macao, where he is Vice-Rector at the University of Saint Joseph. He is the author of 19 books, including, *Taming Randomized Controlled Trials in Education: Exploring Key Claims, Issues and Debates*; *Research Methods in Education* and *A Guide to Teaching Practice* (both with Louis Cohen and Lawrence Manion, several editions of each); *Causation in Educational Research*; *Managing Complex Change in School: Engaging Pedagogy, Technology, Learning and Leadership* (with Alejandro Salcedo Garcia); *School Leadership and Complexity Theory*; and *Management Theories for Educational Change*. He has conducted consultancies for governments, companies, organisations, and institutions in many parts of the world.

Acknowledgements

I am very grateful to the reviewers of the manuscript of this book, for their helpful feedback; thank you. I am very grateful to: Sarah Hyde from Routledge, for her help and support in the preparation of this book; Annette Brown for her help and feedback concerning ethics in replication; Thomas Morrison for his preparation of Figure 6.1. Thanks are due to the following publishers and authors for permission to use materials in the text:

National Science Foundation and Institute of Education Sciences for material from *Companion Guidelines on Replication & Reproducibility in Education Research* (2018): www.nsf.gov/pubs/2019/nsf19022/nsf19022.pdf. Royal Netherlands Academy of Arts and Sciences (KNAW) (2018) for material from: *Replication Studies – Improving Reproducibility in the Empirical Sciences*, Amsterdam, KNAW, for *Table 4. Assessment of the desirability of replication studies*, page 31. Taylor & Francis (tandfonline.com) for material from: *Research Methods in Education* (8th edition), Cohen, L., Manion, L. and Morrison, K. R. B. (© 2018), Routledge, pages 8, 381, 720, Table 44.5 (pp. 844–845). Reproduced by permission of Taylor & Francis Group; *Taming Randomized Controlled Trials in Education*, Morrison, K. R. B. (© 2021), Routledge, pages 56, 125, 165–166. Reproduced by permission of Taylor & Francis Group; Morrison. K. R. B. (© 2019) Realizing the promises of replication studies in education, *Educational Research and Evaluation*, 25(7–8), 412–441, doi:10.1080/13803611.2020.1838300, pages 428, 431 and 429 (Table 1). Reproduced by permission of Taylor & Francis Group.

Introduction

How much trust can we put in research findings and the claims made from them? How sure can we be that something 'works' or does or does not 'work' in serving a particular educational purpose? Should we believe and act on the results of a single research study, however carefully it has been conducted? Will a study which has 'worked' somewhere 'work' here?

If research, policy making, and practice in education are to be secure, then it is dangerous to rely on single research studies. In social sciences, greater confidence can be put in research findings that have been replicated. But what does 'replication' mean? What and how can we plan, do, understand, and conclude from replication studies? This book addresses such issues. It makes cases for and against replication studies and what they can and cannot do. It takes the reader by the hand through all stages of replication research: choosing a suitable study to replicate; deciding what kind of replication to conduct; planning, implementing, analysing, interpreting, and reporting a replication study; comparing it with the original study; judging how successful it has been in confirming the original study; and drawing conclusions from the whole exercise.

Replication studies in education have been advocated for many years, but they have to catch up with their use in other social sciences. An increasingly loud voice argues that their time has come, indeed is long overdue. If educational research is to impact on policy and practice, then, as in other social sciences, education can look to replication studies for validating research findings, their trustworthiness, validity, reliability, and generalisability, and their fitness for declared purposes and aims of education.

Conducting replications is challenging: what happens in education is not only a function of its aims, purposes, and values, but is also acutely contingent on, and intimately bound up with, the rich, complex world of classrooms, students, and teachers. How can a replication study be done in such circumstances? Is it proper even to consider replication studies in the agentic, changing, values-based, individualistic, and social world of education? How to do a replication study? How can the replication's main message – its signal – be identified from the noise of what happens in specific classrooms?

This book addresses such questions. It shows how to introduce, develop, conduct, report, and discuss replication studies in education, their possibilities and their limitations, and the issues that they raise for policy and practice. It covers theory and practice of replication studies in education: how to think about replication studies, how to 'do' them, and how they fit into the landscape and purposes of education.

There are many questions for replication researchers. When and how should we conduct a replication study? What does a replication study in education look like? What should it include? What makes it different from other kinds of research in education? How should it be reported? What are its limits? What can and cannot it do? What does 'replication' mean? What kinds of replication studies are there? What makes a replication fair and genuine? How do we know if our replication has 'worked', and what does this mean?

This book sets out issues for replication researchers to address in ensuring that a replication study is of high quality and sufficiently related to the original research that it seeks to replicate. Its chapters set out different purposes and types of replication, together with how to work with, and in, the world of replication. It identifies challenges in judging how far a replication study has confirmed the findings of the original study. In doing so, it tackles the difficult issue of sameness between the original study and its replication partner, and it guides the researcher on how to handle this. Practical advice is given on how to analyse and compare data from an original study and its replication partner, what conclusions can be drawn from these, and how to write up the findings. From the novice to the experienced researcher, the skill set required to work with replication research is wide-ranging, interesting, and challenging. This book indicates how to develop these. In short, the book shows how to move into, and in, the world of replication.

This book moves methodically through issues, with a clear logic and sequence. It sets the scene for replication studies in education. Then it discusses types and limits of replications and the issues that they raise. It shows how to plan, design, and carry out replications; how to work with findings from the replication study; how to relate these to the original study; and how to report the replication study.

Replications can make an important contribution to educational research. This book indicates how to rise to their challenging demands in education.

1 Why we need replication studies

Overview

This chapter opens up the field of replication studies in education that will be addressed in the present and subsequent chapters. It addresses several matters:

- challenges in defining 'replication';
- types of replication ('exact', 'approximate', and 'conceptual' replications);
- the need for, and benefits of, replication;
- purposes of replication (internal validation, generalisability [external validation], improvements and extensions to an original study);
- the case for replication studies (e.g. from science, for security of findings, for generalisability, for high quality research and meta-analysis);
- the case against replication studies (their view of education and educational research, their limits, utility, and attractiveness to different parties);
- identifying and choosing suitable original studies for replication (what studies can and should be replicated; selection criteria);
- the need to broaden the scope of kinds of original studies that can be replicated (beyond quantitative studies);
- deciding how many replications are needed for an original study (and based on what criteria and for what types and purposes of replication).

The chapter makes a case for replication studies, arguing that single studies on their own are insufficient for educational policy and practice, and it comments on the limits of trust that can be placed in single study findings.

Defining 'replication'

Replication studies in education should be clearly defined. However, simply defining a replication study is challenging (Chhin et al., 2018; Hüffmeier et al., 2016; Patil et al., 2016; Rosenthal, 1991; Schmidt, 2009). There is no clear-cut or unequivocal, agreed-upon definition of replication; of what a replication is; of what constitutes a genuine, reliable, and valid replication; how similar the replication findings must be to the original in order to constitute replication; and how to conduct a replication (Hüffmeier et al., 2016; Schmidt, 2009).

Replication derives from the Latin 'replicare', meaning 'to repeat', 'to unroll', or 'to fold back'. It connotes the repetition of a procedure (e.g. an experiment) in order to reduce errors; to seek confirmation of findings in the original study; to do something again in the same way; to generalise and extend the boundaries of the original study; and to ensure accuracy, correctness, and truth (recognising that 'truth' may be provisional, conjectural, falsifiable, and the best we know at a particular point in time). A general definition of a replication is provided by Mackey and Gass (2005) as conducting an original study again, be it using identical procedures or by making certain changes (e.g. sampling), in order to test the original. Makel and Plucker (2015) note that, in studying gifted education, replication is the 'duplication' (p. 157) of previous research in order to verify the original or to expand it.

However, these are only partial definitions, as they are limited mainly to validation of the original study (reproducibility), and to exact or approximate replications (those that keep as close as possible to the original). The Royal Netherlands Academy of Arts and Sciences (2018) comment that replication as *reproducibility* concerns how far the findings of a replication study agree with those of the original study. If the findings of both studies agree, then those of the original study are deemed to have been reproduced, thereby increasing the likelihood that the original study's findings are valid. Peels and Boulter (2018) indicate that a replication study is independent of the original study but uses similar methods and is conducted in circumstances that are similar. The National Science Foundation and Institute of Education Sciences (2018) defines 'reproducibility' as occurring when another investigator finds similar results when reworking data from a prior study.

However, replications that concern reproducibility are unlike those kinds of replication studies which have a wider embrace, for example conceptual replications that seek to generalise. Here, a replication is that which repeats the test of a hypothesis or the findings of an earlier study but uses different methods in order to see if the 'concept' (see Chapter 3) applies in different contexts and settings (Schmidt, 2009). The National Science Foundation and Institute of Education Sciences (2018) comments that, generally speaking, replication studies involve the collection and analysis of data in order to determine how far the new study yields the same findings as the original study, in part of in whole. In separating this from 'reproducibility', this kind of replication applies an original study to a new context or setting, to see if the 'concept' generalises or extends the limits of the original study.

The term 'replication' is ambiguous. Sometimes it denotes a *type* of research study, whilst at other times it is used as a judgement of how much and where it confirms or does not confirm the findings of the original study. Gelman (2018) comments that terms such as 'successful replication' and 'failed replication' in replicating are misguided and should be replaced by degrees of success or failure on a 'continuous measures' scale (p. 2); the present book frequently uses the term 'how much and where' in judging a replication and notes that this is typically a matter of human judgement which, like a court of law, concerns being 'beyond reasonable doubt'. To say that a study has not replicated the original study (a non-replication) is often to say that it found results that do not confirm those of the original study or which are unclear ('indeterminate') as to whether they confirm those of an original study.

The National Academies of Sciences, Engineering, and Medicine (2019) distinguishes between reproducibility, replicability, and generalisability. Reproducibility concerns reproducing the same results with the same, original data, when re-analysed. This is a significant issue in the age of big data coming from many sources, some of which might be protected and private (e.g. on human subjects) and which use different kinds of computation software, codes, algorithms, and analysis, some of it being proprietary and restricted. Transparency and disclosure are required of the computational methods being used in analysis of the original data. Here, *reproducibility* concerns finding exact agreement between the findings of the original study and the replication study, and if this is not found, it suggests that there is something wrong. This does not guarantee that the original study was correct; both studies could contain the same error(s).

The National Academies of Sciences, Engineering, and Medicine (2019) notes that *replicability* concerns obtaining results that are consistent with those of the original study, using different, new data but similar methods to answer the same research questions as in the original study. Here, the issue is not one of obtaining identical results, as this is impossible, but one of close similarity, that is, a matter of degree rather than a yes/no, binary conclusion. Plucker and Makel (2021) remark that a direct replication concerns a 'robust estimate' (p. 1) of how big and how reliable the original study's findings were. Indeed, statistical analysis of the original study and its replication study are based on probabilities rather than certainties. Here, the task is to ascertain and report the level of closeness to the original study and its findings, together with the degree of certainty and uncertainty in the results of both studies. This indicates that there is no absolute standard for judging replication between two sets of results, there is no absolute, incontrovertible 'truth' here, but, rather, the best that we know at any one time, and based on cumulative studies, replications, and human judgement.

If the replication study finds results that differ from those of the original study, this does not imply that the original study's results were correct or incorrect, just as a single replication study may be unable to confirm or refute the original study absolutely. There are many possible reasons for differences in findings, including: the presence of new factors in the replication study; the absence of some variables in the original study; the inherent variability of factors in the studies; the inability to exert controls on data, particularly on complex variables and factors; poor quality studies; fraudulent practices; differences in the criteria for judging the original study and the replication study.

Replication as *generalisability* refers to how far the results of a study apply to contexts, settings, populations and situations that differ from those in the original study. Here, different methods might be used from those in the original study. The intention here, as in a conceptual replication, is to determine how far the original 'concept' can apply elsewhere, that is, whether the signal that rises above the noise of one context and method can apply to other contexts, regardless of whether the methods used are similar to, or different from, those of the original study.

Chapters 2 and 3 address different types and kinds of replication study. For the present chapter in defining replication, taking the lead from Schmidt (2009), the National Science Foundation and Institute of Education Sciences (2018) identifies two main kinds of replication: 'direct' and 'conceptual', and defines them thus:

> **Direct replication** studies seek to replicate findings from a previous study using the same, or as similar as possible, research methods and procedures as a previous study. The goal of direct replication studies is to test whether the results found in the previous study were due to error or chance. This is done by collecting data with a new, but similar, sample and holding all the research methods and procedures constant.
>
> **Conceptual replication** studies seek to determine whether similar results are found when certain aspects of a previous study's method and/or procedures are systematically varied.
>
> (p. 2)

A direct replication is conducted in order to verify that results found in an original study have been reproduced and were not due to chance, error, or bias; it indicates how reliable the results of the original study are (Chhin et al., 2018). In contrast, conceptual replications deliberately change variables in order to see how far the original study can apply or generalise to other groups, settings, locations, procedures, conditions, contexts, and so on, to see if the original 'concept' holds fast despite other changes to the original study. In doing so, they can identify the boundaries of generalisability (Plucker & Makel, 2021). Deciding whether to conduct a direct or conceptual replication depends on fitness for purpose: a direct replication may be useful if the original study has produced novel findings, and a conceptual replication might be useful if the original findings have already been replicated (ibid.).

To these can be added an 'approximate' replication, which, adhering as far as possible to an exact replication, varies one or more 'nonmajor' variables (Porte, 2012, p. 8), whilst still enabling a close comparison to be made between the replication and the original study. The intention here is to validate the original study whilst also seeking its wider generalisability. An approximate replication might change one variable at a time to see which causes a change in findings from those of the original study (Makel & Plucker, 2015).

Replications must refer to an original study. This might appear to be a statement of the obvious, but, in practice, when one reads replication studies, it is almost as if there were a *post hoc* epiphany in which the researcher realises that he or she has conducted a conceptual replication of an idea which, subsequently, seems to have been raised in a previous study, and then declares that it has been a conceptual replication. This misreads what a replication study is and what it is for: a replication study is a deliberate attempt to work with, and on, a named, identified original study.

The case for replication studies in education

The case for replications appears strong. They claim to overcome the danger of relying on single studies in research-based policy and practice, and they contribute to confirming the reliability of, veracity of, credibility of, security of, generalisability of, applicability of, safety of, and trust in, findings, serving transparency and avoiding the suppression of unpalatable or contradictory findings (Anderson & Maxwell, 2016; Benson & Borrego, 2015; Cai et al., 2018; Eden, 2002; Frank & Saxe, 2012; Ioannidis, 2012; Jones et al., 2010; Melhuish, 2018). Matthews et al. (2018) note that unreplicated research in education does not even meet a minimum requirement for contributing to safe evidence-informed practice. Simply acting on, or abandoning, research on the basis of a single study is dangerous (Stanley & Spence, 2014), even unethical (see Chapter 5), just as failing to publish a statistically non-significant finding can damage knowledge generation and revision. Single studies alone are an insufficient base for educational policy and practice, and replication studies reduce the risk of basing policy on a single study, though not every study might require a replication (Tyson, 2014). For safety's sake and for ethical practice, if a study has significant policy or practical implications, then a replication study should be mandatory. A replication study which fails to replicate might save investing resources into following up on original studies that produced sensational results (Plucker & Makel, 2021).

Replication studies prevent the belief in, and spread of, erroneous findings, and quell doubts concerning researcher bias, even fraud (Slavin, 2018; Travers et al., 2016). A single, isolated study requires corroboration and re-testing to overcome charges of meaninglessness, uselessness, bias, error, exception, outliers, chance, pointlessness, unknown generalisability, measurement errors, other random errors, and singularity of scope (Chhin et al., 2018; Hüffmeier et al., 2016). Makel & Plucker, 2015; Stanley & Spence, 2014). Replication studies can reduce the likelihood of a Type I error (i.e. false positive: failure to accept a true null hypothesis) and a Type II error (i.e. false negative: failure to reject a false null hypothesis), both of which are alive and well (Ioannidis, 2005, titles his provocative paper 'Why most published research findings are false'). Ioannidis (2015) noted that 56 per cent of original research findings may be false positives and, in the absence of replications, a considerable majority are 'unchallenged fallacies' (p. 650; see also Pashler & Harris, 2012), often deriving from small, underpowered original studies (Bakker et al., 2012; Ioannidis, 2015; Pashler & Harris, 2012).

Replication is a defining feature of natural science (Chhin et al., 2018; Gómez et al., 2010; Kane, 1984), its gold standard (Frank & Saxe, 2012) and its 'Supreme Court' (Collins 1985, p. 19), pursuing stability, generalisability, and exceptionless scientific theory, separating the signal from the noise of specific and differing contexts and circumstances, and preserving a discipline's foundation on cumulative empirical evidence (Stout & Heck, 1995). Replications can help to establish a theory (Irvine, 2021) and its generalisability, independent of specific circumstances and local conditions in which the original study was conducted. They test a theory in conditions different from those that gave rise to it, thereby contributing to the objective evaluation of a piece of knowledge (Gómez et al., 2010). They contribute to the self-correcting nature of science (Popper, 1959) and are a routine *sine qua non* of the scientific method in which repeatability is sovereign (Lindsay & Ehrenberg, 1993; Schmidt, 2009). Rather than constituting the imposition of policing the research (Ioannidis, 2015), they are central to the process of discovery (e.g. Chhin et al., 2018), and Plucker and Makel (2021) note that a self-correcting science requires self-correcting scientists. How far education is akin to the natural sciences is, of course, debatable.

Replications in education serve four main purposes:

1   to confirm the validity, reliability and findings of an original study;
2   to establish the generalisability, transferability, and scalability of the original study to different contexts and settings;
3   to make and test improvements and rectifications to the original study;
4   to extend the study beyond the original study's limitations.

With regard to (1), replication studies are validation exercises, testing claims made from the original study and checking its quality and security: was the original study conducted with due rigour (e.g. fidelity to scrupulous procedures) and care? Did it make any unsupported or invalid assumptions? Did it possess construct, content, concurrent, and ecological validity? Were the results reliable and secure? Did the claims made really follow from the evidence provided? Was the data analysis correct? Were the explanations for the findings warranted and secure? Were the implications of these for policy and practice appropriate and a consequence of the findings? This is the field of internal validity in an 'exact' replication, in which as close a replication study as possible reworks the original study to look for flaws in it. Replication guards against false positives, false negatives, and overstated or understated effect sizes. Replications can provide a more reliable effect size than a single study, often reducing it (Brandt et al., 2014). For example, in psychology, the Open Science Collaboration (2015) found that, whilst 97 per cent of original studies reported statistically significant results, this dropped to 36 per cent in replication studies, and effect sizes in replication studies were only half as big as those in the original studies (see also Fabry & Fischer, 2015; Ioannidis, 2015).

With regard to (2), replications can serve generalisability (Gersten et al., 2015; Johnston & Pennypacker, 2009; Travers et al., 2016; Zingaro et al., 2018), seeing if the key idea, the concept, and the findings of the original study hold true in different contexts, for example with different populations, samples, locations, settings, and with different research design, tasks, procedures and metrics, and outcome measures and approaches used to analyse the results (National Science Foundation and Institute of Education Sciences, 2018). They test the concept (as in a conceptual replication), the hypothesis, idea, set of practices, or findings, to see if they hold 'true' independently of contextual or operational matters, that is, they separate the signal from the noise.

With regard to (3), if errors or areas for improvement to the original study have been spotted, then a replication study can correct and amend these, and test the revised version. For example, let us say that the original study had too general and undiscriminating a set of metrics for measuring outcomes; the replication could amend and test these. Or, if the original study did not control sufficiently for extraneous exogenous or endogenous variables in the design and data analysis, then the replication study could correct this shortcoming. Or, if the original study only weakly operationalised the research purposes and research questions, then the replication study could improve these.

With regard to (4), if the original study was regarded as being limited in its scope, then the replication study could extend, broaden, and deepen this, or go into the issues in greater depth, for example adding on independent variables, dependent variables, control variables, mediating and moderating variables (Block & Kuckertz, 2018, advocate adding one variable at a time in an extension study), or adding in a larger or a broader sample.

Replication results can also feed into meta-analysis (Eden, 2002; Plucker & Makel, 2021). Meta-analysis has attracted criticism for not distinguishing sufficiently between high quality and poor quality studies, large sample and small sample studies, studies which differ in kind, and so on (Cohen et al., 2018; Makel & Plucker, 2014; Morrison, 2021; Paterson et al., 2016; See, 2018; Wrigley, 2018). Studies which have strong replication results offer greater security than those which have not, and this can help to ensure that meta-analyses work on quality-assured results of individual studies.

Table 1.1 provides a brief summary of key reasons for having replication in educational research.

Table 1.1 Key reasons for having replication in educational research

Replication research:
- overcomes the danger of relying on single studies in research-based evidence and practice;
- contributes to confirming the reliability of, veracity of, credibility of, security of, generalisability of, applicability of, safety of, and trust in, findings;
- serves transparency and avoiding the suppression of unpalatable or contradictory findings;
- prevents the spread of erroneous findings;
- is a defining feature of the scientific method;
- serves 'exceptionless' scientific theory;
- contributes to the cumulative and self-correcting nature of science;
- overcomes researcher bias;
- reduces the likelihood of a Type I error and a Type II error;
- provides more reliable effect sizes than single studies;
- serves ethical practice when bringing research evidence into practice.

The case against replication studies

The case against replication studies in education operates at many levels. At the level of principle, questions can be raised of the extent to which education is a science at all, rather than being, for example an art, a humanistic endeavour, a craft, a social enterprise, a person-centred act, a valuative exercise, and/or a combination of these, such that to separate out the 'science' element is to misread the intrinsically complex, human-centredness nature of education (e.g. Biesta, 2020; Flyvberg, 2011). Education is a context-rich, context-dependent, variable-dense, causally complex activity which is not susceptible fairly to being regarded solely or largely a science. There are simply too many variables to control in the everyday, agentic, dynamic classroom. What happens in one classroom differs from what happens in another, even with the same teacher and the same subject matter; or in the same classroom with the same teacher, same subject matter, and the same students on a different day of the week, or in the same classroom with the same subject matter and the same students but with a different teacher, and so on. 'What works' with one teacher or one set of students can be a dismal failure with another teacher or another set of students. Experienced teachers bring their accumulated tacit knowledge and wisdom to a teaching and learning situation, rendering a purely or largely scientific approach to education a misguided enterprise. The 'noise' is the 'signal' rather than the signal being the key to understanding what is happening in teaching and learning.

At a pragmatic level, questions can be raised of how far a scientific approach to educational research actually 'works'. For example, whilst randomised controlled trials and meta-analysis – frequently the focus of replication studies in education – currently enjoy their moment in the limelight, Morrison (2021) summarises a wealth of arguments and evidence to advance concerns and critiques of these, the effects of which suggest that such 'scientific' approaches have many serious limitations (see also Biesta, 2020).

At a utility level, there are limits to what a replication study can do and show and to what researchers and educationists can and cannot take from them. For example, whilst some kinds of replication study (e.g. conceptual replications) can confirm and corroborate the original study, they cannot disconfirm or falsify it (Chapter 3). Whilst an exact replication might be able to make good this shortcoming, there are many reasons why it might be impossible to conduct an exact replication in education (Chapter 2).

Even if the case for replications appears strong, and although the 'replication crisis' (Yaffe, 2019) has been averted in some social sciences (Travers et al., 2016), at the time of writing, replication studies in education are relatively few, limited, unglamorous, and unpopular. They have to play catch-up (e.g. Gersten et al., 2015). Makel and Plucker (2014) reported that only 0.13 per cent of articles on education appearing in the top 100 journals over a five-year period were replication studies, only six journals included over 1 per cent of replication studies and 43 published none at all. Coyne et al. (2016) commented on the paucity of replication studies in special education, and Makel et al. (2016), searching in 36 special education journals, reported a total replication study rate of approximately 0.5 per cent (see also Lemons et al., 2016).

Education lags behind other social sciences with regard to replication studies. A problem is encouraging parties to do them and to take notice of them. Many disincentives deter researchers from conducting replications (Alm, 2010; Artino, 2013; Hüffmeier et al., 2016; Ioannidis, 2015; Makel et al., 2016; Makel & Plucker, 2014, 2015; Melhuish 2018; Spector et al., 2015; Yong, 2012). Frank and Saxe (2012) contend that conducting replications is time-consuming, expensive and, because of publication practices, unrewarded, so they wonder who will do them (p. 600). Eden (2002) notes that replications suffer from diminishing returns, being considered as worth less than the original study (cf. Plucker & Makel, 2021).

Replications have a lower status in the research-and-publication stakes in a 'hypercompetitive climate' (Pashler & Wagenmakers, 2012, p. 528) and the rush to be published (Yaffe, 2019); they lack prestige and the cachet of novelty (Ioannidis, 2012). They are unattractive to journals seeking to move forward their fields of concern ('Why publish something that is already known?'; Schmidt, 2009, p. 95). This calls into question the often-heard, optimistic comment that science is self-correcting (Pashler & Harris, 2012). Researchers and aspiring academics seeking career advancement are discouraged from conducting replications because they replace an original, novel piece of research with taking thoughts, studies, methodologies, and plans of others and trying them out in a similar or different context, constituting a mundane, unglamorous, and pedestrian exercise (Lindsay & Ehrenberg, 1993; Makel et al., 2012; Makel & Plucker, 2014; National Science Foundation and Institute of Education Sciences, 2018). Indeed, Ioannidis (2012) jokes that replication is considered 'a despicable exercise' best suited to 'idiots' who are capable only of 'me-too' mimicry (p. 647). Plucker and Makel (2021) note, however, that such views mistakenly confuse novelty with creativity, and that creativity can reside in addressing utility. Indeed, they argue that an original study's research finding that is irreplicable is neither innovative, creative, nor useful (see also Gelman, 2018).

Replication is also a risky business, as, the replication study might obtain a result that differs from, or challenges, the original research; the original or the replication may be at risk or, more personally, the originator or the replicator, calling a person's competence into question. Hence, researchers might be unwilling to share instruments, data, and research processes with others. Pashler and Harris (2012) note that conceptual replications are particularly risky in that, if they find different results from those of the original study, the theory or hypothesis is in ruins, reputations are at stake, the 'failure' may not be published, or nobody will take any notice of it.

Despite the need for, and call for, replication studies in education, they suffer from the 'file drawer' problem (Jones et al., 2010; Rosenthal, 1979, 1991; Travers et al., 2016), which is reinforced by the apparent unwillingness of journals to publish replication studies (Coyne et al., 2016; Frank & Saxe, 2012; Ioannidis, 2012; Makel & Plucker, 2014; Roediger, 2012; Schmidt, 2009; Tincani & Travers, 2019). Indeed, researchers might conduct a replication without calling it such, to avoid being ignored or summarily rejected by editors (Eden, 2002; Jones et al., 2010). (Plucker & Makel, 2021, comment that not calling a replication study a replication study renders it difficult for readers of research to see what the study has or has not replicated.)

If journals do publish replications, then they might publish only those in which statistical significance or large effect size is found, leading to publication bias (Dickersin, 2005; Tincani & Travers, 2019), attracting conceptual rather than direct replications and studies with sensational or surprising results (Pashler & Harris, 2012). Pigott et al. (2013) note that a study reporting a statistically significant outcome was more than twice as likely to be published than one reporting a statistically non-significant outcome; of 79 published reports, only 19 (24 per cent) included all the outcomes originally recorded in the dissertation. Hence, if replication studies are to be published, journals must change their acceptance criteria and practices. Added to this are Spector et al.'s (2015) and Hüffmeier et al.'s (2016) comment that funding grants for replication studies are meagre or non-existent and Chhin et al.'s (2018) comment that money spent on a replication study is money not spent on a 'new study' (p. 603), that is, funding is difficult to obtain. Little wonder, then, that replications are currently unattractive to prospective upwardly mobile academics; the opportunity cost is too great.

However, at the time of writing, the Institute of Education Sciences, the primary federal funder of education research in the United States, is targeting replication studies (http://ies.ed.gov/funding/ncer_rfas/systematic_replications.asp) and Plucker and Makel (2021) note that funding agencies are becoming more attracted to replication research, valuing reliable science over novelty, thereby bringing together what is in the interests of the public good and an individual researcher's career.

What kinds of original studies should be replicated?

Not every original study warrants a replication. How does the researcher or policy maker decide whether an original study should be replicated, on what grounds and for what purpose (e.g. which of the purposes indicated earlier: internal validity checks; external validity [generalisability]; and improvements, rectifications, and extensions to the original study)? There are many reasons why a replication should be undertaken, set out in Table 1.2 (Block & Kuckertz, 2018; Brandt et al., 2014; Ioannidis, 2015; Makel & Plucker, 2015; National Academies of Sciences, Engineering, and Medicine, 2019; Plucker & Makel, 2021; Porte, 2012; Porte & McManus, 2019; Tyson, 2014).

The Royal Netherlands Academy of Arts and Sciences (2018) indicates that the desirability of a replication study can be assessed in terms of four areas: knowledge, impact, cost, and alternatives. Table 1.3 reproduces its guidance.

In short, if an original study is non-trivial, non-parochial, and can make a potentially useful contribution to education policy, practice, and research, then it should be replicated. This includes original studies that have not found statistically significant results or large effect sizes; such studies are not ruled out of

Table 1.2 Reasons for replicating an original study

An original study might be useful to replicate if it:
- is likely to be of interest and usefulness to policy makers and practitioners;
- has an important, major finding that could impact, or has impacted, on policy and practice (i.e. if the results 'matter');
- is an important, timely, and relevant study in the field, with the field needing further investigation;
- is highly and/or widely cited;
- is a major, seminal study in its field;
- has not been already updated, extended, improved, overtaken, and superseded;
- makes a significant contribution to theory, practice, and research in the field;
- makes important recommendations for research, policy making, and practice;
- is a high quality, well-designed piece of research;
- plugs a gap in the field or meets a need for research in that field;
- contributes to contemporary debates in the field;
- contributes to discussions of a controversial matter in the field (e.g. on which there are disagreements and contradictions);
- has surprising, unexpected (e.g. in light of previous studies) and/or interesting findings (e.g. statistically significant or statistically non-significant; large or small effect sizes);
- is interesting and potentially important but limited (e.g. in the variables controlled, failures to control, sampling and populations, methodology, instrumentation, setting [such as laboratory, schools, classrooms, location, physical settings], duration, procedures, metrics and assessment, effects, data analysis, who conducted the original research);
- is worth extending (e.g. for generalisability);
- is capable of generalising;
- is opening up a new field which, at the time, had limited or scarce research coverage;
- has the potential to make a large and/or significant contribution to the field in question;
- is sufficiently important, actually or potentially, to warrant further investigation and testing;
- is written by notable people in the field;
- has perceived flaws but which warrants being amended (e.g. errors of omission, commission, ambiguity, lack of precision, errors or limitations in measures used, data analysis and interpretation, potentially false positives and/or false negatives);
- shows that the findings of the original research are suspect (e.g. biased, unsupported by the data);
- makes potentially exaggerated or unsubstantiated claims that need to be exposed;
- has the potential to challenge the original study and its findings;
- shows that there is reason to believe that the findings of the original study were an artifact of the research design and methods used in the research (i.e. that they were not context free);
- would benefit from being validated in an exact or close replication;
- suggests that there is reason to believe that the original study was biased, weak, flawed, incorrect, and/or limited (e.g. in its design, methods, data analysis);
- might bring significant benefits from confirming an original result;
- might produce findings that disagreed with, or were at odds with, those of the original study;
- is replicable (e.g. not all original studies might be replicable if they lack sufficient detail for a fair replication to be conducted).

Table 1.3 Assessing the desirability of replication studies

Criteria	The desirability of a replication study
Knowledge	• is higher when results from a previous study seem more plausible • is higher when there are more doubts about the validity of the methods or the proper execution of a previous study • is higher when its results may have a major impact on scientific knowledge • is higher when it may help improve research methods
Impact	• is higher when its results may have a major societal impact • is higher when it may help avoid wasting research resources on a scientific dead end • is higher when it might improve the functioning of a whole discipline (replication series)
Cost	• is lower when it requires more resources and time investment by researchers • is lower when it places a heavier burden on human and animal test subjects
Alternatives	• must be weighed against performing innovative studies • must be weighed against taking other measures to improve reproducibility

Source: Royal Netherlands Academy of Arts and Sciences (2018; Table 4)

consideration for replication. A lot might be learnt from replication of an original study that had *failed* to support/confirm a hypothesis (Kim, 2019) or that had a small effect size, though it is hard to find evidence of this currently happening in education (but see Hedges & Schauer, 2019). If an original study does not find a positive result, this may be no reason for not conducting a replication study (Block & Kuckertz, 2018; Kim, 2019). The need for replication studies is considerable, questioning the safety in placing too much confidence on single studies, however interesting or rigorous they may appear to be.

On a practical level, in choosing an original study to replicate, one factor is the level of detail and transparency provided in the original study, as the researcher must be able to determine what and how to plan, focus on, and conduct in the replication study and to see how exact, close, approximate, or distal the replication study is from the original study. An original study that lacks sufficient detail and transparency might prevent a replication study from being conducted, as the replication study may not be clear on what is being replicated, changed, extended, and so on (see Chapter 2).

Further, current literature on replication studies suggests that only one or two types of research appear to qualify for being replicated (e.g. experiments, quasi-experiments). This need not be the case, and Chapter 4 makes a case for qualitative research. One distinguishing feature of current original studies and their replications is their focus on *interventions* in education, to see how well and where they 'worked', under what circumstances and conditions, for whom, in the presence of which factors and conditions and in the absence of which factors and conditions, singly or in combination, for what purposes, with what controls and counterfactuals, in what ways and with what side-effects, how successfully, based on what and whose evidence and criteria, compared with what, with what level of trustworthiness, in whose eyes, and with what fallout? (Morrison, 2021). Whilst the focus on interventions is worthy, the case can be made for replicating other kinds of research (e.g. Plucker & Makel, 2021), for example longitudinal studies and surveys, though these are not addressed in the present volume.

How many replications are needed?

One replication is insufficient to instil confidence in accepting or refuting a finding (Anderson & Maxwell, 2016; Hedges & Schauer, 2019). More than one replication is needed in order to establish credible, trustworthy replication of results and to avoid a Type II error, even with large samples (Hedges & Schauer, 2019). However, caution must be exercised here, as simply piling up studies commits the enumeration error of assuming that the more studies there are, the greater the degree of confidence that can be placed in what they show (Cartwright, 2019); rather, each replication must have demonstrable rigour.

If the replication study finds dissimilar results from those of the original study, then one cannot conclude that the original study was unsafe; one or both sets of findings might have been wrong, biased, or context- and condition-specific, and other factors (e.g. sampling, timing) may have contributed to the different findings in the replication. The original finding might work in its own context and conditions, which were not replicated in the replication study. This argues for multiple replication studies of the same intervention, to separate the signal from the noise (Moonesinghe et al., 2007). Researchers and policy makers might agree that conceptual replications which show similar results across, for example, two, three, or four studies and contexts might suffice to promote credibility and applicability (see also Hüffmeier et al., 2016). However, in principle, changing one or more elements in a conceptual replication, for example using different samples and measures, may require the *new* study to be replicated. Hence, the potential for expanding the number of replications could be infinite, a problem that meta-analysis or theoretical saturation may not overcome (Morrison, 2021). This is the familiar argument of the limits of induction. Systematic reviews and research syntheses might contribute to establishing whether something is a sufficiently 'best bet' (Major & Higgins, 2019) to be worth accepting, and replication research can contribute to these.

To avoid infinite replication, the number of replications of an original study depends on what was found, what type of replication was being conducted, and the significance of the original study. For example, if an exact replication confirmed the original study, then this might be sufficient; if it disconfirmed the original study, then a further replication would be advisable. If the original study was of considerable significance and potentially important contribution to policy, practice, and research, then two or more replications might be needed to increase security of the overall findings (depending on their results).

The same might apply to an approximate replication, but, given that an approximate replication deliberately varies one or more of the variables of the original study, each variation of the original study might need its own replication. Then, depending on the results, if the replication confirmed the original study, this might suffice, unless the replication study was of considerable significance and potentially important contribution to policy, practice, and research, in which case further replication might be warranted.

For a conceptual replication, it is difficult to identify the number of replications that might be required. This is because, in a conceptual replication, a non-replication of findings from an original study does not necessarily mean that the original findings were wrong or false (Makel & Plucker, 2015), since the conceptual replication was not so much a validation exercise of the original study as an investigation into the generalisability of the original concept, regardless of changes made to other parts of the original study (discussed in Chapter 3). If the findings of the conceptual replication differed from those of the original study because of a change of setting, sample, procedure, data collection instruments, data analysis methods, and so on, then this leaves the original findings untouched with regard to their validity. Further, if the findings of the conceptual replication confirm those of the original study, this does not mean that the findings of the original study were correct; the replication study or both studies might be wrong (Chapter 3 argues that a more suitable *validation* of a conceptual replication might be to conduct as exact a replication as possible, with attention to precision and accuracy). Even if the results of the conceptual replication confirm or refute those of the original study, it might still be useful to conduct a further replication, to confirm that result, as, for all the researcher knows, it 'works' only in the original and new study, not everywhere.

There is a need for the exercise of professional judgement in deciding and justifying whether an original study needs one or more replications, and whether a replication study, itself, needs a further replication. Simply because a single replication confirms or disconfirms the findings of the original study does not necessarily mean that the original study is correct or incorrect.

Conclusion

This chapter has argued that challenges in replication studies commence very early, even at the level of definition, as there are many types and purposes of replication studies. Here, the chapter introduced exact, approximate, and conceptual replications and set out four main purposes of replications in education research: for ensuring the internal validity of the original study, for generalisability, for testing improvements and rectifications made to the original study, and for addressing extensions to its scope.

The chapter made a case for conducting replication studies, arguing that single studies on their own are insufficient for educational policy and practice. Replications can increase the trust that can be placed in findings. There is an ethical duty to conduct replication of single studies. Replications are rooted in views of educational research as a science, and its cumulative, self-correcting nature. Replications also serve improvements to meta-analysis by ensuring that high quality, replicated, and validated research findings are included in meta-analysis.

By contrast, arguments were made against replication studies, including their restricted view of the nature of education and educational research, their focus on certain types of educational research that, themselves, are challengeable (randomised controlled trials, meta-analyses), and their limited appeal to researchers, educationists, and journals. The chapter indicated that this book focuses on interventions in education.

If replication studies are to go ahead, then a discerning eye must be cast in choosing which original studies should be and need not be replicated, and in selecting an original study for replication. The chapter provided criteria for making such a selection. In turn, this raised the issue of how many replications were needed, and this was argued to depend on the type and purpose of the replication study.

The chapter sets the scene for greater discussion of types of replication study, and these are addressed in the next two chapters.

2 Types of replication studies and the challenge of sameness

Overview

This chapter serves a double purpose: to identify different types of replication study and, in doing so, to address the thorny issue of sameness. The chapter:

- sets out many types and typologies of replication studies;
- suggests the usefulness of adopting exact, approximate, and conceptual replications;
- suggests that exact replications may be limited in education;
- argues that different types of replication study serve different purposes (e.g. internal validation and generalisability);
- argues that serving generalisability does not relinquish the need for internal validation of the original study;
- suggests that sameness between the original study and the replication study is necessary but uncertain on its boundaries and that it is currently unclear on what are the limits of changes in the replication study before it becomes a different study altogether;
- identifies the scope of changes to the original study that might be made in a replication study;
- argues for a high level of detail and precision to be stated in the original and replication study, in order to determine the degree of sameness;
- argues for the ontological and epistemological bases of the original study and the replication study to be the same;
- questions whether the methodological bases of the original and the replication study should be the same.

The chapter draws on examples from education to illustrate the challenges facing replication studies in education, in principle and in practice.

Types of replication studies in education

Typologies and types of replication studies vary (Aguilar, 2020; Hüffmeier et al., 2016; Lykken, 1968; Melhuish & Thanheiser, 2018). Gómez et al. (2010)

indicate that classifications vary by author, subject discipline, and purpose. Replication types frequently fall into three groups: those that do not vary, or vary very little, from the original study; those that vary from the original study but follow the same method as the original; and those that use different methods from the original study. Replication types vary according to the purpose of the replication, for example: to re-analyse existing data; to generalise; to apply a new statistical model; to change instruments for data collection; to change metrics, sample and population, settings, data analysis, procedures, research design, researchers.

To try to obtain purchase on such variety, types of replication studies can be placed on a continuum, rather than being dichotomous or mutually exclusive; these range from 'exact' to 'relative' to 'conceptual' (Eden, 2002; Rosenthal, 1991). Exact replications concern confirmation of the findings of the original study, whereas conceptual replications concern generalisability (Figure 2.1).

Hendrick (1991) identifies four types of replication:

1   *Exact replication*: keeping as close and identical as possible to the original study in all features. This runs the least risk of failure to confirm the original idea or findings (Jones et al., 2010), because it tests the findings of the original study by using the same methods and measures; on the other hand, if it does not confirm the findings of the original study, then the original research (or, indeed, the researcher or researchers) might be severely damaged.
2   *Partial replication*: changing procedural variables whilst keeping other parts the same, investigating the same construct as in the original study but using a combination of identical and modified methods, instruments, and measures. The replication can also extend the original study while retaining most of its original measures. A partial replication runs a moderate level of risk of failure to confirm the original idea or findings, because it tests the idea by using a combination of identical, previously used, and new methods and measures (Jones et al., 2010). If the partial replication does not falsify the original study – its idea, hypothesis, or findings – then this provides stronger corroboration than that of an exact replication.
3   *Systematic replication*: conducting a replication but making consistent differences, in order to extend the original study to different participants or settings. This might include making changes to the design, sample, methodology, procedures, measures, and so on. A systematic replication runs a moderate level of risk of failure to confirm the original idea, hypothesis, or

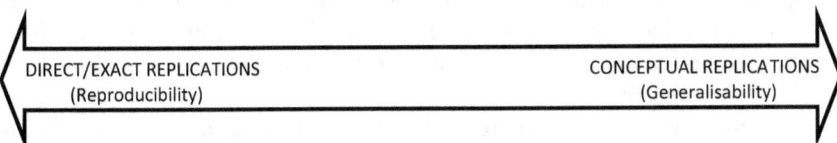

Figure 2.1 The continuum of replication studies

findings, because it changes one or more of the variables and elements of the original study.
4 *Conceptual replication*: changing nearly all but the original concept, hypothesis, or idea. A conceptual replication runs the highest risk of failure to confirm the original concept, idea, hypothesis, or findings (Jones et al., 2010), as it tests these by changing many components from those in the original study. On the other hand, Jones et al. (2010) argue that it can provide the greatest corroboration of the original study's 'concept' (though Chapter 3 questions this).

Tsang and Kwan (1999) suggest six types of replication, organised into two dimensions: *dimension one*, which uses the same or different measurement and/or analysis; *dimension two*, which is the source of the data (same data set; same population; different population). Their six types are:

1 checking of analysis (same measurement and/or analysis; same data set);
2 re-analysis of data (different measurement and/or analysis; same data set);
3 exact replication (same measurement and/or analysis; same population);
4 conceptual extension (different measurement and/or analysis; same population);
5 empirical generalisation (same measurement and/or analysis; different population);
6 generalisation and extension (different measurement and/or analysis; different population).

Dennis and Valacich (2014) identify three types of replication: 'exact', 'methodological', 'conceptual'. Schmidt (2009) notes that there is not a clear-cut or unequivocal definition of replication, of what constitutes a 'successful' replication, what a replication experiment is, and how to conduct a replication. He suggests two types: 'direct replication' and 'conceptual replication' (p. 95); his binary typology is used by the National Science Foundation and Institute of Education Sciences (2018).

Porte (2012) sets out three clear and useful types of replication:

1 *Exact replication* (also termed a 'literal replication' or a 'direct replication'): this keeps as close as possible to the original study in all areas (e.g. research design and methodology, instrumentation, sample and population, intervention and procedures, settings, data types and data analysis), and seeks to confirm the findings of the original study (a validation exercise for internal validity). It recognises that, in the social world, it is not possible to have exact duplication, as people and settings differ, and as the replication typically occurs later than the original study.
2 *Approximate replication* (also termed a 'systematic replication' or 'partial replication'): this keeps as close as possible to the original study in nearly all areas but changes one or more 'nonmajor variables' (p. 8) (e.g. population

and sample, setting, tasks set), in order to be able to compare the original and replication. This type of replication study serves generalisability (e.g. to a new population or setting). It typically retains fidelity to the original research design and methodology.

3   *Conceptual replication* (also termed a 'constructive replication'): this keeps the original 'concept' or idea (Chapter 3 discusses this in greater detail) but makes major changes (e.g. quantitative to qualitative and *vice versa*, research design, methodology, instrumentation, sampling and population) from those of the original study. The purpose of this type of replication study is for generalisability, to see how far, and where, the original concept or idea holds true in different circumstances, settings, and conditions. If its findings agree with those of the original study, then this can suggest that the original concept or idea holds true and that the outcomes are not simply artifacts of the original study's methodology (i.e. they are the signal that rises from the noise).

These are discussed below, and, as a conceptual replication is more widely used than other types in education, Chapter 3 discusses it more fully.

An exact or direct replication strives to duplicate as far as possible the original experiment (Earp & Trafimow, 2015; Makel & Plucker, 2015) in key features, for example research design and methodology, contents and procedures, resources, data collection instruments and timing, measures used, using the same data, data analysis, location, duration and sampling. The intention here is to ascertain how far the findings of the original experiment hold up, thereby reinforcing reliability and validity. This is a confirmatory exercise which attempts to be as exact a copy as possible of the original study (Coyne et al., 2013, 2016; Matthews et al., 2018; National Science Foundation and Institute of Education Sciences, 2018), using and re-analysing the original data or as similar data and methods as possible. This exercise concerns the internal validity of the original study. Whether an exact replication is possible is also contingent on the level of detail provided in the original study (Brown, 2012); sufficient detail may not exist in the original study for an exact replication study to be undertaken. Though it might be possible to contact the author of the original study, whether that author will provide such details is an open question.

Exact replications can validate the original study – a requirement that is not met, or not as straightforwardly met, in approximate or conceptual replications. Such validation is important. As Yong (2012) remarks: if we want to show that X is true, we don't do Y, we repeat X, that is, we conduct an exact, direct replication. An approximate or conceptual replication is no guarantee of the reliability, credibility, validity, correctness of the original, the replication, or both, but only how far and where something 'works', does not 'work', partially works, or is 'indeterminate' (see Chapter 5) in contexts and conditions that differ from those in the original study (Morrison, 2019).

Identical, exact replications in education, however, face many challenges (Morrison, 2019). These include, for example ensuring the same contents, teachers, students, duration, frequency, timing, intensity, strength, quality, contexts, settings, location, presence of sufficiently similar enablers, qualifiers, inhibitors, causalities, conditions, contingencies, and side-effects (Kvernbekk, 2016). This is a formidable list. Illustrating such challenges, Coyne et al. (2016), writing on replication studies in special education, note the unlikelihood of being able to conduct an exact, direct replication (and the social sciences more widely), as it may be impossible to duplicate and replicate all the aspects of, and variables in, the original study (see also Chhin et al., 2018; Frank & Saxe, 2012; Rosenthal, 1991). Conditions are unique, thereby presenting a difficulty for exact replications.

An exact, direct replication requires a precise and accurate process in which the original data are re-analysed or in which new, very similar data are examined in the same way as in the original study. This raises a fundamental issue in education that was raised in Chapter 1: given the high context density, variable density, causal density, person-centredness of education, how realistic, even how desirable it is, to conduct an exact or direct replication study, as education concerns differences between unique individuals, being person-centred, rather than being concerned with averages and overall results (Sacks, 1999), though Plucker and Makel (2021) note that holding to such a view might lead to confining research to case studies and action research with little cumulative or generalisable value. Goldacre (2013) notes the similarity between people and that, in the world of education, even though every student is different, nevertheless they are sufficiently similar for research in education to detect which interventions work best overall, that is, the signal can emerge and rise above contextual noise. However, how far this is either acceptable or practical is an open question. The work of Coyne et al. (2016) is an instance of what may be a wider phenomenon, *viz.* that close replications are not possible in education. Indeed, direct replications are very rare in educational research (Chhin et al., 2018); most are conceptual (Chhin et al., 2018; Jones et al., 2010).

The inability to conduct an exact, direct replication in education may not be a problem. For example, Eden (2002) notes that exact replications, even though they can be useful, do not catch the potential contribution of replication studies, as the *less* similar the replication is to the original study, the greater might be its contribution, by seeing how far and where the 'concept' (in a conceptual replication) holds fast across variations from the original study, that is, generalisability. An exact replication can corroborate the original study but cannot go further (Morrison, 2019). By contrast, an approximate or conceptual replication can provide a more generalisable corroboration. However, in doing so, the risk of non-corroboration is higher, as it introduces one or more possible sources of difference from the original study (Jones et al., 2010; Moonesinghe et al., 2007). Further, once we step out of an exact, direct replication, we can no longer falsify the original study, because the replication is not comparing like with like.

An approximate replication keeps the same research design and methodology and strives to keep close to key original conditions, though it might change other putatively less significant elements of the original study, for example the sample and the population, the setting, procedural matters, details of the instruments and tasks. However, this raises the issue of how to differentiate 'major' from 'nonmajor' features (Porte, 2012, p. 8), and what are the boundaries of each of these components. In approximate replications, like systematic replications, the researcher can change one 'nonmajor' variable at a time. This can be useful in identifying which variable makes a difference between the findings of the original study and the replication study; this method comes at a cost, as it implies the need for several replications not only to identify which variables are causing the difference but also to replicate the relevant replication study.

A conceptual replication keeps the concept of the original study but deliberately changes one or more components in order to test the concept, idea, hypothesis, theory, or set of practices under investigation, for example changing the research design, methodology, sample and population, context and setting, experimenters, intervention components, tasks, independent variables, methods and operationalisation, age groups, procedures, apparatus, data collection instruments, measures and data analysis, outcomes, time points. This is done to test the concept and/or theory underpinning the study, to see if the findings remain the same in different circumstances, settings, and conditions, in other words to see how well it 'works' in settings and conditions that differ from those in the original study. This seeks to address generalisability (e.g. Coyne et al., 2016; Dennis & Valacich, 2014; Earp & Trafimow, 2015; Eden, 2002; Gómez et al., 2010; Hendrick, 1991; Jones, 1978; Jones et al., 2010; Kelly, 2006; Makel et al., 2016; Makel & Plucker, 2015; Matthews et al., 2018; Melhuish, 2018; National Academies of Sciences, Engineering, and Medicine, 2019; National Science Foundation and Institute of Education Sciences, 2018; Rosenthal, 1991). A conceptual replication constitutes a potentially powerful contribution to the 'what works' agenda, as it straddles a range of contexts and conditions and purports to separate the signal from the noise.

Conceptual replications can serve the third purpose of a replication study as set out in Chapter 1 (to make improvements and rectifications to the original study), as, if there is reason to believe that the original tasks, instrumentation, and measures were lacking or erroneous, for example in precision, scope, reliability, validity, then they can introduce improvements to these (Brandt et al., 2014; King, 1995). Conceptual replications serve convergent validity, operating as triangulation (Lindsay & Ehrenberg, 1993) and enhancing the confidence that can be placed in the *conceptual* validity of the study, rather than its findings being an artifact of the methodology, design, instrumentation, or data analysis being used.

An exact replication study, then, is useful for validating the findings of the original study, whilst approximate and conceptual replication studies are useful in addressing the generalisability of the original study, though this is likely to come at the cost of sacrificing the validation of the findings of the original study. Approximate and conceptual replications cannot falsify the findings of the original study, as they have changed one or more variables of the original study, that is, they have not repeated the original study.

Further, replication and generalisability are not the same animal. Strict replication, as Chapter 1 indicated, concerns repeating an original study in order to reduce errors and to seek confirmation of findings in the original study. How far an approximate or conceptual replication can accomplish this is questionable.

Generalisability may be a worthy endeavour, but this does not obviate the need to confirm how far the findings themselves of the original study are safe, and approximate or conceptual replications have difficulty in doing this. Take away the generalisability issue from the exact replication, and we are still left with a replication *qua* validation; take generalisability away from the approximate or conceptual replication, and we are left with nothing except a hypothesis, concept, or idea whose comparability with the original study and validation of the original study's findings remain unquestioned. Replication has two key purposes: (a) validation and (b) generalisability; exact replications are strong on (a) but weak on (b), whilst approximate or conceptual replications are strong on (b) but weak on (a). This suggests, that, for a full replication, we need both (a) and (b), which implies conducting more than one type of replication.

The problem of sameness

A problem facing researchers in education is that if one or more variables are changed in the replication study (as in the partial, approximate, systematic, and conceptual replications noted earlier) and differences from the original study are found in the results of the replication, then it is difficult, if not impossible, to detect the source(s) of the difference, there being more than one possible source. Nor is it possible in partial, approximate, systematic, and conceptual replications to falsify the original study's findings, as the findings in both the original study and the replication might stem from the features and elements of these separate studies. Further, in social sciences, if one changes one variable, then this typically changes another, that is, it has knock-on effects on the entire study, rendering the replication substantially different in causal nature from the original study (Cartwright & Hardie, 2012; Deaton & Cartwright, 2018; Morrison, 2021). It tests something that is different from that of the original study; it is a different study (Morrison, 2021).

Hao (2015) notes that participants, settings for teaching and learning, and a host of uncontrollable factors render replication difficult. Similarly, Raloff (2015) comments that many factors obstruct replication research's confirmation of the original research because of the difficulty in conducting replications. She notes that only 35 out of 100 previously published studies in psychology could be replicated by Nosek and his team of 270 scientists. Replication may be nearly impossible if people or materials vary greatly, and yet such variation is a defining feature of humans; people respond differently to the same conditions, contexts, and environment, thereby changing the study's implementation (Coyne et al., 2016; National Science Foundation and Institute of Education Sciences, 2018; Raloff, 2015). As Ioannidis (2012) puts it, if provocatively, efforts at repeatability and reproducibility of published research have a 'dismal' success rate (p. 647).

These issues raise the challenging task of addressing sameness in comparing the original study and its replication (e.g. Melhuish & Thanheiser, 2018). It is impossible for the original study and its replication to be identical, so what are the limits to sameness? At what point does the replication become too distant or different from the original study for it to be considered as a legitimate replication? What are the boundaries of sameness? Does sameness apply to the research design, to methodology, procedures, tasks in the intervention, sampling, instruments and measures, settings, data collection and analysis methods, findings? Which one(s) of these must be the same as in the original, and which ones can be varied and still count as a fair replication study? Table 2.1 summarises some concerns in considering sameness in a replication study in education.

What defines sameness in considering the intervention, and how can one ensure and judge sameness? At what point, and on what elements, is a replication study sufficiently similar to the original study for it to warrant being termed a replication, and how is this decided? Or, by contrast, at what point and on what elements does a putative replication study become a different study rather than a replication? What must be kept the same between the original study and the replication study, and how realistic or possible is it to hold constant the necessary 'constant' in a replication study, and how far do differences fall legitimately within the scope of a replication study or render it a different study altogether? This raises the need for defining, and holding to, the nature and degree of variability that can be tolerated before a replication breaches sameness. This is a matter of human, informed judgement and decision making; it cannot be cranked out mechanically from a formula.

A simplistic answer to what should be the same and what can differ can be in terms of the purpose of the study and its type. For example, an exact replication

Table 2.1 Concerns in considering sameness in a replication study in education

At what point does a replication cease to be a replication if we change:
- intervention contents and their procedures and tasks;
- timing, time frames, and duration;
- characteristics of the population, sample, and allocation;
- different people, personalities, and behaviours;
- sociocultural, temporal, and locational contexts;
- researcher(s), data collection instruments;
- differences in cultures and curricula;
- characterisation of the dependent variable;
- causal contexts, factors and conditions.

Questions to ask of replication studies:
- How to decide if a replication has ceased to be a replication?
- How far can controls operate in different contexts?
- How possible is it to hold constant a set of variables in addressing sameness, as their interaction, relative strengths, presence and influence of other factors cause a difference or a similarity of findings?
- What if new factors appear in the replication study that were absent from the original study, as one factor in the replication study's context that was absent from the original study may cause similar or different findings?
- What if factors appearing in the original study were absent from the replication study, as one factor in the original study's context that was absent from the replication study may cause similar or different findings?

should keep everything the same – identical – between the original and the replication study (though this may not be possible in social sciences). An approximate replication can change one or more variables, provided that the research design is the same and that only 'nonmajor' variables are changed (though, as argued earlier, what constitutes 'major' and 'nonmajor' is unclear, as changing one variable can affect the entire study). An approximate and a systematic replication study might need more than one replication study in order to replicate the first replication study, and this might be an acceptable compromise between too few and too many replications in addressing sameness. For a conceptual replication, in which everything except the original concept, hypothesis, idea, or set of practices might be changed, the degree of sameness needed to constitute a legitimate replicate is an open question (see Chapter 3).

It is impossible to keep an original study and its replication study identical (Rosenthal, 1991); no two situations are the same, even if they are similar. Replication is relative (ibid.). The National Science Foundation and Institute of Education Sciences (2018) notes that there is no consensus on how to judge whether a replication really is a replication, and what and whose criteria to use in judging this. Rather, it indicates that proposals submitted for a conceptual replication should specify and justify clearly any variations from the original study. Further, the proposal should state whether the *researcher* conducting the replication is the same as in the original study; researchers conducting the replication study should not be the same as those conducting the original study, as this risks bias. As Morrison (2019) notes:

> [T]he 'gold standard' is where a replication is conducted by a researcher who has no affiliation to the original study. Writing on psychology replications, Ioannidis (2015) notes that fewer than half were conducted by researchers who were not authors of the original study, reiterating his earlier finding (2012) that direct replications by authors who were not one of those involved in the original findings were 'exceptionally uncommon' and that 'only a fraction' of these showed similar findings (p. 649). Barshay (2019) notes that replications conducted by the original researchers recorded benefits up to 80 per cent higher than the independent studies, and a huge percentage of studies had 'insider connection' (p. 3). For many scientific fields, high significance or large effects may signal large bias, a problem in both large-scale and small studies.
>
> (p. 431)

Along with addressing transparency in writing proposals for replication studies, the National Science Foundation and Institute of Education Sciences (2018) notes the importance of transparency in respect of variations from the original study, procedures and data, data sharing, data analysis, objectivity and independence of researchers, level of detail to be reported, details of the sample and the context, and fidelity of implementation. Considerable detail is needed in order to ascertain the degree of sameness and when making the data publicly available, the methods for cleaning and processing the data, what statistical treatments are used, and what codebook and analytic codes are used in replication as reproducibility. Researchers should also describe clearly the criteria being used for excluding subjects, data, and results that did not support the main hypotheses and/or findings.

Guidance is limited with regard to the number of components that a conceptual replication might vary before being considered to be not a replication but a new, original study (Coyne et al., 2016). Chhin et al. (2018) found that over half of the conceptual replications investigated varied more than one component of the original, changing the context, methods, and other aspects of the intervention, whilst a smaller percentage varied the outcomes being measured in the replication study. Guidance is currently limited on deciding, for conceptual replications, at what point changes made to an original study render the replication an entirely new study, and how far the original concept, hypothesis, or idea is disturbed or altered in a replication study. However, it is clear that whatever changes to the original study are made in the replication study, these need a full and clear indication, justification, and defence against charges of constituting a different study altogether. This is a matter of human judgement and disclosure, and of being 'beyond a reasonable doubt'.

The nature, extent, and level of sameness required must be disclosed, to ensure that it is a genuine replication, and to hold to these (Hedges & Schauer, 2019), for example in contents, tasks, activities, procedures in the intervention. Stanley and Spence (2014) note that researchers should replace a focus on replicating *results* with replicating *methodology* (see also Jacobson & Simpson, 2019). King (1995), arguing for transparency, detail, and disclosure, suggests that the only way in which the researcher can understand and evaluate an empirical analysis fully is to know exactly how the data were generated and how the analysis was conducted. As part of this, when changes are made in the replication study (e.g. in a conceptual replication), there needs to be a clear indication of what is constant, similar, and different between the original study and the replication study and, where there are differences, how 'theoretically important' these are (Coyne et al., 2016, p. 246), and what they are, for example in the context, conditions, independent and/or dependent variables.

Sameness also raises questions of how far specific and required controls can actually operate in different contexts and how to control for factors appearing in the replication that were absent in the original study, or for factors that were present in the original study but absent in the replication, either of these leading to two different stories being told. Addressing sameness requires the identification of changes made in the replication study and what should be held constant (Coyne et al., 2016; Morrison, 2021). Such items are set out in Table 2.2, for judging the degrees of similarity and difference between the original study and the replication study (there remains the problem of unknowns: other factors which might be at work in a replication, which have not been controlled [error factors]).

In comparing the original study with the (proposed) replication study, Brandt et al. (2014) set out comprehensive comparison questions and items which can be used to judge how, and on what elements, the original study and replication

Table 2.2 What should remain constant and what the replication study might change

Contents of the intervention:
- aims and substance of the intervention;
- procedures, tasks, and instructions;
- focus of the intervention (e.g. knowledge, skills, procedures, attitudes, competencies, behaviours);
- scope of the intervention (e.g. broad, narrow);
- characterisation of the independent and dependent variables;
- pre-testing and post-testing, and the consistency of the focus and coverage of these;
- reliability, validity, and the elimination of bias;
- ontological and epistemological bases of the replication;
- timing, time frames, and duration of the intervention;
- duration of each session of the intervention;
- number of intervention sessions each week and in total;
- 'dose-response' component of the intervention: its nature, diagnosis, frequency, intensity, quality, strength, amount, pacing, variation over time, sequence, inception and follow-up, risks, side-effects, other relevant factors, differentiation for different participants, procedures;
- fidelity to the contents, procedures, tasks, timing matters, and instructions;
- timing and frequency of the data collection;
- support for the participants (preparation, training, and development);
- pedagogy, feedback, and assessment;
- task(s) nature (e.g. incremental, revision, application, reinforcement, correction, extension); conceptual, practical; and demand (low to high, what is being demanded);
- resources (human, temporal, locational, material, physical, equipment, administrative, financial);
- novelty of/familiarity with the intervention.

Research design:
- research design and research methodologies;
- statistical power;
- allocation to group (e.g. control or intervention) where relevant;
- counterfactuals and controls;
- calculations of, and allowances for, attrition;
- population and sample (strategy, size, type, nature, inclusion and exclusion, subgroups);
- ethics;
- data collection instrument(s) and their alignment/independence to the intervention;
- measures and metrics used, reliability and validity (e.g.: construct, content, cultural, ecological, concurrent).

Setting(s) of the intervention:
- geographical, sociocultural, temporal, and locational;
- school type(s) (where relevant);
- school location (where relevant);
- school organisation (where relevant);
- school size (where relevant);
- class size (where relevant);
- group size and nature (where relevant);
- location of the intervention (e.g. in class, out of class);
- causal contexts, factors, and conditions.

Participants:

- learners/recipients of the replication: age, ethnicity/race, socioeconomic status, background, gender, ability/disability, language(s), levels of education, academic levels;
- teachers/those conducting the intervention: age, ethnicity/race, background, gender, ability/disability, language(s), levels of education, qualification, years of experience, academic levels taught, amount and nature of training undertaken for the intervention, experience in the particular field of the intervention;
- researchers/those conducting the replication: age, ethnicity/race, background, gender, ability/disability, language(s), levels of education, qualifications, years of experience in the field, amount and nature of preparation undertaken for the intervention, experiences in the particular field of the intervention, research training completed.

Data analysis:

- selection and organisation of data for analysis;
- data analysis methods (qualitative and quantitative);
- statistical tests;
- standardisation;
- level(s) of analysis (e.g. individual, group, class, school, region);
- multi-level analysis.

---

study are similar and different, and by how much (e.g. exactly the same, to 'close', to 'conceptually different', p. 219), set out in Table 2.3. Whilst several of these items from Brandt et al. (2014) concern only or largely the reporting stage of the replication study, these are included here to retain the coherence and integrity of the original.

For sameness to be assured, a considerable level of detail and precision should be present in the original study and the replication study, including definition, focus, operationalisation, setting, conditions, conduct, instructions to be followed, isolation and control of variables, holding items constant and manipulating certain variables, degrees of intervention, nature and duration of the intervention, dose-response, metrics, and so on. Whether such detail is available in the original study and the replication study in education may not be possible, but their absence or variance can have important effects on the findings of the two studies, together with the judgements made and conclusions drawn from them. Teachers might not use an intervention as it was originally conceived; rather, they tailor it to their own situations, settings, contingencies, conditions, and circumstances (Kim, 2019; Morrison, 2021; Thomas, 2012).

For an exact, approximate, or conceptual replication study to be fair requires both the original study and the replication study to possess and disclose a high level of precision and detail, particularly in exact and approximate replications, so that the researcher can see what kind of replication study is most fit for purpose, how to conduct the replication study, what to focus on in the replication study, which parts of the original study can be improved and/or extended, and how to validate the findings of the original study. The original study and the replication study should include fine-grained details of the contents of the intervention, the

Table 2.3 Comparing the replication study with the original study

The effect's nature
- effects that the replication is attempting to replicate;
- effect size sought, and why;
- confidence intervals in the original study;
- sample size, strategy, and nature in the original study;
- location of the original study;
- how the original study was conducted.

The replication study's design
- access to the materials of the original study;
- if the original materials are unavailable, how will the replication study create the materials;
- assumptions made in the original study;
- location of the researcher during the data collection;
- researcher's knowledge of the intervention and its setting;
- researcher's knowledge of the purposes and hypothesis of the research;
- targeted size of the sample, and the rationale for this.

Similarity and differences between the original study and the replication study
Identify and judge the similarities and differences, and the closeness of the similarity in question (exact, close, conceptually different):
- instructions;
- measures;
- stimuli;
- procedures;
- location;
- remuneration (where relevant);
- participant populations;
- anticipated differences between the original study and the replication that might affect the direction and size of the effect;
- action taken to test whether those anticipated differences will influence the outcomes of the replication study.

Analysing and evaluating the replication
- criteria for excluding outliers, certain potential or actual participants, and so on;
- plan for the data analysis;
- criteria for judging whether the replication is a success.

Pre-registering the replication study
- what is being registered (e.g. plan, procedures, materials, analysis proposal), and where.

Reporting the replication study and its findings
- the effect size found in the replication;
- the confidence interval of the effect in the replication;
- comparison between the effect size of the original study and the replication study;
- decision on whether the replication is successful or a failure, and based on what criteria;
- access to data from the replication study;
- all the analyses undertaken are included;
- limitations of the replication.

Source: Brandt et al. (2014)

research design and its components, the setting(s) of the intervention, the participants, and the data analysis.

Brandt et al. (2014) argue that, for a close or exact replication to be convincing requires attention to the details and the implementation of the original and the replication study, including:

- careful definition of the research design, areas of focus, and measures in the original and replication study;
- details of the methods and effects that the original study and the replication study seek to replicate;
- as close as possible adherence to key elements of the original study (e.g. methods, population and sample, procedures and instructions, contents and operations of the intervention, setting and contextual features of the intervention, tasks in the intervention, instrumentation and measures used, methods of data analysis);
- ensuring transparency, disclosure, and availability of the details of the study, for external evaluation, including syntax, data, and analysis;
- how to compare the results of the replication study and the original study (e.g. effect sizes and their direction, confidence intervals, distributions and contexts [see Chapter 6]);
- conducting the replication study by independent researchers.

There must be a sufficiently high level of specificity and detail on these items in both the original study and the replication study in order for the replication study to be genuine and fair. In selecting an original study to replicate, a high level of detail and transparency is necessary in the instructions for the conduct of the intervention, so that the researcher can see how exact, close, approximate, or distal the replication study is with regard to the original study.

If the level of detail, transparency, and precision are low or absent in the original study and/or the replication study, then what can be taken from either study or both of these studies is uncertain, even if the findings of the original study and the replication study are similar or, indeed, different. The National Science Foundation and Institute of Education Sciences (2018) requires statements of procedures in replications, but their levels of specificity are not stated, nor are the criteria for judging sufficiency of similarity in the elements of the original study and the replication study. The extent and limits of these should be disclosed and justified.

Patil et al. (2016) counsel caution in deciding how far a replication study confirms the original study, for many reasons: the complex nature of some interventions; differences in populations, samples, and researchers; and the time lapse between the original and replication study (Pashler and Harris, 2012, note that the median time lag between original and replication studies was four years, extending beyond ten years, i.e. they were 'long-lag', p. 534). Further, simply holding constant a set of variables is insufficient in addressing sameness, as it is their interaction, *relative* strengths, together with the presence and influence of other factors, that make a difference or, indeed, a similarity: one factor in the replication study's context that was not present in the original study might bring similar or different findings in the replication study. This challenge also surrounds large-scale, multi-site interventions or studies: how to take account of differences and variances in the contexts of the several sites.

In judging the significance of similarities and differences between the original study and the replication study, the question is raised of whether ontological, epistemological, and methodological differences can be tolerated between the two studies (e.g. Markee, 2017; Plucker & Makel, 2021). Ontology and epistemology are contentious matters, open to many interpretations. They are the object of debate and vary according to the disciplines and fields of knowledge in question. How they are interpreted in, for example, classical philosophy, might differ from how they are interpreted in social sciences. A useful stipulative definition here is provided by Guba and Lincoln (1991) who, writing about their use in education, define ontology as the nature of the reality in question and epistemology as how we can be sure that we know what we purport to know about the matter in question.

The ontological and epistemological bases of the original study and the replication study should be the same, as to change these is to fundamentally change the nature of the research in question (Jacobson & Simpson, 2019; Stanley & Spence, 2014). Whilst these are more or less guaranteed in an exact and close approximate replication, it is a different story for conceptual replications, where major changes are possible (see also Chapter 3). Keeping the ontological and epistemological bases of the original study and the replication study the same strives to ensure that the replication is a fair test, comparing like with like. If they differ between the original study and the replication study, then this calls into question how fair the test can be, as the replication study is testing something fundamentally different from the original study, and the canons of 'proof' in the two studies differ. If these two differ, then how can the replication study confirm or disconfirm the original study, as the original study and the replication study are playing by different rules?

The ontological and epistemological bases of the two studies should be transparent, as, if they are unclear, unstated, lacking in sufficient detail, or, indeed, if they differ, then this questions whether replications, particularly conceptual replications, are actually replications at all, and, if their epistemological bases differ, whether and how we can *know* whether they are or are not replications. Detail and precision must be provided on the ontological and epistemological bases and assumptions of the two studies, including how the original study and the replication study define the concept, hypothesis, idea, set of practices in a conceptual replication (Coyne et al., 2013, 2016; Gersten et al., 2015; Jacobson & Simpson, 2019; Melhuish, 2018).

Epistemologically speaking, what if a replication study appeals to an objective reality, with generalisability – external validity – and 'proof' achieved through precision, accuracy, lack of ambiguity, universality, the isolation and control of variables, manipulation of variables, hypothesis and theory generation and testing (Gersten et al., 2015; Jacobson & Simpson, 2019; Melhuish, 2018), whereas the replication study, being faithful to some social and human sciences, appeals to hermeneutic understanding of the role and significance of interpretation, agency, individuality, uniqueness, multiple interpretations, subjectivity, ambiguity, context-situatedness, complex conditionality, high causal density and complexity (Morrison, 2019, 2021)? In the former, the plausibility, legitimacy, and generalisability *qua* transferability are stated by the researcher; in the latter, these are accorded by the readers of the findings rather than solely the researchers.

If the epistemological foundation of the original study is that of an external, objective reality and existence that can be known and understood through objective measures, does this rule out, for example, qualitative, naturalistic, ethnographic replication studies? If the epistemological foundation of the original study is that of multiple subjective realities, values, and attitudes that can be known and understood only through the situationally specific, subjective views and definitions of the situation by participants, does this rule out a replication study that is based on 'reality' as having a singular, objective existence?

If we consider the 'reality' of the original study to reside in pluralistic constructions of it that are made by participants, that is, a constructivist view (Guba & Lincoln, 1991), then a replication study which is a randomised controlled trial might be epistemologically out of step and incommensurate with the assumed ontological nature of the original study. Further, if we regard replication research in education as somehow a science (which is open to question, e.g. Lucas et al., 2013; O'Leary and Chia, 2007; Reed, 2008), then Kuhn's (1962) view of science as paradigm-driven comes into play, and to replicate an original study requires fidelity to that paradigm (Glazerman et al., 2002). The paradigm embraces: the ontology; the constituents of the phenomenon; its epistemology and ways of working, knowing, and claiming to know; and truth tests.

If one subscribes to an objective view of an external, absolute reality, then this might legitimise experimentation and quasi-experiments, randomised controlled trials and their meta-analysis but proscribe qualitative, naturalistic, and subjective research of purportedly unique situations. By contrast, if one subscribes to a view of the 'reality' of a phenomenon as being subjectively defined, context-dense, causally complex, and variable-rich, then randomised controlled trials and quasi-experiments may be ruled out and phenomenological, interpretive, and naturalistic research studies of individual cases, featuring subjective, multiple interpretations and views, may be ruled in.

With regard to methodology, at the time of writing, cross-methodology replications are neither ruled out nor ruled in (e.g. Coyne et al., 2016; Glazerman et al., 2002; National Science Foundation and Institute of Education Sciences, 2018; Schmidt, 2009). However, making changes to methodology, from that used in the original study, can muddy the results (Glazerman et al., 2002; Makel & Plucker, 2015; Plucker & Makel, 2021). Currently, for a distant, conceptual replication, open season is declared for almost any kind of replication study's research design and conduct. This questions how acceptable it is to conceptually replicate an original study which used a randomised controlled trial or experimental approach with a qualitative case study replication study, or *vice versa*, as these are incommensurable and categorically different, with different paradigms, purposes, foundations, ontologies, epistemologies, methodologies, and canons of falsifiability.

This raises the further question of whether replication studies are, in principle, impossible or unfitting in that branch of qualitative research which celebrates the *unique* nature of the phenomenon in question, including classrooms, student groups, and individual students (e.g. Coyne et al., 2013, 2016). The challenge here is to establish sufficient commensurability between unique studies to the extent of being able to conduct a fair replication of a 'unique' original study (e.g. a case study).

A replication study which is based on a different ontology and epistemology from that of the original study, maybe even a different methodology, might be unable to falsify the original study, and the counterfactuals for the replication study and the original study might differ. This raises the question of whether the counterfactuals should be the same in the replication study and the original study.

In short, how far does a replication study, particularly a conceptual replication, permit *any* type of research design and conduct that the researcher wishes to use, to be ruled in, regardless of the original study, as long as the theory, hypothesis, concept, idea, set of practices, main features of an intervention – the 'concept' – remain intact? If they differ between the original study and the replication study, then how fair can the comparison be between them? The replication is reduced to seeing if X occurs in another situation. That is an impoverished view of replication.

At the time of writing, replication studies are mainly experimental studies (Coyne et al., 2013, 2016; Dennis & Valacich, 2014; Earp & Trafimow, 2015; Gómez et al., 2010; Makel & Plucker, 2015; Plucker & Makel, 2021; Schmidt, 2009; Travers et al., 2016). The National Science Foundation and Institute of Education Sciences (2018) provides examples of only randomised controlled trials. The call for qualitative studies is increasing. For example, Makel and Plucker (2015) and Plucker and Makel (2021) comment that replications need not be limited to experimental studies, and that qualitative research, for example action research and case studies, can and should be used. Indeed, Lucas et al. (2013) note that replication of qualitative studies is a fundamental requirement for growing a theory. Aguilar (2020), Melhuish (2018), and Melhuish and Thanheiser (2018) provide examples of qualitative replication studies in education. However, it is an open question whether, where, or how far quantitative studies and methodologies can be replicated with qualitative studies and methodologies, and *vice versa*.

Conclusion

There are different typologies and types of replication study in education. This chapter has argued for fitness for purpose in selecting an appropriate type of replication study, and that two purposes of replication studies (internal validation and generalisability) should not be mutually exclusive. To address these implies that more than one replication study of the original study is needed for securing generalisability. Generalisability, as in approximate and conceptual replications, raises issues of what can and cannot be changed between the original study and the replication study, and at what point changes made in the replication study render it a different study from the original.

This argued for a high level of detail, precision, and transparency to be stated in the original and replication study, in order for the level of sameness to be determined, and these matters must be taken into account when selecting an original study for replication. The chapter argued that changing the ontological and epistemological bases of the original study in a replication study exceeds the boundaries of sameness. Whether this extends to methodological sameness is an open question. This raises issues concerning the boundaries of sameness in a conceptual replication, and the next chapter addresses conceptual replications in greater detail.

3 Conceptual replications in education

Overview

Conceptual replications feature strongly in replication research in education. This chapter sets out key features, attractions, and limitations of conceptual replications. It raises a range of issues for conceptual replication researchers to address, and it provides guidance on how to ensure that the necessary requirements of a conceptual replication study are met. The chapter:

- identifies definitional matters in conceptual replications: what is a 'concept' and what is 'conceptual' in a conceptual replication study;
- clarifies differences in type and purpose between an exact replication and a conceptual replication;
- sets out key features and requirements of a conceptual replication and how these differ from those of an exact replication;
- identifies attractions and limits of a conceptual replication, including issues of construct validity and reliability;
- argues for detail, precision, and transparency in the concept, the original study, and the conceptual replication, what details should be provided and how these impact on choosing an original study to conceptually replicate;
- addresses the constituents of a fair conceptual replication, potential threats to, and difficulties in, ensuring fairness, and how to address these;
- identifies problems of sameness in a conceptual replication, how to address them, and what elements of the original study must be kept the same in the conceptual replication;
- identifies consequences of making changes between the original study and the conceptual replication;
- indicates the limits of conceptual replication in terms of validation and verification, and examines consequences of the elision of replication with generalisability and applicability;
- suggests that conceptual replications are unable to falsify an original study, and why, and why they can only trivially verify or validate the findings of an original study;

- examines the significance of context and causality for a conceptual replication study and their implications for under-determination and over-determination of findings from a conceptual replication;
- indicates what can and cannot be drawn from the findings of a conceptual replication study and why.

The chapter raises concerns and issues in planning, conducting, and analysing data from conceptual replications, and what they can and cannot do and show.

The field of conceptual replications

A conceptual replication can serve the 'what works' agenda, as it seeks to determine how much and where, with whom, and under what conditions and in what settings a 'concept' in the original study 'works' elsewhere (Matthews et al., 2018). In particular, it seeks to determine how far, and where, the original study's 'concept', hypothesis, idea, set of practices are confirmed in a different setting, when one or more variables in the original study are changed. Coyne et al. (2016) give an example of an original intervention that 'worked' with second graders with learning disabilities but did not 'work' with older students with intellectual disabilities. The findings of the original study were not necessarily called into question; they were simply less generalisable. This is both the strength and the weakness of a conceptual replication: as introduced in Chapter 2, it can serve generalisability, but it cannot validate the original study. A conceptual replication can indicate how far an original study is confirmed, partially confirmed, not confirmed, or is indeterminately confirmed (is unable to confirm or disconfirm) elsewhere; this is useful in identifying boundaries of generalisability (Earp & Trafimow, 2015; Schmidt, 2009).

Conceptual replications do not need to be a close or exact copy of the original study. Instead, they *apply* the original idea – the 'concept' – in settings, contexts, conditions, and contingencies that differ from those of the original study. Conceptual replications have received considerable attention (e.g. Coyne et al., 2013, 2016; Gersten et al., 2015; Hao et al., 2019; Hawe et al., 2015; Hendrick, 1991; Rosenthal, 1991; Shanahan, 2017; Schmidt, 2009; Therrien et al., 2016; Tyson, 2014; What Works Clearinghouse, 2018). They test the generalisability and applicability of a 'concept', however defined (see below), from the original study to see how well and where it 'works' elsewhere.

A conceptual replication study purposefully adjusts one or more aspects of the original study (Matthews et al., 2018). These might be, for example, grade level, the student population, the setting of the study, essential components of the instruction and measurements. Conceptual replications employ different methods to address the same hypothesis as that of the original study (Spector et al., 2015). The changes that they make to the original study can be considerable, raising the question of what a conceptual replication must include from the original study in order to count as a replication rather than being a different study altogether.

If it oversteps boundary conditions to what can be changed, then the conceptual replication ceases to be a fair replication, discussed below.

A conceptual replication investigates how far the 'concept' 'works' when one or more aspects of the original study are changed, for example: research design; methodologies and methods; contexts and settings; population and sample; components of, and tasks in, the intervention; procedures and instructions for the intervention; duration, timing, intensity, amount, and frequency of the intervention; data collection instruments; measures and metrics used; data analysis methods; variables that are controlled; variables excluded and new variables introduced. (Coyne et al., 2016; Dennis & Valacich, 2014; Earp & Trafimow, 2015; Eden, 2002; Gómez et al., 2010; Hendrick, 1991; Jones et al., 2010; Makel et al., 2016; Makel & Plucker, 2015; Matthews et al., 2018; Melhuish, 2018; Morrison, 2019; Rosenthal, 1991).

One concern in a conceptual replication is whether, in fact, a conceptual replication is a replication at all if many features of the original study are changed, and whether a concept can be separated from the context that gave rise to it or in which it was originally tested. Table 3.1 summarises some components that the conceptual replication study can change from those in the original study, deliberately excluding ontological and epistemological foundations (see Chapter 2). The conceptual replication strives to keep the original 'concept' intact but to vary the conditions and settings under which it is tested.

The attraction of a conceptual replication is its appeal to the wider applicability and generalisability of the 'concept'. However, conceptual replications encounter difficulties with regard to definition and constitution; scope and limits; ontology, nature and quiddity; epistemology; whether they test a theory; inability to falsify the original study and limited ability to verify the original study; methodology and methods; the significance of context, conditions, settings, and contingencies; changes to causality; and precision. These are explored below.

Table 3.1 Making changes in a replication study

Conceptual replications can vary:
• research design;
• methodology;
• sample and population;
• context and setting;
• experimenters;
• intervention components;
• independent variables;
• methods and operationalisation;
• procedures;
• apparatus and equipment;
• data collection instruments;
• measures and data analysis;
• outcomes;
• time points and duration.

Conceptual replications do not constitute a test of the *validity* of the findings of the original study (Coyne et al., 2016). Instead, they concern applicability and generalisability, to see how far the findings of a replication concur with those of the original study, under different conditions (Cai et al., 2018). However, it can be argued that, before one proceeds to a conceptual replication study that tests applicability and generalisability, the validation of the original study should be conducted (e.g. a direct replication). This is in order to avoid the risk of conducting a conceptual replication of an original study whose validity (e.g. construct validity) has not been ensured (Aguilar, 2020; Cai et al., 2018; Chhin et al., 2018; Coyne et al., 2016; Makel & Plucker, 2015; Spector et al., 2015; Yong, 2012). Chhin et al. (2018) report that, at the time of writing, although no direct replications had been funded by the Institute of Education Sciences in the United States, direct replications are a critical stage in replication studies, as they help to determine the veracity and validity of the original or previous studies.

Defining the 'concept' in a conceptual replication

Conceptual replications must be clear on the meaning of the key term 'concept': whether a concept really is a concept, or a theory, a hypothesis, a statement, an idea, a set of practices, that is, the quiddity of the 'concept'. Further, the question here is how to judge how far a conceptual replication study sufficiently replicates the original study, and what are the limits of a 'concept': whether almost anything that is related to a given general 'concept', idea, or set of practices might be considered a conceptual replication. In other words, the boundaries and limits of the conceptual replication need to be clarified, and in relation to the original study. This requires clarification of what constitutes a 'fair test' of the original study in a conceptual replication, and the chapter addresses this.

Conceptual replication is a *portmanteau* term, with many meanings, interpretations, types, and purposes (Chhin et al., 2018; Coyne et al., 2016; Schmidt, 2009). For example, is a conceptual replication a *way of thinking about* replication, an *approach* to replication, a *type* of replication, a way of *conducting* a replication, or some combination of these? What is the meaning of the 'concept', and how it is being used in the original study and its conceptual replication? The conceptual replication must clarify how the term 'concept' is being used (Bienefeld et al., 2020).

Should the replication researcher simply accept and assume the veracity or validity of the original 'concept' as a given, and just go ahead and apply it in different settings, samples, conditions, contexts, and contingencies, or should a conceptual replication require a previous exact or close replication of the original study in order to validate the original concept? A conceptual replication risks sidestepping the validation of the original study, such that the validity of the original study cannot be guaranteed. For this, a conceptual replication study can consider being as close to an original study as possible, recognising that an exact replication – a *reproducibility* study – is unlikely to be possible in the social sciences (National Academies of Sciences, Engineering, and Medicine, 2019). Further, for a conceptual replication to be a secure test of the original study, both the original study and the replication study must provide sufficient detail, transparency, and precision for the researcher to be able to interpret the findings (see Chapter 2).

There are many differences over the definition and meaning of 'concept' and 'conceptual'. A 'concept' here can be a construct, a hypothesis, a theory, a belief, an intervention, an idea, a set of practices, an effect, and so on. Concepts can be mental representations and images, abstract objects and abstractions, thoughts, theories, general ideas, sets of practices, hypotheses, linguistic representations, abilities, notions (Margolis & Laurence, 2019). It is not always easy to identify the definitions of 'concept' and 'conceptual' that are being used in a conceptual replication in education, as they may be stated imprecisely or unclearly in the original study and/or the conceptual replication study, risking the two studies operating on the basis of different assumptions, thereby failing to be fair replications.

The term 'concept' is broad and polysemic, and, therefore, it risks being too all-permitting a term. Simpson (2018) illustrates this in the example of the word 'tea' (p. 899), which, in some cultures, denotes a drink of infused leaves whilst in others it is a full early-evening meal. If the original study used the former definition whilst the conceptual replication used the latter, then, even if a result was found, this would constitute an unfair replication, as it would not be comparing like with like.

A 'concept' *qua* theory can be considered to be the signal that rises above, and is an abstraction from, the contextual noise surrounding it (Lucas et al., 2013), that is, it is irrespective of location, setting, or time. However, how far a 'concept' or 'theory' can divest itself of context in social sciences is an ontological and epistemological question (Biesta, 2020; Flyvberg, 2011), discussed below.

Studies in education (original or replication) need clarity in how the terms 'concept' and 'conceptual' are being used (but see Melhuish, 2018); authors use catch-all or general definitions, for example Schmidt (2009) and the National Science Foundation and the Institute of Education Sciences (2018). Whilst Makel and Plucker (2015) comment that conceptual replications test the 'underlying construct' (p. 158) of interest to the researcher, this leaves unexplored and unchallenged what the 'concept' actually is that is being replicated, other than in a general, potentially ambiguous, sense (Morrison, 2019).

Definitions of 'concept' and 'conceptual' raise issues of (a) *ontology*: what exactly is the 'concept', and what is 'conceptual' in the conceptual replication in question (just as we can ask what is the 'what' in the 'what works' agenda); (b) *epistemology*: how we *know* what is the nature of the 'concept' and 'conceptual', and what are the warrants, procedures, and canons of proof in demonstrating that we know what the concept is and what is 'conceptual' in the conceptual replication; and (c) *methodology*: how we investigate the 'concept' and what is 'conceptual' in the conceptual replication, discussed below (Dennis & Valacich, 2014; Earp & Trafimow, 2015; Guba & Lincoln, 1991; Hendrick 1991; Rosenthal, 1991) (see also Chapter 2).

The term 'concept' in a conceptual replication is often a hypothesis or 'theory', or a set of practices (e.g. Melhuish, 2018), though equating a 'theory' or a hypothesis with a 'concept' is contested (Lucas et al., 2013; Margolis & Laurence, 2019). There is a risk of lack of clarity in identifying what, exactly, is the 'what' in 'what works' and when the 'what' constitutes a 'concept' in a conceptual replication. For example, the conceptual replication *qua* hypothesis testing or theory testing might be to test a set of practices, construct, abstraction, representation, idea rather than a concept.

If the conceptual replication is testing a hypothesis or theory, this leaves open what is meant by a 'theory' and a theory of what, what it is and how it can be tested, what warrants underpin it, and how far the original study and the conceptual replication agree on the definitions of 'theory' and the warrants underpinning it. A fair test of the original study needs clarification and agreement on these. Just as with the term 'concept', the term 'theory' is, itself, open to many interpretations (Hammersley, 2014; Kerlinger, 1970; Kettley, 2012; Lucas et al., 2013; Merton, 1967). For example, a theory might be: that which can be tested and falsified, a hypothesis, idea, belief, set of normative principles; a conjecture; a suggestion or proposition; a bundle of internally coherent concepts that form a framework; a set of interrelated constructs or statements that rise above contextual noise and which can explain phenomena; an explanatory framework or an explanation for a single event or set of events; an abstraction, generalised and generalisable statement or set of principles which hold true across different contexts and conditions; that which brings together and specifies a systematic *relationship* between elements or component parts, concepts and constructs; that which *describes* and/or *explains* (tentatively/conjecturally) and/or *predicts*.

Hence, calling a concept a theory, whilst it might suggest something that is, or needs to be, tested in an intervention, does not solve problems of clarity and precision of, and agreement on, definition and what is being tested. Whether one calls a concept a theory, hypothesis, idea, or set of practices in a conceptual replication, the indicators of the concept in the original study and the conceptual replication need precision, detail, transparency, and clarity on what, exactly, is being tested, and certainty of what the indicators are actually indicating (a validity issue).

Ontology and epistemology in conceptual replications

Chapter 2 indicated that a conceptual replication and its original study must make clear their ontological and epistemological foundations, to ensure that these are the same and in order to be testing like with like. For example, if the original study is based on a singular, external, objective reality and existence which can be known and understood through objective measures, or if it operates on the basis of multiple subjective realities, values, and attitudes which can be known and understood only through the situationally specific, subjective views of participants, then these bases must hold fast in the conceptual replication in order to be comparing like with like. If we consider 'reality' to reside in pluralistic constructions of it, as defined by the statements made by participants, that is, to be situationally specific and constructivist (Guba & Lincoln, 1991), then an objectivist approach in a conceptual replication might be out of step with the assumed ontological nature of the phenomenon in the original study. Further, replication in education arguably cannot avoid accepting a realist ontological position.

If the original study's ontological basis is of an objective, absolute reality, then to replicate it in terms of subjective definitions of the situation would be to commit a category error, a paradigm error, incommensurate with the founding ontology, and *vice versa*. The ontology and epistemology of the original study and its conceptual replication must be the same for the replication to be 'fair'.

Detail and precision in the concept, the original study, and the conceptual replication

Considerable precision and detail in original studies and conceptual replication studies are important: what, precisely, is the concept in the original study and the conceptual replication study; what are its key components, tasks, procedures and instructions, methods and instrumentation? Are the indicators that are being used sufficiently precise and accurate to be valid and reliable? For an exact replication, the requirement for precision and accuracy are a *sine qua non*, and this should also apply to a conceptual replication.

A key issue in choosing an original study for replication is the original study's level of precision, transparency, and detail provided, for the conceptual researcher to be clear on what is being replicated, what is being changed, what remains the same, what is being excluded and included and so on. This argues for transparency (Schoenfeld, 2018; What Works Clearinghouse, 2018), to determine whether the concept as set out in the original study is suitable for a conceptual replication study at all (Aguilar, 2020; National Academies of Sciences, Engineering, and Medicine, 2019). Considerable attention should be given to several components in judging whether a conceptual replication study sufficiently addresses the original study for it to be considered a fair replication. These include definition and constitution of the concept, for example: a concept, construct, abstraction, idea, hypothesis, theory, set of practices; the scope of the study; ontology, quiddity, and epistemology; research design, methodology and methods; tasks and procedures; timing and duration; controls; counterfactuals and causality; contexts and settings; precision and accuracy; in short, the many points provided in Chapter 2.

Human and social sciences differ from other sciences. For example: one of the defining features of studies in the natural sciences is their high degree of precision, detail, and accuracy in definition and focus; operationalisation and procedures; conditions and settings; conduct, processes, and instructions to be followed; identification, isolation, and control of variables; identifying which items to hold constant and which to manipulate; what degree, frequency, intensity, duration, timing, and nature of intervention; what metrics and measures to use; what indicators to use and their fitness for purpose (National Academies of Sciences, Engineering, and Medicine, 2019). By contrast, in the social and human sciences, including education, such precision, detail, and accuracy of these elements in the original study and the conceptual replication study may not be present, possible, or even desirable, and educational research may be more of a hermeneutic activity, concerning understanding rather than 'proof' (Biesta, 2020; Flyvberg, 2011). However, too much imprecision and variance in the original study and its conceptual replication affect the trustworthiness of the findings of the conceptual replication and the conclusions that are drawn from it.

In undertaking the conceptual replication, one or more features of the original study can be altered, provided that the 'concept' remains the same. As Chapter 2 indicated, teachers rarely, if ever, take an intervention and use it in its original form; rather, they adjust it to their own circumstances and situations, conditions and contingencies. This raises the question of what constitutes a fair conceptual replication. For instance, where are the controls in the intervention between the original and the replication study, for example: the teacher's personality and behaviour; student characteristics, motivation, and engagement; the conduct and tasks of the intervention (frequency, nature, intensity, duration); the presence or absence of factors; the time of year and day; the weather? All of these might feature differently in the original and replication studies and affect the findings. What differences between the original study and its conceptual replication can be tolerated before the conceptual replication becomes an unfair conceptual replication of the original study?

Teachers involved in a replication study are unlikely to adhere identically to instructions for the replication, its contents (e.g. their amount, frequency, and quality), pedagogy, intensity, duration, teacher behaviour and reactions, sequence, timing. The teacher modifies the intervention in response to the classroom situation that obtains at a particular time, including student characteristics singly and in combination, class management, student motivation, curricular demands, differences in students' abilities and interests, and causal factors operating in the class (Morrison, 2019, 2021). How far such modifications threaten a replication study's requirement of fidelity to the procedures of the original study raises the question of at what point the replication study becomes, in effect, a different study, an unfair conceptual replication.

How much modification to the intentions and contents and procedures of the replication study can be tolerated before fidelity to the original study is undermined? How can the researcher judge how far fidelity to the intended procedures is sufficient, optimal, or under-addressed? The easy answer is that the components of the original study as set out in Table 3.1 can be adjusted in the conceptual replication, and that this is a fairer test of the conceptual replication than would be the case if those features were the same (i.e. incapable of separating the signal from the noise). However, this raises the question of how much the 'concept', context (however defined), and causality are symbiotically, inextricably interlinked in the original study and the conceptual replication. In short, how far is the conceptual replication, like its original study, a function of bundling together context, causality, and 'concept' and seeing how they fare in the conceptual replication? The 'success' of the 'concept' may turn out to be a composite of several factors, not simply the 'concept' alone.

Many original studies in education would benefit from greater precision transparency and detail, for example in the instructions for the conduct of the intervention (Morrison, 2021), as, without these, it may be unclear how close to the original study its conceptual replication actually is. If such details are lacking, then conceptual replication researchers might try to contact the author(s) of the original study in order to address fidelity in the replication (Brown & Wood, 2019; National Science Foundation and the Institute of Education Sciences, 2018). If detail, precision, and accuracy are understated or lack transparency in the planning, conduct, and reporting of the original study and the conceptual replication, then it is unclear what can be drawn with certainty from the studies, even if the findings of the conceptual replication confirm or refute the original study. The National Science Foundation and Institute of Education Sciences (2018) requires statements of procedures in replication studies; however, the level of specificity required is not stated, nor are the criteria for judging what similarity there must be in the conceptual replication's findings. The original study and its conceptual replication must decide, disclose, and justify these.

The conceptual replication researcher must be sure that she has described the concept precisely, clearly, and in sufficient detail, for agreement to be certain on its consistent use and meaning in both the original study and the conceptual replication, and for construct validity to be assured. In short, the definitions of a 'concept' and 'conceptual replication' should be the same in the original study and its conceptual replication.

Pre-registering a conceptual replication can request judgements from peer reviewers with regard to what counts as sufficient similarity. As indicated in Chapter 2, there are boundary conditions in a conceptual replication with regard to similarity and changes that it makes to the original study. These include the need to keep constant between the two studies their interpretation and applications of terms such as 'concept' and 'conceptual' (e.g. Melhuish & Thanheiser, 2018), the scope of the two studies, and their ontological and epistemological bases. As discussed later in this chapter, questions are raised of how close must be the similarity between the causalities and counterfactuals at work in the two studies and of the significance of contexts and settings in determining the prospective results.

Coyne et al. (2016) suggest that a conceptual replication study must indicate how important, theoretically speaking, are changes made between the original study and its conceptual replication, and where they lie, for example in the context, conditions, independent and/or the dependent variables. Writing on special education, they identify six main areas in which constants or deliberately varied 'dimensions' from the original study can be considered (p. 248): 'participants', 'settings', 'intervention' (the independent variable), 'outcome measures' (the dependent variable), 'research design', and 'analyses'. These purport to keep the original concept undisturbed. However, as is argued later in this chapter, if the conceptual replication changes one or more of these, this can affect the entire conceptual replication and what is found from it. The effect of this can be profound, such that, if similar or different results are found between the original study and the conceptual replication, it may be unclear what these indicate, what they say about the original study, and how far the conceptual replication has confirmed the findings of the original study, or, indeed, if it is impossible to say ('indeterminate' findings). Whether making such changes affects the validity of the original concept is a moot point.

Conceptual replications can consider changing one variable at a time (Makel & Plucker, 2015), thereby enabling the researcher to suggest how much such-and-such a single change has contributed to a change in the findings between the original study and its conceptual replication. This would require several conceptual replications to be conducted, changing, each time, for example: the sample, context and setting, conditions, instrumentation, procedures, methodology, instrumentation, controls, to see which makes a difference to the result in comparison to the original study. As Chapter 2 argued, this must exclude changes to the ontological and epistemological bases of the original, as these are founding elements and constituents of a fair test, discussed later in this chapter, without which the conceptual replication study is akin to comparing oil and water.

The limits of a conceptual replication

Conceptual replication elides replication with applicability and generalisability. In doing this, it risks overlooking key issues of testing the construct validity and reliability of the original concept. Further, changing one or more conditions of the original study render the conceptual replication incapable of falsifying the original study's findings; indeed, as argued later in this chapter, they might only trivially verify the findings of the original study. Conceptual replications replace internal validation with external generalisability, leaving untouched the question of how far the findings of the original study are valid, safe, trustworthy, and reliable. This renders a conceptual replication as being a limited, somewhat impoverished interpretation of 'replication'. By overlooking internal validation of the original study's findings, a conceptual replication is only, in fact, a partial replication, even if, nevertheless, it is useful.

Whereas exact replications can support internal validity by repeating the study under as many of the original conditions, contents, and procedures as possible, conceptual replications change these, and, hence, can support only external validity *qua* applicability and generalisability (recognising, of course, that theory can derive from observations of applications in different contexts). Conceptual replications accept as 'givens' or 'assumed' the construct-, content-, and criterion-related validity of the original concept (Lucas et al., 2013). This avoids the interrogation and validation of the original study. However, as Yong (2012) remarks, there is a need to conduct as close a replication as possible before a valid conceptual replication can be assured, and this may not be possible in education. Without this, a conceptual replication cannot guarantee the reliability and validity of the original study, the original concept, and the replication. Rather, all that the conceptual replication study can aver is how far a particular intervention 'works' in contexts, settings, and conditions that differ from those in the original study (Morrison, 2019); indeed, as discussed below, even this is open to question. Whilst it is unworthy to criticise a conceptual replication for not doing something that it is not designed to do, nevertheless it is important to see what a conceptual replication can and cannot do.

Conceptual replication studies test the *application* of a *given* concept, idea, theory, hypothesis, set of practices, intervention, findings under circumstances and conditions that differ from those in the original study. To test the veracity or validity of a concept *qua* hypothesis or theory, a theory should be tested in circumstances that differ from those that gave rise to it. However, a conceptual replication does not do justice to this; rather it is more a test of the concept's applicability, generalisability and scalability than of its veracity or validity. Further, it might not be possible or desirable to rule out, isolate, and control the number and range of factors and variables – contextual, causal, mediating, moderating, exogenous, and endogenous – that are present in the original study and the conceptual replication (and which might differ in each), even in the face of the claim that, for example, a randomised controlled trial can attenuate this problem through random selection and random allocation (Morrison, 2021). The issue here, indeed the quandary for education, is that, if the original concept is not tested in an exact as possible replication, then it is unclear how, and if, its veracity and validity can stand, but a conceptual replication, because of its very nature, is unable to secure this. A conceptual replication is light on, and differs from, being a validation study.

The findings and theories of a study are conjectural, provisional, tentative, subject to change, and the best that we know at a particular point in time; the veracity/validity of a theory is not absolute but is open to change as knowledge advances and earlier ideas and theories are replaced. Here, conjecture and refutation, falsifiability, hypothesis generation and testing are intrinsic to science (Popper, 1962); that is what makes a science a science. Education's appeal to being a science, that is, where it does appeal to being a science at all (and, indeed, such an appeal is contested, see Biesta, 2020, and Flyvberg, 2011), is called into question in conceptual replications in education, as how far it can and should meet such requirements and constituents of a science is questionable. Conceptual replications simply concern the *applicability* of a given concept which is neither interrogated nor is required to be. The ability of a conceptual replication to verify or falsify a concept or theory is limited. It leaves the status of the concept itself largely unquestioned, whilst focusing, instead, on how far it 'works' elsewhere. Again, this is not to criticise a conceptual replication for not doing something that it was not designed to do; rather, this is to indicate what it can and cannot do.

Changing one or more conditions of the original study renders the conceptual replication incapable of falsifying the original study's findings; indeed, they might only trivially verify the findings of the original study. Conceptual replications cannot safely falsify the original study because they have changed key variables and factors; the original study might still be 'true', even if the conceptual replication study finds different results. If the findings of the conceptual replication differ from those of the original study, this does not necessarily invalidate, call into question, or falsify the concept, as the validity of the concept is not being tested, only its *application* in a different setting, that is, how far something whose similarity to an original study may or may not be strong, has 'worked' elsewhere (Coyne et al., 2016).

A conceptual replication cannot *falsify* with any certainty a concept that might have been 'proved' in the original study, because, having made one or more changes to the original study in the conceptual replication study, there may be one or more explanations or causes of a failure to replicate or, indeed, to be successful, and for different results from the original study to be found in the conceptual replication study. We might not know what has caused the findings of the conceptual replication to be what they are. To ascertain how far a conceptual replication succeeds or fails in replicating the original study, both the conceptual replication and the original study must be examined, to determine possible reasons for this (National Academies of Sciences, Engineering, and Medicine, 2019).

A conceptual replication muddies the waters in differing from the original study (Makel & Plucker, 2015; Yong, 2012); whilst it might be able to confirm the findings of the original study, it might not be able to falsify the original study. Further, the conceptual researcher has difficulty in understanding why or how far the conceptual replication did or did not 'work': what caused the results. Yong (2012) notes that conceptual replications permit weak findings to support the original study, and, in so doing, they risk confirmation bias. A conceptual replication study might confirm the findings of the original study, but for reasons and causes which are opaque, because there are many possible causes, different variables present, and because it has changed, for example removed, altered, and/or added variables. How far this constitutes a problem for a conceptual replication which largely, or, indeed, only, seeks to discover how far a concept 'works' in a new setting, is an open question.

The problem here is in knowing how far the conceptual replication has really confirmed, partially confirmed, or disconfirmed the concept, hypothesis, idea, theory, or set of practices from the original study, or, indeed, whether the results are 'indeterminate', that is, we cannot be sure whether they confirm or disconfirm the original study. As Morrison (2019) writes:

> The What Works Clearinghouse (2018) notes that there is no consensus on how to judge whether a replication really is a replication, and what and whose criteria to use in judging this, though it offers its own reporting guidelines, e.g.: variations from the original study; transparency of procedures; objectivity; detail to be reported; sample; context; fidelity of implementation; budgets; data sharing; data analysis etc.
>
> (p. 420)

At issue here is the point that, if replication is limited to generalisability and applicability to other contexts, then this neglects the validation of the concept in question, however it is framed (e.g. a concept, hypothesis, idea, theory, or a set of practices). For this task, an exact or close replication is needed (Brandt et al., 2014). In turn, this raises the question of whether the conceptual replication should have the same controls and counterfactuals as those in the original study, and whether, given the significant causal role of contexts and conditions in an original study and its conceptual replication, this is possible. Counterfactuals and controls in the conceptual replication are likely to differ from those in the original study, and this affects causality in the conceptual replication. It is to this that the chapter turns.

Context and causality

In a conceptual replication, the concept comes out of one context – that of the original study – and it is tested to see how well and where it 'works' in a different context (though it is unclear what are the cut-off points and criteria for judging these, and the replication study should set and disclose these). 'What works' in one situation, setting, or set of conditions may not 'work' in another. Context can exert a major influence on how much the concept 'works', fails to 'work', or is indeterminate (Cai et al., 2018; Gelman, 2018; Irvine, 2021; Lucas et al., 2013; Morrison, 2021). This raises the question of what, actually, is being replicated in a conceptual replication study and what the replication is testing. The simple answer might be that it is testing how much and where the concept, however defined, 'works', or whether the result is indeterminate. However, the matter is much more complex and causally complex than this. As Hao (2015) remarks, the scarcity of replications in educational research may be due to their complexity, as differences between participants, settings, pedagogy, and other factors contribute to rendering replication difficult.

The relative failure of many social science replications to replicate successfully (e.g. Coyne et al., 2016; Open Science Collaboration, 2015) suggests that research in education, rather than trying to control out or override contextual features, should take serious account of including them. What happens in classrooms is context-specific, contingent, context-dense, interaction-rich, variable-dense, causally dense, dynamical, evolutionary, emergent and changing, non-static, time-bound, situationally specific (as evidenced in thickly descriptive accounts and case studies), with generalisability being transferability as determined by the readers and users of the research in their own contexts (Cohen et al., 2018; Morrison, 2021). This questions Silver's (2012) comment that 'truth' resides in the signal, whilst the noise is that which distracts us from the 'truth' (p. 17); rather, the noise might be the signal, and the truth does not possess the singular, somewhat antiseptic conception that Silver suggests. How much the conceptual replication 'works' or does not 'work' in a different context could be because both the concept itself *and* the role of context and conditions contribute to making it 'work' or not 'work' respectively.

Conceptual replications might strive to embrace this complexity by simply attenuating it (e.g. in randomised controlled trials), but, in doing so, this raises challenges in deciding what has caused a conceptual replication to find similar or different results from those of the original study. Further, it is too glib an answer to state that conceptual replications are not concerned with detailed factors and causes, being concerned only with whether a concept can 'work' in a different setting, as this offers little help to the teacher who is considering whether to try out a practice that has been found to 'work' in a conceptual replication. That teacher wants to know *why* something did or did not 'work'.

The issue of causality is difficult in a conceptual replication, as, indeed, it is in the original study and educational research more widely (Morrison, 2009, 2021): what has caused the findings to be what they are; what has caused the findings of the conceptual replication study to be similar to, or different from, those of the original study. Indeed, the question can be raised of how far a replication study must replicate causality/causalities. On the one hand, proponents of a conceptual replication might contend that causality does not matter so long as something 'works' in a different context and in different conditions, which is the whole purpose of the conceptual replication. On the other hand, neglecting issues of causality impedes the understanding of why a concept has, has not, or has only partially 'worked' in a conceptual replication.

The causalities at work in the context-dense, variable-rich, highly contingent world of education (Morrison, 2021), in both the original study and the conceptual replication, frustrate attempts to understand why an intervention 'works' or does not 'work' (Cartwright & Hardie, 2012). The findings of a conceptual replication study might tell us very little of use if we do not know why (even though the conceptual replication might not be concerned with *why* but only with *how much* something 'works' or does not 'work', i.e. with *applying* a concept rather than unpicking causes). The findings of a conceptual replication study are of limited utility if the causes of success, partial success, indetermination, or failure to generalise are not explored.

Cartwright and Hardie (2012) and Deaton and Cartwright (2018) report that an intervention that 'worked' in one context (i.e. the original study) failed to 'work' in a different context (i.e. the conceptual replication), even though the content of the intervention (the concept) was the same. This was because the context of the conceptual replication caused the outcome – the failure. The concept remained intact but simply did not 'work' in a different context because of the causal factors operating in the conceptual replication study's context. They comment that an intervention (the concept) may not travel well from one context to another because of causal differences operating in the new context. A conceptual replication might not be concerned with this, being concerned only with the applicability and/or generalisability of the original concept, regardless of context, but this is a limited, impoverished view of replication.

The significance of causality cannot be understated, and conceptual replications may not be adept in addressing this. If we are to understand, explain, and use the findings of the original study and the conceptual replication, how they 'work', and the extent of their applicability and generalisability, then we need to understand the causal factors operating; teachers want to know the likelihood of something 'working' in their context, and this involves examining the causal conditions at work.

For example, let us say that the original study tested the hypothesis (the 'concept') that teaching about desertification through first-hand video narrative accounts of the effects of desertification improved students' understanding of desertification more than that of students who relied on textbooks. The original study comprised a randomised controlled trial with 200 14-year-old students in eight elite, selective-entry schools in a city, using a cluster trial of four schools as the control group and four as the intervention group. The findings of this original study, based on a written test on desertification, showed that the results of students using first-hand narrative accounts were higher than those of students using textbooks. Then the conceptual replication was conducted with 200 18-year-olds in four post-school colleges in an inner city, using a different, mixed-methods research design: a quasi-experiment with under-performing students, with two colleges in the control group and two in the intervention group, using convenience sampling and three case studies. The findings of the conceptual replication were very similar to those of the original study.

The researcher can ask how far this confirms the original hypothesis – the 'concept', the theory, idea, set of practices – and how much the results of the conceptual replication 'prove' the generalisability of the original study. Here, the answer is 'very trivially' or 'weakly', if at all, since the causal factors at work have changed considerably between the two studies. For example: the students in the conceptual replication studied desertification through a wide range of media, of which narrative accounts were but a tiny element; the students had an enthusiastic and inspiring teacher; the study lasted for longer and with more time given to the topic each week; the assessment contributed to the high-stakes college graduation project; the students worked in small groups, and each group created a multi-media project about desertification, which was reported in the local media. They arranged online interviews with national and international parties who were working to combat desertification, and they assembled a vast array of data and multi-media information.

If the findings of the conceptual replication study confirm those of the original study, what can we infer from this, given that the instruments, the sample, the methods, the procedures and instructions, and so on were different? The concept, set in the contexts and conditions of the conceptual replication, contained a wide range of possible causes, any of which might have brought about the results, suggesting that the 'concept' itself was not being tested much, if at all. The concept might have been comparatively minor or incidental in contributing to the confirmation of the findings in the conceptual replication, and the findings were over-determined by other factors obtaining in the conceptual replication or, indeed, both studies.

In the conceptual replication study, the concept under-determined the results; the results derived from many causes and were over-determined by many other factors. The mixed-methods research, including interviews with the participants, found the results to be a result of their motivation and their engagement, the high-stakes assessment, the opportunity to work online and to engage international people experiencing desertification directly, and multi-media exposure to the event. The use of first-hand video narrative accounts was comparatively trivial for the students; it was only one factor in a multi-factorial causal setting. The conceptual replication found similar performance results to those of the original study, but the absence of controls in the conceptual replication and the presence of a substantial number and type of confounding factors obscure the causality at work, to the extent that the findings of the conceptual replication were of little use. The findings of the conceptual replication could neither falsify the original hypothesis nor verify and confirm it other than trivially. All that the conceptual replication could do was to indicate the *presence* of the concept in the conceptual replication study, and not its significance. Neglecting the interrogation of causality meant that teachers, for example, would not know how far the original concept 'worked' or did not 'work' with sufficient certainly for them to do it themselves; it was literally useless.

If the conceptual replication study obtains similar or dissimilar results from the original study, it is unclear what can be inferred from this, given that the instruments, the sample, the methods, and so on are different in the conceptual replication. We can neither falsify nor do more than minimally confirm the findings of the original study, and what the conceptual replication can offer is of limited practical use, as many factors might have caused the conceptual replication to confirm the findings of the original study. A conceptual replication that confines itself to seeking applicability, generalisability, and scalability often gives rise to more problems than solutions; it does not tell us important matters such as what has caused something to 'work' or not to 'work'.

Let us take the issue further. Imagine that, in the previous example, the conceptual replication failed to confirm the findings of the original study, and that the results of the college students were considerably worse than those in the original study. Does this refute the generalisability of the original concept? Not necessarily, as the concept was still present, but the presence of many confounding, inhibiting factors and conditions led to the poor results of the college students. It was not that the conceptual replication failed to generalise the concept from the original study; it was that the original study's concept was present but lost in a sea of other factors and their causal powers; the original concept was present, but trivially so. This suggests that the conceptual replication researcher should specify the cut-off points and criteria for judging how far, and where, a concept has or has not 'worked' in the conceptual replication, and what to include and exclude in coming to a judgement on this.

If the findings of the conceptual replication study did not confirm those of the original study, this does not invalidate the concept; rather, it indicates that, given the contexts, setting, contingencies, conditions, and other causal factors at work in the conceptual replication, the concept was or was not found. As with the conceptual replication which did confirm the original study, what can be inferred from this is limited and unclear, given that the instruments, the sample, the methods, the tasks, and so on differed from those of the original study. The 'concept' might have been present but was not found because it had been swamped by other factors present in the situation, that is, as suggested earlier, the noise was the signal, the message. The presence of the concept was under-determined because of the presence of other factors, even though the concept remained intact. Presence alone does not necessarily imply generalisability or applicability; nor does it indicate utility.

In the event of non-confirmation of findings from the original study, the conceptual study researcher is advised to study causality and the significance of context; as Kim (2019) remarks, there is a lot that can be learnt from non-replication. Indeed, Block and Kuckertz (2018) note that non-significant results, or replications that do not confirm the original study, can be important in furthering the development of theory, and authors should strive to explain finding that deviate from those of the original study. The conceptual replication researcher can learn a lot from a study that has failed to confirm a hypothesis or concept (and this can apply to both the original study and the conceptual replication study), yet it is currently difficult to find evidence of this currently happening in education (but see Hedges & Schauer, 2019). An original study that finds no positive result might still benefit from a conceptual replication (Slavin, 2018, notes that failure to replicate might be due to a weakly devised original study, not necessarily the concept in question).

An intervention in the original study might 'work' because of the force of the teacher's personality or the willingness of the students to make it work, whereas in the conceptual replication study, it might not work for the very same reason, that is, the 'concept' is not being tested in a conceptual replication, only its application; this is both the claimed strength and yet the weakness/limitation of a conceptual replication. Whilst the replication researcher might say that similar results have been found despite differences in context and conditions, and that this is a useful test of a conceptual replication, extending applicability and generalisability, the researcher does not know which variables, factors, conditions, and so on contributed to an outcome; hence, the research might have limited utility.

A conceptual replication study is a well-intentioned but somewhat limited animal. It tells us only how far something – which may lack clarity of definition – 'works', does not 'work', or is indeterminate, in a different setting with different factors present. Its contents and findings leave us uncertain of what they are an indicator, and the conceptual study researcher works with a phenomenon and with findings whose validity is unclear, untested, and unproven, simply being accepted as a given. This raises the question of how useful it is to say that, regardless of such-and-such a set of causal factors or contexts, settings, conditions, contingencies, and circumstances, something does or does not 'work', only partially 'works', or is indeterminate. A conceptual replication study can neither falsify nor explain how much something does or does not 'work' in the original study or its conceptual replication. A failure to replicate findings from the original study does not necessarily mean that the original findings were wrong or false (Makel & Plucker, 2015). A conceptual replication, therefore, appears to have serious limits on what it can tell us, only that something 'worked', did not 'work', partially 'worked', or is indeterminate, but not why, and, indeed, it is maybe unclear what that 'something' is. In these respects, a conceptual replication, whilst it offers some potential benefit, faces several challenges and has a bounded usefulness for education and teachers. Whether a finding applies to yet another setting is something upon which it cannot comment; a further conceptual replication is needed.

Some key concerns in conceptual replication, then, are:

- Replications cannot falsify the original study.
- Replications might be able to verify the original study, but weakly, often trivially and/or uncertainly.
- The elision of replication with applicability and generalisability overlooks construct validity and reliability.
- A conceptual replication does not test the validity of the original study, its 'construct', 'concept', idea, sets of practice, theory, only its generalisability and applicability.
- A conceptual replication is an impoverished, one-sided view of replication.
- Replications are affected by causal and contextual conditions, and the effects and significance of these are unclear.
- The original study's findings might be intact and correct in their own contexts and conditions but not necessarily in the conceptual replication.

These points suggest that there is a need to identify some constituents of a fair test for a conceptual replication, and these are set out below.

Ensuring a 'fair' conceptual replication

A fair conceptual replication study must ensure sameness between the original study and the conceptual replication study in terms of what is meant by 'concept' and 'conceptual'. However, sameness does not end there. If a conceptual replication is to be fair, then robust and transparent limits should be placed on what a conceptual replication can change from the original study (Morrison, 2019), what it must not change, what new variables can be included, and what variables from the original study can be excluded. Any changes made between the original study and the conceptual replication study must be made clear and justified, indicating how the conceptual replication still retains sufficient conceptual likeness to the original study for it to be considered a fair test of replication.

The National Science Foundation and the Institute of Education Sciences (2018) indicates that changes can be made to the population and sample, components of the intervention and its implementation, outcome measures, and data analytic approaches. However, these are given only as examples, and no limits are set on what can and cannot change. Whilst Porte (2012) indicates that nonmajor changes can be made, Chapter 2 noted that clarity was lacking on what these might and might not include. This rehearses the issue introduced in Chapter 2: at what point does a conceptual replication cease to be a fair replication of the original study, because it has changed many or important components of the original study?

Chapter 2 indicated that sameness must apply to the ontological and epistemological bases of the two studies, leaving open the question of whether changes could be made to the methodology (Chapter 4 addresses changes to methodology). Here, the discussion concerns how far a conceptual replication is a fair test of the original study if it changes different elements of the methods, for example of research design, sampling, tasks, instrumentation, tasks, procedures, data collection, data analysis.

How much variance and changes in methods from the original study is tolerable in a conceptual replication is an open question, as making changes to these can influence how far the outcomes of the replication study confirm, refute, qualify, partially confirm, and so on the findings of the original study, or even render the replication a different study altogether from the original study, even if the claim is made that the 'concept' is independent of the context in which it was originally located, or, indeed, in the conceptual replication. Whether and what a researcher decides to change from the original study must be disclosed fully, clearly, and justified, and, as indicated in Chapter 2, these raise several questions for the researcher to address, for example:

- What are the implications and effects of making changes, on what can be taken from the conceptual replication, both *per se* and with regard to the original study?
- What threats do the changes make to the fairness of the replication study, and how are these addressed?
- What steps are taken to minimise and mitigate the threats to fairness of the conceptual replication and to maximise its fairness?
- What criteria are being used to judge fairness in the conceptual replication, and how and where are these being applied?

Let us say that the researcher changes the sample and/or the setting from that of the original study. The researcher has created a new study. This raises the question of whether this new study, itself, needs to be replicated. Or let us say that the researcher changes the instruments for data collection; this constitutes a new study and, therefore, it, too, should be replicated in order to validate it. At issue here is whether, if a researcher changes one item from the original study, then this new study itself needs a replication. Each time we change a variable, it creates a new study which, in turn, should be replicated. Clearly this can easily lead to the researcher having to conduct many replication studies; it is a runaway problem (see also Hedges and Schauer, 2019, on the need for more than one replication).

Further, changes to methods can affect the results of the conceptual replication. This defines the possible 'success' of the conceptual replication narrowly, in terms of an outcome: how far the intervention has 'worked', for example whether the intervention, intended improvements to practice, achievement, performance, and so on have materialised. But, for example, Simpson (2018, 2019, 2020) demonstrates that in a randomised controlled trial, the sampling, measures, instruments, and study design influence the results: the effect size calculated. Effect size, he shows, is a product of the whole research, not simply of the calculations of the outcome data. Hence, change one or more items between the original study and the conceptual replication, and it is hardly surprising if the findings of the conceptual replication differ from those of the original study. Or, indeed, if the results of the conceptual replication are the same as those of the original study, what caused this? Was it the power of the concept or the changes in parts of the methods? We cannot be sure, and, as discussed earlier, attributing causality is a challenge in a conceptual replication.

Does changing one or more items concerning 'methods' contaminate and/or compromise the fairness of the conceptual replication, that is, fail to compare like with like in terms of the 'concept', or, given that the conceptual replication is only a test of the 'concept', to what extent is this a non-problem? The conceptual replication study researcher has to answer and justify the answer to this challenging question.

Coyne et al. (2016) note that a conceptual replication in special education could change (or, indeed, keep constant) one or more of the following: research design, sample and population, components of the interventions, setting, outcome measures, and data analyses. Chhin et al. (2018) note that, with regard to Special Education Research Grants for conceptual replications in the United States, of the 107 studies that they reviewed, 48 per cent varied one or more components of the interventions, 54 per cent varied the context, 58 per cent varied the methods; 30 per cent varied the outcomes, and 67 per cent varied one or more dimension of the original study. Should we be alarmed by this, as constituting unfair replications? Do we celebrate it as an attempt at extended applicability and generalisability? Do we accept that the benefits of testing the applicability and generalisability of the concept trump the need for a close or exact replication of the features of the original study? Has fairness been compromised? It is for the conceptual replication researcher to make and defend the case.

If a conceptual replication permits changes to the original study, then, whilst it might address generalisability of application, this enables almost any kind of study to be termed a replication as long as it tests the same 'concept'. As mentioned in Chapter 2, this declares 'open season' on any kind of study to become a conceptual replication. Indeed, Lucas et al. (2013) argue that adopting such a broad embrace of a conceptual replication study means that not only are many conceptual replications not called this by their authors, but also they are more common than is often believed to be the case. This raises the concern that conceptual replications, thus construed, are too permissive, insufficiently demanding in terms of what a replication study should comprise and the rigour with which it should be conducted.

How far changes to research design, methods, and instrumentation for data collection are acceptable is an open question. For instrumentation, since the instrument often frames the results (Cohen et al., 2018), it raises the question of the extent to which a different instrument but of the same type, for example different versions of a test or varying the number of items in a test (Simpson, 2018) or of a different type altogether (e.g. changing from a written test to an interview or an observation) can avoid finding different results. Further, is a 'successful' replication that which finds the same results as the original study (see Slavin, 2018)? It is for the conceptual replication study researcher to make and justify the case.

To be a fully-fledged *replication*, rather than an *application*, conceptual replications should constitute a fair test of the original study, and they can be considered fair only if key matters and components such as those set out in the preceding discussion are not only clarified but also conform sufficiently to those of the original study. However, as this discussion has indicated, the criteria and boundaries of 'conforming' are currently unclear. This argues for greater transparency and justification of making changes to the original study, together with greater definition and justification of the meaning of 'fair', and how 'fairness' is operationalised, applied, and ensured in the conceptual replication study.

For a conceptual replication to be fair:

- the ontological and epistemological bases, quiddity, and falsifiability of the 'concept' in the original study and the conceptual replication should be the same, comparing like with like, as to change these is to change the nature of the 'concept' in question (Jacobson & Simpson, 2019; Stanley & Spence, 2014). In turn, this requires the original and the replication study to make clear their ontological and epistemological foundations and pedigree;
- the original study and its conceptual replication should not differ with regard to their definition, interpretation, and applications of the terms 'concept', 'conceptual', and 'theory';
- both studies should have sufficient detail, precision and accuracy for comparisons to be made on similarity and difference;
- the conceptual replication should indicate and justify what it holds constant, or is closely or distantly aligned to in the original study, on what it differs and why, and why and how significant theoretically, ontologically, and epistemologically such differences are;
- the conceptual replication should indicate and justify what controls and counterfactuals are present or absent (Bienefeld et al., 2020), what must be held constant or similar to the original study, and what is justifiably different from the original study in the conceptual replication;
- on a statistical note, for precision in a quantitative original study and its conceptual replication, the effect sizes, distributions, kurtosis, skewness, confidence intervals, and range should be similar (however stipulated), and the conceptual replication should have high statistical power. Confidence intervals should be kept narrow (e.g. 95 per cent), error margins should be small, and the conceptual replication study should have high statistical power (e.g. 0.80) that can come from a large sample, the p-values (if one holds with the [contested] use of null hypothesis significance testing) and effect sizes should be pre-set (Hedges & Schauer, 2019; Morrison, 2019; National Academies of Sciences, Engineering, and Medicine, 2019). Gorard and Gorard (2016) suggest that the number of counterfactual cases needed to disturb a finding should be calculated. Holme (2019) notes that comparing results of the original study and its conceptual replication must account for how close the

results are ('proximity') and how certain are the results ('measurement variability', p. 2359). These are discussed further in Chapter 6;
- transparency and disclosure are key requirements (on how far the context, setting, procedures, tasks, causalities, conditions, contingencies, research design and implementation, controls, and so on at work in the original study and the conceptual replication contribute to its outcomes), so that the reader can judge how fair a replication the conceptual replication really is;
- how far the 'concept' is a strong or weak feature of the original study and the conceptual replication, under-determined or over-determined by contextual factors, contingencies, and causalities operating in the studies;
- the conceptual replication should make clear what it does and does not, and can and cannot, demonstrate and what the findings show with regard to extended applicability and generalisability, that is, its boundaries;
- the criteria and grounds for judging the 'success' of the original study and the conceptual replication should be stated, similar, and, in some replications, even identical;
- the conceptual replication should justify the validity of the indicators of the 'concept' being used, indicating their closeness to those of the original study.

Whilst these can be requirements of a fair test, there remains the need for greater guidance on making *judgements* of fairness, as there are no absolutes here. At the time of writing, there is limited guidance and no regulatory authority with regard to the 'cut-off' points for judging how far the conceptual replication is a fair test, how far and where its findings confirm or do not confirm those of the original study, and how far the conceptual replication stays within the limits of what it can and cannot claim to show. The replication researcher must address this task.

Conclusion

This chapter has suggested that a conceptual replication should provide clarity, detail, transparency, and precision in terms of definitions and components of the concept, contents, and procedures of the replication, tasks in the intervention, and in what respects they are similar to, and different from, the original study and what can safely be taken from them. Levels of detail, transparency, and precision also affect choosing the original study that is to be conceptually replicated.

Conceptual replications differ in contents and purpose from exact replications, but this does not obviate the need for exact replications, or, given that exact replication – reproducibility – is impossible in education and the social sciences, a sufficiently close replication. The chapter has argued that there are limits on what can be taken from a conceptual replication in terms of validation. Conceptual replications say little about construct validity and reliability; the limits to their power of validation and verification are, in part, consequences of the elision of replication with generalisability and applicability. Alongside this, they bundle together concept, context, and causality, such that it is difficult to determine what, exactly, a conceptual replication shows. Conceptual replications are unable to falsify an original study and they can only trivially verify or validate the findings of an original study.

A 'fair' conceptual replication is important but problematic. The chapter indicated components of fairness. Conceptual replications make changes to the original study, and the chapter identified constituents of, and threats to, a fair conceptual replication, difficulties in ensuring fairness arising from issues of sameness, and how to address these. It indicated components of the original study that should be kept the same in the conceptual replication study (their ontological and epistemological bases), and it identified consequences of making changes between the original study and the conceptual replication. Conceptual replications must make the case for any changes made to the original study and demonstrate that such changes do not interfere with the concept in question and its significance. They must demonstrate that the findings, however much they confirm, fail to confirm, or are indeterminate with regard to the original study, are not artifacts of the methods used in the conceptual replication. In other words, researchers must ensure that it is not the tail of the research design, methodology, and conduct itself, or, indeed of matters of context, settings and causality, that is wagging the dog of the concept.

The chapter indicated the significance of context and causality in a conceptual replication study and what could be taken from it in comparing its findings to those of the original study. In doing this, it raised issues of under-determination and over-determination of the findings of a conceptual replication. In turn, this suggested that there are limitations on what can and cannot be drawn from the findings of a conceptual replication study and how useful they can be for teachers. Yes, they can tell us whether the concept in setting A can 'work' in setting B, but not why and how, and not beyond contexts A or B. Hence the chapter has argued for exercising realism in deciding what can be taken from a conceptual replication, what it really tells us, and how useful its findings are for other settings and/or teachers. A conceptual replication which concerns applicability, generalisability and scalability has many limitations.

Conceptual replications, carefully planned and conducted, can contribute to educational research, but that contribution is quite limited because of limits on what they can and cannot do and what they can and cannot tell us. This is a matter that is not confined to conceptual replications alone but more widely to the heavily contextual, agentic, reflexive, recursive world of education as an open, uneasily predictable, dynamic, and emergent system within which researchers in education operate.

4 Quantitative and qualitative replications in education

Overview

This short chapter discusses how far a replication study can vary the methodology of the original study and its paradigm basis, in addressing the issue of sameness between the two studies. It argues that, whilst exact replications prevent this, how far this can apply to approximate and conceptual replications is more open. Accepting that replication is intrinsically never identical, the chapter addresses two questions: (a) how far an original study which has been rooted in one paradigm can be replicated in a study that is rooted in a different paradigm; and (b) how far an original study which is qualitative can be replicated in another qualitative study. In addressing these, the chapter sets out two paradigms – quantitative and qualitative – and, whilst each of these embraces a wide range of study types, argues that:

- in meeting the demands of fair comparison, fidelity to the paradigm base of the original study must be maintained in the replication study;
- a conceptual replication is more akin to an extension, enrichment, and application study than to a fuller replication study;
- claims made in qualitative research for the uniqueness, context-rich, variable-dense, uncontrollability of variables in each study of education call into question how far replication is possible and meaningful;
- claims made in qualitative research for the uniqueness of each study do not preclude using qualitative studies in replication research, but this raises challenges in indicating how far the replication has 'worked';
- deciding how far a replication study has been successful is a matter of degree and judgement 'beyond a reasonable doubt', and these call for detail, disclosure, and transparency in criteria, indicators, trustworthy evidence, and judgements of the original study and the replication study.

Whilst there is no absolute and single standard for deciding (a) whether sameness is sufficient between the original study and the replication study, and (b) how far the replication study has confirmed the findings of the original study, the chapter argues that replication, as a matter of degree, requires replication researchers to identify and justify their judgements on what the replication study shows.

DOI: 10.4324/9781003204237-5

In discussing qualitative research, the chapter limits itself to case studies of an intervention. It indicates that, even this one type of qualitative research usefully illustrates issues found in other types of qualitative research, as the nature, definition, and scope of a case study are broad.

Two questions on methodology

Earlier chapters have suggested that replication studies must consider the limits of changes that can be made before a putative replication ceases to be a replication, and, in doing so, this engages issues of ontology, epistemology, and methodology. It argued that the replication researcher must make a case for claiming that the replication study is fair and sufficiently close to the original study. Chapters 2 and 3 argued that the ontological and epistemological bases of the original and replication study should not differ, and it left open to professional judgement the question of whether this should also apply to methodology. The argument concerned the paradigmatic nature and bases of research studies, suggesting that these should remain the same between the original study and the replication study. However, as Chapter 3 indicated, conceptual replications did not appear to abide by such constraints, as, provided that the 'concept' remained the same, how they are tested in a replication study is less significant an issue. Here, replication is more a matter of degree than of being absolute (Peels, 2019; Plucker & Makel, 2021).

This chapter pursues the topic of sameness further, by considering two main questions:

1 How far can an original study which has been rooted in one paradigm (e.g. a scientific, quantitative, experimental study) be replicated in a study that is rooted in a different paradigm (e.g. a qualitative study)?
2 How far can an original study which is qualitative be replicated in another qualitative study?

The issue here is how far the replication researcher can compare like with unlike with regard to the methodologies of the two studies in question. This is particularly the case if the methodology of the replication study departs from that used in the original study or, in the case of qualitative studies, if claims are made for the intrinsic impossibility of replication, as each case is different and unique (but see Plucker and Makel, 2021, for a questioning of this). One difficulty here is that the term 'qualitative study' is very broad, ranging from, for example, using words and visual data instead of numbers, to a range of types of study: case study, action research, ethnography, ethnomethodology, phenomenological research, interactionist research, narrative methods, interpretive methods, and so on. Even within each of these there is immense variety. For example, a case study, as a 'bounded unit' (Cohen et al., 2018, p. 375), can be of one person, a group, an institution, an event, a phenomenon, a situation, a group of institutions, events, phenomena, situations, and so on. Further, Plucker and Makel (2021), arguing for qualitative methods, note that debate currently surrounds the issue of whether they can be used at all in replication research, though Leppink (2017) argues for replacing thinking in terms of qualitative-quantitative divides with 'more-less replicable distinctions' (p. 100).

The two questions raise issues facing the replication researcher in changing methodologies of the research and in working with qualitative studies, and how to respond to these.

How far can a quantitative study be replicated in a qualitative study, and *vice versa*?

To address this question invokes the significance of paradigms. Cohen et al., 2018) state:

> A paradigm is a way of looking at or researching phenomena, a world view, a view of what counts as accepted or correct scientific knowledge or way of working . . . a shared belief system or set of principles, the identity of a research community, a way of pursuing knowledge, consensus on what problems are to be investigated and how to investigate them, typical solutions to problems, and an understanding that is more acceptable than its rivals. . . . Paradigms are not simply methodologies . . . they are ways of looking at the world, different assumptions about what the world is like and how we can understand or know about it. This raises the question of whether paradigms can live together, whether they are compatible or, since they constitute fundamentally different ways of looking at the world, they are incommensurate. . . . One cannot hold two distinct paradigms simultaneously as there are no common principles, standards or measures.
>
> (p. 8)

If we accept Kuhn's (1962) view, then each paradigm has its own ontological, epistemological, and methodological bases. At issue here is the matter of commensurability of research bases and its consequences. For example, can a qualitative case study constitute a replication study of what was a quantitative, experimental original study, and *vice versa*? Is the answer 'no', because it is akin to comparing apples and oranges; they are different species, even if they are both in the family of 'fruit'? In the sense of being replications, statistical findings are not comparable to qualitative findings, and *vice versa*. Experimental findings differ from ethnographies and case studies; they do different things, serve different purposes, and are of different natures; they are different in kind, kith, and kin (e.g. Cohen et al., 2018; Glazerman et al., 2002; Slavin, 2018). A qualitative study cannot be a 'true' replication of a quantitative experimental study or *vice versa*, even though they are both members of the family called 'research study'.

At the risk of condensing and artificially characterising the complexity of quantitative and qualitative research types, for heuristic clarity some distinguishing features (or stereotypes) are summarised here. On the one hand, quantitative researchers, be they in a positivist or post-positivist tradition, appeal to the 'scientific method' which includes, experiments; hypothesis testing and testing of an *a priori* theory; quantification; precision, control, and manipulation; empiricism; determinism; objective, tentative, falsifiable, and probabilistic 'truths'; objective reality independent of individuals; nomothetic purposes, with generalisability and replicability (Cohen et al., 2018). In so doing, with regard to studies of interventions, such researchers use controlled experiments or quasi-experiments, working with averages and calculations of probability, in seeking to prove, explain, and generalise to populations.

On the other hand, qualitative researchers appeal to, the interpretive approach, seeking to understand, respect, make sense of, and construct narratives of a *unique*, non-generalisable, idiographic situation which is fluid, evolutionary, dynamic, multilayered, changing, and situationally and contextually specific; the complexity of specific situations; intentionality, agency, creativity, and meaning making; subjectivity; the social construction of reality; multiple interpretations of 'reality' as 'realities'; emergent, rather than *a priori* theories; and an orientation to cases rather than populations (Biesta, 2020; Cohen et al., 2018; Flyvberg, 2011). Here, researchers study situations in their natural setting and work with fine-grained analysis and in-depth, multiple accounts and interpretations. Qualitative researchers seek to understand, interpret, and make sense of phenomena rather than to generalise. Markee (2017) argues, however, that this does not necessarily rule out the search for similar phenomena elsewhere. Qualitative studies can contribute to an overall finding in a conceptual replication, as it can constitute an extension, enrichment, application study. For example, a qualitative replication can provide a rich picture of the concept in question, and it can indicate how far the original study 'works' elsewhere and in other kinds of studies, that is, contributing to the cumulative contribution of a concept.

If progress is to be made in educational policy making and practice (e.g. from the cumulative nature of research findings), then a broad church is helpful, with quantitative and qualitative studies complementing each other and extending applicability, though not necessarily confirming or replicating each other. At issue here is how far the quantitative approach can embrace the complexity, mire, and significance of human behaviour, and of context, settings, cultures, conditions (witness the comparative failure of the worldwide replication study by the Open Science Collaboration, 2015, in psychology). Some aspects of human behaviour and the social world are not susceptible to measurement and quantification. On the other hand, there are also features of the social world and human behaviour that extend beyond the beliefs and meanings of individuals (Mingers, 2004), and on which it might be useful to conduct quantitative research. In this respect, the two types of study, though not replicating each other, serve a useful complementary function.

Mahoney and Goertz (2006) remark that quantitative and qualitative researchers come from two different cultures and traditions; they pursue different goals in their research and operate on the basis of different norms for conducting research. This is not to say that the two are mutually exclusive. Far from it: statistical data have to be interpreted; they rely on words for such interpretation. Case studies can include numerical data; there is no apartheid here. There is some complementary possibility or common ground between quantitative and qualitative researchers with regard to replication studies, in that researchers operating from differing ontological and epistemological positions often end up doing similar things, such as making comparisons between research findings and seeking to find out how far similar results can be found in different contexts, for example issues of applicability.

Question (1) from earlier asked 'how far can an original study which has been rooted in one paradigm (e.g. a scientific, quantitative, experimental study) be replicated in a study that is rooted in a different paradigm (e.g. a qualitative study)?' The argument here is that they cannot replicate each other but they can discover how far and where the overall findings from one type of study agree with those in another. However, this not the whole story of replication; at best it is mutual confirmation of two instances, one of which, possibly because of sampling issues, might have greater generalisability than the other, whilst the other might provide an indication of how far a concept 'works' in one or more different contexts, and why. This is not to privilege one type of study over another; they are simply different. This is the case, whether the original study is quantitative or qualitative, and similarly so for the replication study. Together, these two types can give a richer picture of how far, how, and where an intervention has 'worked' than would have been the case if only one of these types was used, but whether they constitute replication is a moot point. For example, replication *qua* replication rather than application and generalisability, argues for fidelity to the original methodology, as the methodology is the incarnation – infleshment – of a paradigm which is not commensurate with another paradigm.

How far can an original study which is qualitative be replicated in another qualitative study?

The previous question concerned paradigmatic differences between quantitative and qualitative research studies; the present question concerns the *same* paradigm. At issue here is how far the claim for the uniqueness of one qualitative study prevents fair comparison with another unique qualitative study or contribution to a replication-as-generalisation. For example, Markee (2017) argues that there is a widely accepted orthodoxy that it is impossible to conduct replication studies which are rooted in qualitative research paradigms. Further, answering the question of whether qualitative research can be replicated in exact, approximate, and conceptual replications, he notes that the standard response is often a 'resounding "No"' (p. 367).

This raises a much deeper issue than simple practicality. It concerns the entire enterprise of replication studies in education. Is it really possible or desirable to conduct a trustworthy and usable replication in education at all, given that education is highly contingent, agentic, emergent, conditionally rich, context-dense, variable-dense, with multiple causal density, and a with myriad of uncontrolled and uncontrollable variables operating in every situation which, as Morrison (2021) notes, cannot be overridden by randomisation and random samples?

Here, education is taken to be, in its essence, a person-oriented enterprise, and this engages diversity, uniqueness, differences, and context-specificity, which a qualitative study seeks to address and incorporate. In this qualitative view, education is not about the average child in an average classroom in an average world. Whilst a case study might catch complexity in thick descriptions and high-granularity analysis, the outcome of this is the production of findings on a unique instance, with unique people in unique situations and unique settings, with unique causal factors and conditions operating. Not to recognise this is to overlook the intense and overriding human-ness and 'person-ness' that constitutes teaching (Thomas, 2016, p. 403), a feature which, Thomas notes, is all too often sorely neglected. Against this backcloth, what can, in truth, be replicated with any reliability or validity?

Is replication here a misguided exercise in the futile, regardless of what findings it may provide? Or is it the case that a qualitative study of a unique situation does not preclude the possibility of findings that might generalise (though, as argued earlier, generalisability is not a full test of replication)? On their own, qualitative studies might not advance generalisability very much, but cumulatively, they might (Plucker & Makel, 2021). Further, qualitative studies, for example case studies, might advance generalisability through 'analytic' generalisability rather than statistical generalisability (Yin, 2018). This is where the qualitative research study contributes to the expansion, exposition, clarification, and generalisability of the theory, thereby helping researchers to understand other similar cases, phenomena, or situations, that is, there is a logical connection between the study/case and the wider theory. Qualitative case studies can contribute to generalising to a broader theory (rather than to populations) which can be tested in one or more empirical studies or cases. Cohen et al. (2018) note that case studies can contribute to generalisation in several ways, for example:

- from the single instance to the class of instances that it represents (e.g. a single-sex selective school might act as a case study to catch significant features of other single-sex selective schools);
- from features of the single case to a multiplicity of classes with the same features;
- from the single features of part of the case to the whole of that case;
- from a single case to a theoretical extension or theoretical generalization.

(p. 381)

They argue that case studies are variable rich, but that multi-variable phenomena are often more homogeneous than highly variable. Indeed, a large sample qualitative study might be useful. This challenges the assumption that qualitative studies must be small-scale in order to catch the in-depth data and richness of the situation in question; this is not a necessary, axiomatic characteristic or tenet of a qualitative study (see, e.g., the large-scale qualitative data analysis of Miles & Huberman, 1984, 1994). Indeed, coding large-scale qualitative data can be regarded, in part, as an exercise in generalisation.

If researchers can conduct case studies that catch the range of variability, then they can demonstrate generalisability. As qualitative case studies unavoidably include universals, they can provide 'exemplary knowledge' (Thomas, 2010, p. 576) of a wider phenomenon; they may have wider resonance with, and significance for, contexts and situation beyond their own. Whilst this does not constitute replication, nevertheless it argues that the unique nature of qualitative studies (in this instance, case studies) does not preclude them from contributing to generalisability. As Peels (2019) notes, there might be many instances of common features across different original, unique studies. As Chapter 3 indicated, generalisability *qua* transferability can be determined by the users of the research in their own contexts, and qualitative studies are not ruled out of the replication-as-generalisation field simply because they happen to study a unique instance.

Qualitative replication might not have sufficient similarity to the original qualitative study for exact and approximate replications to be conducted; hence, having both the original study and the replication study as qualitative studies might be possible only in a *conceptual* replication. Further, whilst the ontological and epistemological bases of the qualitative studies might be the same, qualitative studies might differ in type, for example case studies, action research, ethnographic research, phenomenological research. Indeed, in addressing fitness for purpose, it might be that the qualitative research confines itself to the kinds of data collected (e.g. observational data, interview data, words, visual data, oral and aural data), whilst operating in what otherwise would be a quasi-experiment (e.g. with control and treatment groups), that is, replacing metrics and statistics with word-based data, as in process evaluations.

Qualitative studies can feature in conceptual replications, as they are concerned more with replicating the concept than adhering to one particular methodology and set of methods; they seek to rise above such noise. If so, then this raises issues of what standards of comparison are needed to ensure that the replication has 'worked'. Such judgements reside in the replication researcher and reader as judges. Such judgements might include, for example, comparing the original study and the replication study with a view to identifying their similarity/closeness and differences in the following, and the importance of these, together with changes made to:

- the purpose and type of replication;
- the type of qualitative research in the original study and the replication study;
- research design, research questions, sample/groups receiving the intervention, focus of the studies, instrumentation, contexts and setting, constraints, conditions, controls, data types, data collection, additional data, excluded data, frequency of intervention: each week, in total, and in the number of sessions each week;
- data analysis methods and their application;
- intervention: 'concept', contents, treatments, procedures, instructions, tasks;
- causality;
- findings and conclusions.

Table 4.1 Judging the replication of qualitative studies

- On what areas of the original study and the replication study are you focusing in considering replication?
- What criteria, indicators, and evidence are you using to come to a judgement on how far the replication study really is a replication study, that is, its level and contents of sameness between the original study and the replication study?
- What criteria, indicators, and evidence are you using to come to a judgement of how far the replication study really has confirmed the findings of the original study?
- At what point does your replication study cease to be a fair replication, and what standards and criteria are you using to come to this judgement?
- At what point does your replication study cease to confirm the findings of the original study, and what standards and criteria are you using to come to this judgement?
- On what are you focusing in deciding how far the replication study has been successful in confirming the findings of the original study?
- What factors are you considering in deciding how far the replication study has confirmed, partially confirmed, disconfirmed, or indeterminately found, the original study?
- What are the *critical* factors in deciding whether the replication study is a reliable and valid replication?
- What are the *critical* factors in deciding whether the *findings* of the replication study are reliable and valid?
- What levels of sameness, and on what, must there be between the original study and the replication study, and why?

The dangers of this (e.g. relativism) can be attenuated by triangulation, transparency, and disclosure of the standards, criteria, indicators, and evidence used in reaching a judgement about the degree of replication. At issue is the need for the replication research to disclose and justify several matters, set out in Table 4.1.

The questions in Table 4.1 are not exclusive to qualitative studies; they also apply to other kinds of replication study. They indicate that judgements of replication cannot simply be read off mechanistically from a result but reside in the case made by the replication researcher, how defensible that case is, what degree of replication has been shown, based on what criteria, standards and evidence, and with regard to what; how much similarity is 'beyond a reasonable doubt'. Replication is not absolute; whilst statistically based replication studies deal with probabilistic findings and interpretations, for qualitative studies (case studies in this chapter) the degree of replication is a matter of judgement that is based on transparency, trustworthiness, and the provision of sufficient detail and justification for the replication researcher and the reader to judge how far, and where, a replication has or has not been demonstrated, or whether the findings are indeterminate.

Conclusion

The chapter has argued that, in order to meet the demands of fair comparison, fidelity to the paradigm of the original study must be maintained in the replication study. The extent to which changes of paradigm, for example in a conceptual replication study, constitute a breach of such fidelity, calls into question whether a mixed-paradigm conceptual replication is a genuine replication at all, or only in a very limited sense. The concern of the conceptual replication is the 'concept', somewhat regardless of the research methodology that it adopts (and a conceptual replication is more an extension, enrichment and application study than a complete replication study).

Whilst the chapter argued against changing paradigms between the original study and the replication study, this leaves under-addressed the issue of the claims made for uniqueness of each situation studied in a qualitative original study and a replication study. The chapter argued that the uniqueness of one situation does not prevent the replication researcher from comparing the findings of qualitative original studies and qualitative replication studies, as each case study is the bearer of issues, themes, factors, theory that can transfer from one study to another and contribute to the accumulation of data on generalisability.

The question was raised of whether or how far, in fact, it is possible and desirable to conduct a meaningful replication of an original study in education, given the context-specific, variable-dense, causally complex, person-centred, and person-dependent world of education, and in the presence of uncontrolled and uncontrollable exogenous and endogenous variables in classrooms. In other words, it questioned the fundamental premise of replication research in education: its legitimacy, meaningfulness, fairness to the complex world of classrooms, and utility. The answer? Qualitative replications can be legitimate, meaningful, fair, and useful.

Even if one accepts the arguments that quantitative and qualitative replication studies endeavour to identify the signal from the noise of classrooms, this does not overcome easily the challenge of deciding what a replication study has *really* replicated rather than what it has purported to replicate and how far the replication has 'worked'. This concerns what the replication researcher can infer from the findings of the replication study and how to judge how far the replication study confirms, disconfirms, partially confirms, or cannot confirm or disconfirm the findings of the original study. Confirmation and disconfirmation are matters of degree, requiring transparency and disclosure of details, criteria, indicators, and evidence for claims made. The replication researcher has to make and defend the case for the judgement made about what the replication study has shown, 'beyond a reasonable doubt', in relation to the original study. Replication requires, and is, a human judgement, and this confirms the nature of education as a human-centred enterprise.

5 Planning a replication study in education

Overview

This chapter takes the reader through a range of issues in planning a replication study in education, with guidance, practical advice, and examples. It sets out four main stages in planning a replication study in education, identifying considerations to be addressed at each stage:

Stage One: Address the original study and justify the replication study
Stage Two: Identify and align the purposes and types of replication study
Stage Three: Change and compare the components of the original study and the replication study
Stage Four: Plan the operationalisation and conduct of the replication study

The chapter addresses these in sequence, for planning a replication study:

- how to find and choose an original study to replicate;
- who and what to evaluate in the original study, in order to clarify what needs to be replicated, why, and how to conduct the replication;
- the type of replication study to adopt, and for what purposes, how to justify decisions made on these matters, and how to align the purposes of the replication study with its type and contents;
- what to focus on in the replication study and what it will do;
- how to operationalise the replication study and what issues to consider in this;
- what changes to make between the original study and the replication study, where, why, and how to make them;
- how to compare the original study and the replication study with regard to sameness and difference, and the significance and consequences of these;
- how to identify the measures and success criteria in the replication study;
- what to include in the research design of a replication study;
- ethics in the research;
- the need for constant reference to the original study.

The chapter provides the replication researcher with an indication of what to consider in planning a replication study, what to include in the plan, and how to compile and organise the plan.

DOI: 10.4324/9781003204237-6

A staged approach to planning the replication research

Stage one: address the original study and justify the replication study

This section moves from identifying an original study to evaluating it in order to decide whether it is suitable for, and capable of, replication. It indicates how to find and select a possible original study, the criteria for evaluating its suitability for replication, and how to decide whether, in practice, it can be replicated. This section argues for a clear statement of the criteria for the replication researcher to use in searching and choosing an original study for replication, and how to justify the choice of the study. Here, the researcher must describe, evaluate, and critique the main features of the original study; evaluate its research purposes, questions, areas of focus, and what it was striving to do and 'deliver'; check the meanings and interpretation of terms and concepts in the original study (e.g. to see if they need to be refined and clarified in the replication); and evaluate how and how effectively the intervention and its original concept and/or hypothesis were tested. Then the section indicates the need to identify the areas of the original study on which the replication study should focus, why and how.

The starting point for a replication study is the original study. It is important to spend time finding one or more potentially suitable original studies and then review, evaluate, examine, interrogate, and critique those which are contenders for replication, in order to decide whether they are worth replicating, and then to select one of these for replication. The researcher can use search engines and search terms to locate and review potential studies for replication, noting, for example, a range of factors set out in Table 5.1.

Chapter 1 suggested that an original study might be worth replicating if it meets one or more of the criteria which are summarised in Table 5.2.

The purpose of focusing on the original study is to evaluate its potential, worth and suitability for replication. If the original study meets one or more of these criteria, then it can be considered for replication. In addressing this, the replication researcher should conduct a deep, critical, and interrogative analysis, examination, review, and evaluation of the original study, to identify and understand,

Table 5.1 Finding and selecting an original study for replication

---

Original studies might be considered for replication in light of:

- their sources and formats (e.g. are they in highly cited, prestigious, and high impact sources and are they peer-reviewed or not peer-reviewed);
- what kind of publication they are (e.g. a journal article, a book, a book chapter, a report, a conference paper, a working paper) and the number of citations received;
- where and when they were published and cited (recency might be important);
- where they are referenced (in what other sources);
- their up-to-date-ness;
- who are the authors (e.g. well known);
- whether any other studies have already updated, extended, and overtaken them;
- the type of study conducted (e.g. experimental, quasi-experimental; quantitative, qualitative, case study, action research).

Table 5.2 Criteria for evaluating an original study with a view to replication

An original study can be considered for replication if it:
- commands attention because it had a major finding that could impact, or has impacted, on policy and practice;
- is of interest and usefulness to educationists, those working in the field and/or policy makers (e.g. if it makes important recommendations for research, policy making, and practice);
- is timely and relevant;
- is highly and widely cited;
- is a major, seminal study that makes a significant contribution to the field and to knowledge and/or plugs a gap in the field, meets a need in it and contributes to contemporary debates in the field, and has not already been updated and/or overtaken and superseded;
- has surprising, contentious, and/or interesting findings;
- makes a significant contribution to theory, practice, and research in the field;
- is an important, timely study in the field that could advance and/or open up the field, or if it is interesting and potentially important but currently limited (i.e. worth extending and investigating further, in order to improve the original study and/or to ascertain its generalisability);
- has high quality research which is well designed or, by contrast, if there are flaws, weaknesses, and limitations that warrant being amended and extended;
- would benefit from further data to refine and extend the study;
- gives a reason to believe that the findings of the original study were an artifact of the research design and methods used in the research (i.e. that they were not context-free);
- gives a reason to believe that the original study makes questionable claims and/or is biased;
- can provide data that might refine and extend the study;
- would benefit from being validated further;
- has the potential to challenge the original study and its findings.

for example, what it does and does not include, what is missing in the original study, what it does, and what needs to be improved or looked into further. It is important to check the internal validity of the study and to evaluate its quality, strengths, weaknesses, and limitations; the claims made from it; and whether they are supported by the evidence provided. The replication researcher should consider whether there is sufficient detail, transparency, and precision for a replication study to be able to operationalise and conduct a fair comparison with, and replication of, the original study and to be able to identify what needs further investigation in the replication study, what kind of replication is required, and what, if anything, needs to be changed in the replication, and why.

Having found what might be a suitable original study, the replication researcher should examine and evaluate key components in the original study to identify what the purpose, focus, nature, and contents of the replication study should be, what it should do, why and how. Many original studies contain a range of areas for replication. These include, but are not limited to, the following, and these depend, in part, on the nature and scope of the original study (see also Table 2.2):

- purpose and research questions;
- research questions and hypotheses;
- research design, methodology, and statistical power;
- population, sampling, sample size, and attrition;
- focus, contents, scope tasks, conduct, procedures and instructions for the intervention;
- concept (for a conceptual replication);
- independent and dependent variables in the study;
- key components of the intervention (e.g. the frequency, intensity, quality, strength, amount, pacing, variation over time, sequence, inception and follow-up, risks, side-effects);
- timing, time frames, and duration of the intervention and each of its sessions, and number of sessions each week and in total;
- methods, resources, and materials used in the intervention;
- the setting, context, and conditions in the study;
- piloting of the study;
- pre-test and post-test and their timing;
- data collection instruments, measures, and data analysis methods;
- what the original study found, reported, and 'delivered'.

Given this range (see also Tables 2.1 and 2.2), the replication researcher must decide which of these areas (and/or, indeed, others) to focus on, and why. What, exactly and precisely, does the replication study seek to replicate and/or exactly duplicate from the original study, and why? What does it not necessarily seek to replicate and/or exactly duplicate, and why?

The replication researcher interrogates and evaluates the original study in order to not only justify the need for, and worthwhileness of, a replication, but also to see where improvements to, and refinements of, the original research might be made in the replication study and what the replication study can do, for example to test the internal validity of the original study or extend, apply, and address its generalisability. Plonsky (2012) indicates three areas of the original study (he raises these in the context of meta-analysis, but they can apply more widely): the introduction and literature review; the methods of the research; and the results and their discussion.

With regard to the introduction and literature review, Plonsky (2012) suggests evaluating the clarity of the focus and definition of purposes and questions asked of it, how well and sufficient the potential and actual moderator variables have been identified and explained, whether the relevance of the study (theoretically and practically) has been stated, whether potential biases of researchers have been indicated, whether the strengths and weaknesses of studies referenced have been identified and explained, and whether sufficient explanation has been provided of the data collection instruments.

With regard to the methods of the research, Plonsky (2012) raises several questions which, in slightly modified form, can be asked (adjusted here in order to refer to an original study rather than meta-analysis): how exhaustive is the search for primary research studies in the background to the original study; how explicit and unambiguous are the criteria for including and excluding studies and variables; how effectively has publication bias been assessed; was inter-rater reliability assessed and sufficient; was the quality of the studies included in the literature review assessed; did the original study contain a self-evaluation of its strengths, weaknesses, and limitations; were effect sizes reliable; how well were issues of missing data handled; how well were outliers handled; how transparent, appropriate, and available was the coding of data. Plonsky's items are useful but not exhaustive, and it is important for the replication researcher to add to these a range of components of the research and the research design identified in the present chapter. Evaluating the methods of the research in the original study calls for a fuller and more detailed, close-grained analysis of the components of the research in the original study, in order to identify what, specifically, the replication study should focus on, change, modify, improve, correct, extend, or apply.

With regard to the results and their discussion, issues raised by Plonsky (2012) in relation to meta-analysis can be applied to the original study, for example: how well are the findings and their summary presented; how far and where the study adds new knowledge concerning the construct in question; how effectively the findings are contextualised, how acceptable is the interpretation of them, and how well they are referenced to the theories and models that are being tested in the study; how useful, practical implications are discussed; how well the findings of the study provide suggestions for future research, for example concerning methodology and substance of the research in question.

While the worth and worthwhileness, causes of, reasons for, and potential benefits from replicating the original study are important factors, the replication researcher must also address the practicality of conducting a replication. Relevant considerations here are set out in Table 5.3.

Table 5.3 Practical questions in deciding whether a replication is possible

Practical questions concerning whether a replication study is possible include:
- Is the research replicable and feasible? (Not all original studies might be replicable if they lack sufficient detail for a fair replication to be conducted.)
- Does the original study contain sufficient detail, clarity, transparency, and precision for a replication to be able to be conducted?
- Are the original/raw data available and easily accessed (in an exact replication)?
- Are charges made for access to the original data?
- Does the researcher have the resources (e.g. time, people, finance, administrative and research support, equipment, facilities and materials) to be able to conduct the research?
- Does the researcher have sufficient background, expertise and research methods ability, language and other requirements to be able to plan and conduct the replication?
- Does the researcher have access to participants?
- What conditions or constraints are there in terms of access, permissions, and conduct of the replication, and what effects do these have on the replication study?
- Can the researcher plan and conduct the research alone?

It is important for the replication researcher to identify and justify the reasons for conducting the replication, and what has caused or given rise to the need for the replication. Why conduct the replication? Why is it needed? Why is it important to conduct a replication? What is it about the original study that warrants or merits a replication study? For example, this might be a concern about the need to validate and corroborate the original study and its findings, to address a possible weakness in, or limitation of, the original study, to improve the methods and intervention in the original study. It might be to work with refined instrumentation and clarified meanings of words and concepts, to improve the conduct and contents, tasks and procedures of the intervention. Or it might be to try a new approach to the concept in question, to test the same hypothesis in different settings, to adopt new methods of data analysis, and so on. The need for a replication study might stem from recognition of the need to investigate potential benefits from seeing how far, where and how an important finding is transferable and generalisable to another context, setting, group of people, and field of study. It might also arise from recognising the potential benefits of extending the scope of the original study.

Stage two: identify and align the purposes and types of replication study

Emerging from the choice and examination of the original study and warrant for conducting a replication should be the operationalisation of the replication study. This can commence with a clear statement of the purposes of the replication, which has a direct influence on the type of replication being proposed. As set out in previous chapters, the purposes of the replication might be: (a) to validate the original study and to confirm its findings; (b) to expand the generalisability and applicability of the original study; (c) to improve on weaknesses and limitations of the original study, amending flaws and refining the study to make its conduct, analysis, and findings more acute and rigorous; or (d) to extend, in breadth and depth, the scope of the original study. In turn, these different purposes suggest different types of replication study:

- A validation study (a) is well served by an exact or direct replication.
- An original study seeking generalisability and wider applicability (b) is well served by a systematic, approximate, or conceptual replication, each of these increasing the number of variables that can be changed from the original study (discussed below) (e.g. a systematic replication might add or change one variable at a time from an original study, whereas an approximate replication might change more than one at a time, and a conceptual replication might change several simultaneously).
- Weaknesses in, or limitations of, an original study (c) can be addressed in a close replication, as this type strives to maintain and refine key features of the original study.
- Extending, broadening, and deepening scope of the original study (d) can be addressed in a close, approximate, systematic, or conceptual replication.

74 Planning a replication study in education

In addressing these matters, the researcher must interrogate the original study in detail (as indicated earlier, some original studies do not provide sufficient detail for the replication to be conducted securely, i.e. to compare the original study with the possible replication). The close analysis of the original study should enable the researcher to identify what, precisely, the replication must do, to justify changes to be made in the replication study, to indicate what improvements, rectifications, refinements, and changes the replication will make to the original study, and why. These might include:

- if the original study omitted or sidelined important variables, and/or its instrumentation could be improved;
- if the intention of the replication is to move towards testing the generalisability of the original study (e.g. moving from an efficacy to an effectiveness trial or from an internal validity check);
- to add one change of item at a time (to see which variable or variables make a difference to the results);
- to identify the degree of replication possible between the original and the replication study;
- to change the setting of the intervention;
- to change the person/people who is or are carrying out the intervention, moving away from the original researcher to an outside, independent party;
- to change the sampling and sampling strategy (e.g. if the original study's sample was small, underpowered, selective, and biased, or to widen the sample);
- to test for false positives and/or false negatives in the original study;
- to increase the duration and intensity of the intervention to see if these made a difference to the findings;
- to vary the task/intervention variables to see if these made a difference to the findings;
- to adhere to explicit instructions and procedures (e.g. if the original study had substantial variability of treatments and instructions);
- to change the measures, metrics, and methods of data analysis (and their timing) being used (e.g. for refining these with regard to the original study);
- to change the methodology, features of the intervention, instrumentation (e.g. to remove possible bias detected in the original study), data collection, and data analysis (to determine how far the findings of the original study might be due to the methodology, duration of the intervention, instrumentation for data collection, data analysis, etc.);
- to have more refined, fine-tuned, and detailed data collection instruments, with more data collection points, including delayed data collection after the end of the intervention to test for longer-term impact;
- to check findings against baseline data;
- to improve the data analysis (e.g. moving from significance testing to the use of effect size, confidence intervals, range and distributions) and to have greater in-depth analysis of data;
- to offer alternative interpretations of the findings of the original study;
- to confirm or change the findings of the original study.

The replication study should indicate what the replication study should investigate and test further, and why (specific points and areas from the original study, the hypothesis, intervention, conduct, data analysis, findings, etc.). In doing so, the replication study should also indicate its intended 'deliverables', why these are important, and how they relate to the original study, so that it becomes clear and transparent what the replication is for, what it is designed to do, and what are its potential benefits, for what and for whom.

Stage three: change and compare the components of the original study and the replication study

Close, systematic, approximate, and conceptual replications change variables, excluding some and including others. They make changes to the original study, with conceptual replications indicating this sharply. The replication study must indicate and justify the reasons for, and purposes of, what to keep constant between the two studies.

The replication study must also indicate: what, where, how and why it has made changes between the original study and the replication study, with regard to variables; contents, tasks, and procedures of the intervention; research design; methodology, methods, and instrumentation; population, sampling, and sample size; participants (e.g. students, teachers, researchers); conduct of the research; timing, time frames, and duration of the intervention; features of the intervention: its nature, frequency, intensity, strength, amount, pacing, variation over time, sequence, inception and follow-up, and so on; resources; settings, contexts, and conditions; data collection, data types, measures, metrics, and data analysis. This rehearses the details provided in Chapter 2 (see also Brandt et al., 2014; Coyne et al., 2016).

The criteria used in making changes must be transparent and defensible, indicating how they render the replication study more fit for purpose than the original study and how they address, for example, the purposes of generalisability of, and improvements and extensions to, the original study (and how, where, and why), how they address reliability and validity, and how they engage the issue of whether these 'new' or 'revised' replication studies will, themselves, need replicating in the interests of validation. This involves identifying and judging how close or how distant, and where, are the similarities between the original study and the replication study, and the significance of these (Brandt et al., 2014).

In a close replication, Brandt et al. (2014) confine such changes to: instructions and procedures; measures; stimuli; location; remuneration (where relevant); participants: population and sample; possible changes to the direction and size of the effect size, and whether such differences are likely to influence the findings of the replication study. In a conceptual replication, which can change many factors, the replication researcher must suggest and justify how much the changes made might affect the findings of the replication and its comparison to the original study. A clear and defensible justification of changes should be provided, indicating how they render the replication more fit for purpose, what that purpose is, and why the changes are important. There is little value in simply changing for change's sake.

Brandt et al. (2014) argue that, for a *close* replication to be convincing, it requires rigorous implementation by independent researchers, including: (a) careful definition and indication of the methods and effects that the replication study seeks to replicate, including the design, areas of focus, and measures in the original study and replication study; (b) adhering as closely as possible to the methods that were used in the original study, with the same participants, instructions and procedures, interventions, measures, and methods of data analysis; (c) ensuring disclosure and making available the details of the study, for external evaluation (e.g. syntax, codes, data, and details of the analysis); and (d) critical and evaluative comparison of the results of the replication and the original study, including effect sizes and their direction, confidence intervals, range and contextual factors. They also suggest that it might be necessary or useful to contact the author(s) of the original study in order to ensure fidelity to the original study in the replication study (see also National Science Foundation and the Institute of Education Sciences, 2018).

This rehearses the need for sameness between the original study and the replication study, and the burden of proof is on the researcher to demonstrate that the sameness between the two studies is sufficient.

Stage four: plan the operationalisation and conduct of the replication study

The extent of the similarity of the replication to the original study, and changes made in the replication study, will affect how the replication study is operationalised. Here, the replication study must address several points:

- the need for the replication;
- the benefits stemming from doing the replication study;
- the usefulness of the replication study;
- a review of the original study to identify the purpose of the replication study;
- how the replication study relates to, springs from, and compares with the original study;
- a review of the relevant literature in the field, in order to locate the replication study in an appropriate context, to provide a theoretical warrant for the replication, and to inform the research purposes and research questions;
- the purpose and objectives of the replication;
- what the replication will do and 'deliver';
- the type of replication, and how that type is fit for purpose;
- the significance of the replication: why it is important;
- what the replication will keep the same as the original study, and why;
- what the replication will change, and why;
- what the possible effects of the changes might be on the replication study and its findings;
- the research questions for the replication;

- the focus and contents of the replication, with justifications provided for decisions on these;
- the research design and the justification for its elements;
- the ethics of the replication;
- reporting: to whom, and who owns the data;
- the indicators/success criteria for the replication (discussed below);
- progress reporting in the replication study (where relevant).

Differences between the original and the replication study are inevitable, and this frustrates easy conclusions being drawn from the replication's findings (Patil et al., 2016). For example: no two samples are identical other than in an exact replication of the original data (replication as reproducibility); sampling error and measurement error exist in any study. As with other kinds of research, a replication study is not always straightforward or simple (Jacobson & Simpson, 2019). Replication requires key elements of the intervention (see 'replication condition' in Schmidt, 2009, p. 97) – those factors that might bring about changes in the dependent variable (e.g. procedures, tasks, activities, and contents) – to be repeated in the replication. However, this may be difficult, even impossible, in the 'real world' of classrooms. The teacher, for example, brings to the situation her or his accumulated, tacit, professional knowledge of the students, pedagogy, curricula, and so on (Morrison, 2021; Sternberg, 1995) and, therefore, tailors the key elements of the intervention to the situation in hand. Indeed, not to do so could be regarded as unprofessional, even unethical (Morrison, 2021). The replication study would need to indicate how such factors featured in, and influenced the planning, conduct and, subsequently, the findings of the replication.

Further, in planning the replication study, the researcher should accept that replication in education and social sciences is challenging, given the high causal density and rich context-embeddedness of the intervention and significant teacher influence in classrooms. For example, if the intervention is a randomised controlled trial, then the researcher should recognise that randomised controlled trials operate in an environment of considerable causal density and in the presence of many hidden or known conditionals, thereby rendering replication studies challenging (Manzi, 2012). Very high causal densities, Manzi avers, such as those found in education, operate with statistical statements that are 'extremely conditional' (p. 204). Similarly, differences in teachers and students (e.g. their heterogeneity or homogeneity), and settings, number of lessons, procedures, background and characteristics of teachers, levels of support and training provided to teachers during implementation, render replication difficult (Gersten et al., 2015; Morrison, 2021). Whilst this is not exclusive to replication studies, nevertheless it is challenging.

For example, causal contexts and the interactions of context-specific causal factors ('causal cakes', Cartwright & Hardie, 2012, p. 61) – different combinations of ingredients which make different causes operate in the original and replication studies – differ from one context to another and influence the intervention's effects (see also Deaton & Cartwright, 2018). Indeed, to suppose that 'what works' in one context will transpose itself straightforwardly into another context might be ill-advised, even in a conceptual replication. Of course, conceptual replications are designed to address this very problem, and this is a major source of their contribution to education, *viz.* to see where results hold fast, regardless of specific contexts, how far they can generalise, and how far context makes a difference. However, if a replication study subsequently does or does not find the same or similar results as the original, then this raises the question for the researcher of what are the causes of this (Morrison, 2019).

Contextual variables exert a strong influence in education, hence, the attribution of *simple* causality risks overlooking or downplaying the many degrees of freedom and confounders between a cause, or combination of causes, and effects (Aguilar, 2020; Biesta, 2020; Kim, 2019; Morrison, 2009, 2021). This supports the use of conceptual replication studies to identify where effects generalise to other students, settings, and so on. As in other types of research, expecting straightforward replications and straightforward interpretations of their findings is unrealistic, as contextuality and rigour in measuring, analysing, and interpreting sources of variation feature here.

In planning the replication study, consideration should be given to statistical power. Many replication studies have low statistical power (Hedges & Schauer, 2019; Hüffmeier et al., 2016; Ioannidis, 2012, 2015; Lortie-Forgues & Inglis, 2019; Pigott et al., 2013), that is, insufficient power to avoid Type I or Type II errors and/or to detect a very small but important effect size (see Simonsohn (2015) on the need to protect true findings from underpowered replications). Lortie-Forgues and Inglis (2019) report that, of 141 trials that they reviewed in education, only 6 per cent had statistical power of 0.80 (a common setting) and the average statistical power was 0.23, with a median of 0.17, that is much lower than 0.80. Small, underpowered studies and significance-chasing studies are legion, leading to false positives (Ioannidis, 2015).

Statistical power is the probability that a study will detect a true effect, separating this from random chance, correctly rejecting a false positive (a Type I error) and a false negative (a Type II error). Statistical power is a function of four elements (Ellis, 2010): sample size and nature, the alpha (α) statistical significance level (typically set at 0.05 or lower), the setting of an acceptable beta (β) level (overcoming the probability of a false negative), and effect size sought. The larger the sample is, the greater is its potential statistical power. Cohen et al. (2018) suggest that, for statistical power: the sample should be large; the effect size should be set to be large; the alpha (α) should be low (in order to reduce the chance of a false positive); the sample should be homogeneous, or, if this is not possible, the sample size should be increased in order to take account of heterogeneity; a one-tailed test should be used (which predicts the direction of the findings, e.g. a positive correlation); high reliability coefficients should be required (e.g. the Cronbach alpha), if necessary, adjusting items in the instruments in order to achieve this; and parametric measures should be used. They indicate that, even with the frequently used alpha (α) setting of 0.05 and beta (β) setting of 0.20, yielding a power level of 0.80, small samples (e.g. below 100) may undermine the claims made for the research.

If the power level is set at 0.80 with an alpha of 0.05, for a pre-specified effect size of 0.8 (a moderately large effect size), the sample size should be 25 in each group (e.g. the control and treatment groups in a randomised controlled trial), giving a total of 50 participants (Lehr, 1992). For a pre-specified effect size of 0.5 (a moderate effect), the sample size should be 64 in each group, giving a total of 128 participants; for a pre-specified effect size of 0.3 (a small effect), the sample size should be 178 in each group, giving a total of 356. The smaller the pre-specified effect size, the larger is the sample size required in order to be able to detect it (Torgerson & Torgerson, 2008). Cohen et al. (2018) note that statistical power varies according to the test and measures used and that because statistical power is affected by effect size, alpha levels, and beta levels, changing any one of these may require making changes to the sample size.

The proposal and plan for the replication should include a clear statement of what constitutes a successful replication. Chapter 6 addresses this in greater detail, for quantitative and qualitative research, emphasising that the judgement of replication, non-replication, or indeterminate replication, whilst informed by data, is a human act based on the principle of 'beyond a reasonable doubt'. This does not prevent the researcher from pre-defining (indeed, pre-registering) the criteria, cut-off points, and evidence required, so that judgements can be made of how far and where the replication study has confirmed the original study.

A successful replication might be that which confirms or, indeed, disconfirms the results of the original study (e.g. if there was reason to suspect the findings of the original study). It might be deemed to be successful if it has been able to conform closely to key components of the original study. It might be considered to be successful if it has indicated whether the concept tested in the original study can apply to, and generalise to, different settings, contexts, samples (where and how well), or if it has confirmed or, indeed, disconfirmed, the original study when it has been tested in different circumstances, conditions, using different research designs, methodologies, samples, data collection instrument, data analysis methods, and so on, that is, if the concept holds true as being the signal arising from the noise of the research design and conduct, indicating that the findings are not simply an artifact or consequence of the methods of the study. A replication study might be deemed to be successful if it has identified new areas for further research. Table 5.4 indicates several concerns in defining 'success' in a replication study.

Table 5.4 Deciding 'success' in a replication study

Some concerns in judging 'success':
- Does 'success' mean finding the *same results* as the original study?
- Does 'success' mean finding *different results* from the original study?
- Does 'success' mean following the same *methodological and procedural* requirements?
- Does 'success' mean following different *methodological and procedural* requirements?
- What if the replication results differ from those of the original study?
- How 'close' must 'close' be with regard to results, and which results (e.g. effect sizes, distributions, means, confidence intervals, range, standard error, statistical significance)?

The replication study must identify success criteria, what they are, how they will be applied, what are the indicators of success, what evidence will be needed to indicate the success of the replication, and in what area(s), and what the replication study must do in order to meet the criteria for being successful. Put simply, a replication study will be considered a 'success' if it has achieved its stated purposes.

The proposal and plan for the replication might also include a clear statement of what constitutes an unsuccessful replication, and reasons for this. This is not confined to the absence of, or poor performance in, the factors that constitute a successful replication. Whilst it can be simply a matter of *absence* or poor achievement of its purpose, in terms of the stated success criteria, it might also be because of the *presence* of other factors in the replication study. This has its parallels in the school effectiveness literature, in which an effective school is that which not only does not have certain negative characteristics but also possesses key positive characteristics (Morrison, 1998). A replication study might be deemed to be unsuccessful for many reasons, such as a failure: to confirm or disconfirm the findings of the original study; to generalise; to have validated the original study; to have identified areas for further research; to have conducted a reliable, valid, rigorous, trustworthy, and error-free replication. Failure might be due to the presence of other exogenous and endogenous factors which were not controlled sufficiently and/or the presence of causalities and counterfactuals that differed from those in the original study.

The replication researcher must exercise caution in identifying success criteria and planning for their achievement, as 'success' is a slippery term here, for example some 'failures' might not necessarily be construed negatively. For instance, finding that a concept does not generalise to a different setting or to a different sample may not necessarily constitute a failure, as it has succeeded in identify a boundary limitation of the concept. This suggests that judging success or failure should be in terms of the achievement of what the researcher wished to take from the replication study and the achievement of the purposes of the research, for example which were to test a concept, hypothesis, idea, finding, set of practices, and not necessarily to duplicate the results of the original study. If we confirm a result of an original study in a replication study, this is important; if we do not confirm the result of an original study in a replication study, this, too, is important. Chapter 6 returns to issues of 'success', replication, non-replication, and indeterminate replication in a replication study.

Research design

In addressing the components of the research design for the replication study, Table 5.5 sets out a perhaps formidable checklist of requirements to assist in clarifying and justifying the replication study, identifying what remains the same as in the original study and where differences are made, and enabling readers of the subsequent research to evaluate the study.

Many of the features of operationalising the replication study in Table 5.5 are standard components of a research proposal and research plan, but here, additionally, these are constantly referenced to the original study and/or the original

Table 5.5 Components of the research design in a replication study

Components of the research design	Closeness to the original study (e.g. no change, small change, major change)
Purposes of the replication study	
Intended outcomes and deliverables of the replication study	
Research question(s)	
Ontological basis of the issues in question	
Epistemological basis of the study	
Ethical issues (e.g. informed consent, rights to withdraw, anonymity, confidentiality, non-traceability, non-maleficence, sensitivity, rigorous research) Farrimond	
Methodology or methodologies of the research	
Constraints on the research	
How the research will be conducted	
Contents of the intervention and tasks in it	
Timing, time frames, and duration of the intervention	
Duration of each session of the intervention	
Number of intervention sessions each week and in total	
Frequency, intensity, strength, amount, pacing, variation over time, sequence, inception of the intervention, and any differentiation made for different participants	
Any differentiation made for different participants	
Identification of possible risks and side-effects, and how the replication study will address these	
Indication of any follow-up to the intervention	
Procedures and instructions for the intervention	
How the replication study will ensure fidelity to the contents, procedures, tasks, timing matters, sequence, and instructions of the intervention	
Population and sampling: sampling strategy, type, size, nature, purpose	
Preparation of, and support for, the participants (e.g. training and development)	
Setting(s) of the intervention, its contexts, contingencies, conditions, key features	

(Continued)

Table 5.5 (Continued)

Components of the research design	Closeness to the original study (e.g. no change, small change, major change)
Access to participants in the research	
Types of data collected	
When data collection will occur, and why then	
Methods of data collection: instrumentation and conduct of the data collection	
Details of the pre-test and post-test (where relevant)	
Validity and reliability of the data collection instruments	
Elimination of bias at all stages of the replication	
Resources (human, temporal, locational, material, physical, equipment, administrative, financial)	
Data analysis: measures, metrics, methods, statistics, coding, thematic analysis, and so on, and a justification for the methods of data analysis	
Positionality and reflexivity of the researcher	
Relationship of the researcher to the original study (e.g. the same researcher, related to, independent)	
Summary of the sequence of the research	

concept. Table 5.5 includes the need for the replication study to indicate how close it is to the original study on a range of features, and where it differs (on the issue of sameness, see Chapter 2).

In turning this list in Table 5.5 into an action plan, a possible sequence is set out below, which adheres to the sequence of Table 5.5 (the arrows at the end of each subsection indicate the next step in the sequence):

Background: select the original study for replication → analyse and evaluate the original study →

Approaching the replication study: identify the purposes, intended outcomes, and deliverables of the replication study → identify the type of replication study in order to meet its purposes, intended outcomes, and deliverables →

Components of the intervention: identify and justify what is unchanged between the original study and the replication study and what changes are made to the original study in the intervention → ensure that the ontological and epistemological bases of the original study and the replication study are the same → address ethical issues in the intervention → identify and justify the methodology of the intervention → identify the constraints on the replication study → identify the areas of focus, contents, tasks in the intervention → identify key features of the intervention (frequency, intensity, strength, amount, pacing, variation over time, sequence, inception of the intervention, and any differentiation made for different participants, together with risk analysis and risk control) → identify the 'delivery' of the intervention (timing, time frames and duration, duration of each session, number of intervention sessions each week and in total, follow-up) → identify the procedures and instructions for the intervention, fidelity to its requirements, and how the intervention will be conducted → identify the population and sampling → identify the access to the participants → indicate how to prepare the participants in the intervention → indicate the resources required for the intervention → identify the setting(s), conditions, contexts, and contingencies of the intervention → identify the data types and, if relevant, the measures needed (i.e. plan with data analysis and intended outcomes in mind) → identify the procedures for, process of, and timing of data collection → identify and devise the instruments for data collection, pilot and test them, check their validity and reliability → indicate the data analysis technique and procedures in the intervention →

Issues in the entire replication study (as distinct from the intervention alone): identify how the ethical issues in the replication study will be addressed → identify the areas of focus, contents, tasks in the replication study → indicate how bias will be avoided in the replication study → indicate the resources required for the replication study →

Reporting: how to report the key features of the intervention and its findings → identify and justify what is unchanged between the original study and the replication study, what changes are made to the original study in the replication study, and why → address issues arising from the positionality and reflexivity of the researcher and the relationship of the researcher to the original study → indicate whether/how the replication study will be pre-registered and reported, and where → indicate the success criteria, indicators, and the nature of the evidence for the replication study and how much, where, and how the replication study has been successful →

Summarise the sequence of the research: summarise and present clearly the sequence of the replication study.

The entire sequence is long and large, and whilst there may be variations and recursions in the sequence (e.g. due to constraints arising), it strives to be practical. Chapters 6 and 7 address in greater detail the issues of data analysis and reporting, respectively.

Once the plan for the replication has been completed, pre-registration of research studies can be considered in order to avoid publishing only statistically significant results (i.e. avoiding 'confirmation bias') (Ioannidis, 2005). Details to be included in the pre-registration should indicate variations between the original study and the replication study, for example: goals and their measures, context, setting, location, conditions, sampling, methods, instrumentation, research design, outcomes and outcome domains, measures and metrics (and cut-off points), statistics, time scales and timing of data collection points, components of the intervention, and implementation features (Anderson & Maxwell, 2016; Chhin et al.,

2018; Plucker & Makel, 2021). Further, data on the replication researcher can be included to indicate if it is the same researcher as in the original study or a new, independent, outsider researcher (Eden, 2002). Consideration can also be given to sharing share raw data (e.g. the Open Science Framework: http://OSF.io for pre-registration) in the interests of transparency and non-selective reporting of research results (Moonesinghe et al., 2007).

Ethics in replication studies

Replication research must be ethical. Different parties are involved in replication research, and ethical behaviour applies to all of them. Whilst replication researchers have great responsibility here, they are not the only party. Chapter 1 noted that conducting replication is risky, as the replication study might obtain results that differ from, or challenge, those of the original research, and that this can be taken personally by the author(s) of the original study, even calling into question their competence. Writing on psychology, Sundie et al. (2019) contend that replication studies risk accusing the original researchers of poor practices in their research and 'questionable ethics' (p. e9), particularly in the case of sensitive research. Replication researchers should take care to remain objective, dispassionate, and secure in their integrity; they should avoid having an axe to grind or seeking to 'maliciously contradict' (Morrison et al., 2010, p. 285) the original study or its author(s). Replication researchers must act disinterestedly, for the sake of the work, not its authors, and must avoid conflicts of interest.

Ethics permeates the research endeavour (Cohen et al., 2018). Every stage of the research process must ensure that ethical behaviour takes place, with informed consent where appropriate, respect for individuals, non-maleficence, avoidance of harm, beneficence, anonymity and non-traceability of individuals, transparency and disclosure, safeguarding and protection, protection of vulnerability and sensitivity, and responsible behaviour by both the replication research and ethics review boards (ibid.). The replication researcher must have sufficient expertise to work expertly and with due fairness in both the original study and the replication study; that is an ethical duty.

Brown and Wood (2019), writing on development studies, comment on occasional 'angry responses' from the authors of the original study (p. 922) and serious tensions in replication research, noting the need to work on the choice of wording used in, and the tone of, the report, in order to ensure that it is 'non-combative' (p. 919). Similarly, Plucker and Makel (2021) comment that replication does not need to be 'adversarial' (p. 6). Brown and Wood (2019) comment on the desirability of telling the authors of the original study the replication results and giving them the opportunity to write a response, sometimes to be issued simultaneously with the publication of the replication study. Brown and Wood (2018) also advocate caution in stating that the original study contains an 'error' or a 'mistake' (p. 16), rather than a difference stemming from different methods of data analysis between the original and the replication study, unless, of course, there is a genuine error, in which case its source should be identified (see also Brown & Wood, 2014).

Personal feelings can run high with regard to exact or close replications which find different results from the original study (Brown & Wood, 2019). This might occur less in conceptual replications, as Chapter 3 indicated that they concern testing applicability and generalisability rather than the validity or security of the findings of the original study.

At issue here are the principles of *primum non nocere* (first of all, do no harm) and beneficence: ensure that the replication study is for the greater good (though this can be uncomfortable if the greater good trumps an individual's reputation). Ethical behaviour must ensure that the replication study focuses on the original study and not its author, that the replication researcher reaches out to the authors of the original study in advance of, and during, the replication study (a matter of 'basic, professional courtesy', Brown & Wood, 2018, p. 17), and that the tone of the replication report is suitably cool and dispassionate. The replication study stands by the quality of its work, analysis, and argument, not their temperature. The replication study report should avoid any hint of personal affront, and the author(s) of the original study should have the right of reply (which is often a matter for journal editors, discussed below).

Brown (2021) also comments that the involvement of a third party to support replication studies and mitigate potential conflicts between the authors of the original study and the replication study can sometimes be helpful, though she notes that, with regard to the project 'International Initiative for Impact Evaluation', plain sailing was not always the case for her and her co-author:

> What we learned from that program is that the third party role can end up being a common enemy for the original authors and the replication researchers. There were several cases where original authors (and their supporters), angry about replication studies, claimed to support replication research as a practice but were highly critical of our program. A few replication researchers also faulted the program for some of the tensions. Nonetheless, we think that the processes and policies that we established did lead to better outcomes in terms of the research and the relationships than would have been otherwise.
> (Personal communication)

Brandt et al. (2014) note that, if possible, collaboration between the author(s) of the original study and the replication study can help to understand fully how the original study was undertaken. Replication researchers must be prepared for authors of the original study to be unwilling to share their data, for various reasons that vary from safeguarding and ownership of the data, protection of individuals and confidentiality, to an unwillingness to have their work re-scrutinised, having already been peer-reviewed.

Replication researchers have an ethical responsibility and duty to conduct their study with rigour, transparency, ensuring the highest quality of the study, the trustworthiness of the data and its findings, and propriety. Poorly designed and conducted research, and/or with untrustworthy results, is unethical (Farrimond, 2013; Hammersley & Traianou, 2012).

Sundie et al. (2019) make the case for replication studies to avoid 'weak manipulations' (p. e7) of, and making unnecessary changes to, the research methods used in the original study, and to ensure that the research study has construct validity and cultural validity. The replication must be a fair, unbiased test, reporting the findings of both studies, warts and all, be the replication study successful, unsuccessful, or indeterminate (Block & Kuckertz, 2018). Block and Kuckertz comment that the data in the replication study must be comparable to the quality of the data in the original study or even higher, with tables of original and replication data presented for comparison, and that the replication study should be sufficient to enable a fair comparison to be made with the original study. These matters are ethical, not simply procedural, part of the ethical duty of the researcher to conduct high quality research. This extends to the desirability of pre-registration of the replication study and which items are included in the pre-registration, for transparency (Brandt et al., 2014; Van der Zee & Reich, 2018).

Transparency and disclosure are important ethical factors here. Honesty, openness, and consent to make data sets public come to the fore, with open access to data repositories (e.g. American Political Science Association, 2012). This extends to sharing methods of data analysis, for example codes, syntax, and scripts (Van der Zee & Reich, 2018) and sufficient details for a fair evaluation to be undertaken of the replication (Brandt et al., 2014). Data intended for subsequent sharing, for example for subsequent re-analysis in further studies, should be anonymised and steps taken to remove any possibility of individuals being identified, to be consistent with any prior commitments of confidentiality and non-traceability, and to avoid any actions which could damage an individual's well-being (British Educational Research Association, 2018). The balance between privacy and openness can be delicate (Van der Zee & Reich, 2018), and protecting individuals must be uppermost.

In order to avoid charges of plagiarism and breaches of copyright, replication researchers who use data from an original study must ensure that they have permission for such use (where required), and they should disclose that these data are not their own and whose they are. This involves acknowledging the sources of the data (and any other materials) and permissions obtained. In abiding by academic integrity, plagiarism must be avoided (American Political Science Association, 2012; Morrison et al., 2010), which involves full disclosure of sources and how they have been used, with due acknowledgement of permissions. It is important to adhere to reporting guidelines and protocols (see Chapter 7).

Ethical practice in data analysis, includes:

- using appropriate data analysis techniques, ensuring that the data analysis is fit for purpose;
- analysing, rather than judging the data without supporting evidence;
- in statistical analyses, using appropriate statistics and being faithful to the assumptions underpinning them, presenting results which fairly represent the situation (e.g. not showing it in a better or worse light than is really the case; exerting suitable controls in the data analysis; not collapsing, aggregating and

summarising data unfairly; and including outliers unless there is a defensible reason not to do so);
- using all the relevant data and not being unfairly selective in the data used in the analysis, not omitting or concealing data that do not 'fit' what the researcher wishes to show and not according undue priority and weight to some data;
- not falsifying and/or making up data;
- not (ab)using data to support a preconceived or preferred view;
- being fair to the data and what they show (e.g. not making false, exaggerated, sensationalised, unsubstantiated, unsupported or over-stated claims or misrepresenting what the data show, and not biasing or distorting the analysis by projecting one's own values onto the data and their interpretation);
- removing data that identify individuals who have not given their permission to be identified, yet giving sufficient and appropriate 'voice' to participants (e.g. in qualitative research);
- considering rival interpretations and explanations of the findings.

Honesty, fairness, integrity, transparency, completeness, trustworthiness of the quality of the research and its findings, and freedom from bias are essential, even if the findings and their consequences are not what might have been hoped for (Ioannidis, 2015).

In short, ethical concerns must be addressed at all the stages of the research: selecting the original study for replication; deciding the type of replication to conduct; designing the research and the components of the research design; conducting the replication study; data analysis and interpretation of the original study, the replication study, and the comparison of the findings of both studies; and the reporting of the replication research.

Ethics also extends to journal editors who, as Chapter 1 suggested, are often unwilling to accept replication studies or are only interested in publishing replications that have sensational or surprising results, large effect sizes, or strong statistical significance. Editors have an ethical duty to open their doors wider to replication papers and not to suppress such papers or to dissuade researchers from conducting and submitting replications. The argument goes wider, involving issues such as whether publishers should levy charges for accessing research that has been funded by public sources (such as local or national governments) or whether access to such research should be free (Biesta, 2020). Replication research is part of the political economy of academic publishing of research (ibid.), and publishing is a multi-million-dollar business that relies on readers having to pay to read research that has been publicly funded, and this raises ethical issues.

Ethics, as one anonymous reviewer of this book pointed out, raise the ethical responsibility for publicly funded original research to be tested in a replication to ensure that its results are trustworthy. This also involves ensuring the quality of the replication study itself and its findings. The same reviewer also suggested that, in addressing ethical behaviour, funding agencies or parties should make it a mandatory requirement for research studies and their related educational programmes which have been shown to have a positive impact (e.g. a high effect size) in a single study to conduct a replication study before exposing children to the programme or intervention in question.

Replications can overcome researcher bias; they can reduce the likelihood of a Type I error and a Type II error, and they can provide more reliable effect sizes than single studies, as many original studies, particularly small-scale studies conducted by individual researchers, tend to overstate the findings and the effect sizes of randomised controlled trials. This is part of the ethical responsibility for safeguarding: children and teachers should not be exposed to programmes and interventions that are based on flimsy, under-tested, and one-off studies, however strong the findings of the single study happened to be.

Results must be demonstrated to be trustworthy before being launched onto educational institutions, and replication studies have a part to play here. It would be unwise, even unethical, to devise policy in education on the basis of insecure evidence, and evidence must move beyond single studies, as, on their own, we don't know how secure or generalisable are their findings; there is a need for replications in education as in other disciplines to ensure that what we think we know is secure. There is a need for healthy scepticism in considering research evidence (See, 2020). Ensuring that research is of high quality is an ethical duty.

Conclusion

Planning a replication study must consider a wide range of matters, some of which emanate from the original study and some of which concern the purposes of the replication. The rootedness of the replication study in the original study or concept is central to the planning of the replication study, including its purposes and type. The replication study might be to validate, remediate, extend, refine, apply, improve upon, and generalise from the original study or concept. In turn, these affect the type and conduct of the replication study, what to hold the same as in the original study, and what to change, and how and why.

These points argue for a close-grained analysis and evaluation of the original study, in order to identify and justify where to make changes in its replication study and what to hold constant between the two. The chapter has indicated what to include here and what to address in the replication study, what the replication study is for and what it will do.

Planning the replication study must operationalise its purposes, research questions, types, areas of focus, and conduct: what to consider and how to turn a purpose into a concrete piece of replication research. In addressing this, the chapter argued for the need to make constant reference to the original study, in order to understand, justify, and work with the levels and areas of sameness and difference.

The chapter indicated that, whilst it is important to plan for what constitutes a 'successful' replication and to identify success criteria in the planning of the replication study, nevertheless terms such as 'success' and 'failure' in a replication have varied meanings. Here, the chapter has suggested that, whilst success and failure might concern the confirmation or refutation of the findings of the original study, or its generalisability and applicability in contexts and settings that differ from those of the original study, it is a moot point as to whether these constitute success or failure, as the replication's findings have made a positive contribution to understanding the boundaries and limits of the original study, its hypothesis, idea, and concept. This raises the issue of relating the outcomes and findings of the replication study to its intended purposes in judging whether, where, and how far the replication study has succeeded or failed. It is for the researcher to decide 'beyond a reasonable doubt', and to indicate on what grounds, how far the replication study has or has not 'worked'; 'success' and 'failure' are a matter of degree, rather than being an absolute.

The replication researcher must provide an inclusive, justified, and complete picture of what has been considered in planning the replication study, and how this has led to its compilation and the contents of what is included. The researcher must behave ethically, with integrity, transparency, honesty, fairness, the provision of sufficient detail, and the avoidance of bias. To complement this, the replication research itself must be of the highest standard and meet rigorous demands of quality, trustworthiness, and fitness for purpose throughout. Research is an ethical endeavour.

6 Data analysis and interpretation in a replication in education

Overview

This chapter argues that the data analysis in the replication study must be conducted both in terms of the replication study itself and in comparing it with the original study. In terms of the replication study itself, the chapter addresses several points:

- the need to focus on the achievement of the purposes of the study in itself (e.g. to see how successfully the intervention has 'worked');
- the need to clarify, disclose, and justify the criteria for judging how far the study has been successful – a replication, non-replication, or an indeterminate replication – and difficulties in judging with any certainty how far the replication has been successful;
- the kinds of statistical analysis that can be conducted and tools for this: standardised means, difference tests; effect size; confidence intervals, standard error, distributions, skewness, range, direction;
- tools for qualitative data analysis, some of which derive from grounded theory, and what qualitative data can and cannot do;
- issues in combining qualitative and quantitative data analysis.

The chapter argues that, when focusing on the findings of each study, each study should define with precision and accuracy what are the exact areas of focus in the findings: what the findings are about and exactly which findings. In comparing the findings of the two studies, the chapter addresses several issues:

- the need to determine how similar or different they are, and with what level of certainty, given that no two studies are the same;
- the challenges in comparing two studies that differ from each other in many respects;
- the argument for conducting an exact replication and the challenges of comparing the findings of an approximate, systematic, and conceptual replication (i.e. that which is not an exact replication);

DOI: 10.4324/9781003204237-7

- the need to define the criteria for similarity, difference, a 'successful', 'unsuccessful', and 'indeterminate' replication;
- using a set of questions for comparing the findings of the original study and the replication study;
- identifying challenges in comparing and interpreting the original study and the replication study and what their findings show; what one can and cannot conclude if the findings are similar or different; and how far, and where, the replication study has been successful.

The chapter focuses on issues, and gives examples, of analysis, interpretation, statistical tests, and tools of qualitative data analysis, indicating what these are and how and why to use them. Central to the data analysis is the question 'what is the replication researcher looking for in the findings?', and the chapter addresses this question.

Purposes of the data analysis

Data analysis has two main purposes. Firstly, it seeks to identify how far the replication study itself, on its own, has 'worked' and succeeded in its intention. Secondly, it seeks to identify how far the replication study has found similar or different results from those of the original study, for example how far and where it confirms, refutes, and qualifies those of the original study or yields an 'indeterminate' result. The first of these is confined to the replication study alone, whilst the second is the purpose of the entire exercise.

The data analysis is informed by, and must be aligned to, the purposes and type of replication study and should provide answers to the research questions. Typically, the replication researcher is looking to see how similar or different the results – the findings – of the replication study are to those of the original study, with what level of certainty, and where the results of the replication confirm, partially confirm, do not confirm those of the original study, or whether it is impossible to tell. For an exact replication, this is in order to confirm the validity and security of the original study and its findings; for a close, approximate, systematic, or conceptual replication, this is to determine whether the original study can be generalised and applied beyond its original bounds, for example to other settings, samples, methods, and instrumentation. At issue here is the study of similarity and difference and the level of certainty and uncertainty with which claims for such similarity and difference can be made.

Variability occurs naturally within and between the original study and the replication study, frustrating attempts to draw easy conclusions from the replication's findings (Patil et al., 2016). Indeed, a full replication study in education might be impossible (Holme, 2019). Except for an exact replication using the original data and identical procedures, a replication cannot give exactly the same answer, as no two samples and settings are identical. Sampling error and measurement error exist, producing differences in measured outcomes, for example of effect size, and this renders it uncertain as to how far a replication has or has not shown the same findings as the original (Stanley & Spence, 2014). Hence, the degree of uncertainty that is tolerable must be decided, which is typically a matter of human judgement. The chapter sets out several concerns in deciding the tolerance level, for example statistically and in terms of human judgement.

Certainty of similarity and difference is not only a statistical matter: as indicated in previous chapters, given the context-rich, variable-dense, causally complex nature of classrooms and social settings, the level of certainty that can be accorded to findings of similarity and difference is unclear. Human judgement is needed.

To fulfil its purpose, an exact replication, concerning the internal validity of the original study, can rework the original data, re-analysing the data to check for different findings. Here, the researcher can use the same or different statistics or methods to analyse the data, to determine whether different results from those of the original study are found, and, if they are, what to draw from this. However, in other replications it is likely that using different methods of analysis and different statistics will produce differences in outcomes, for example in effect size. Hence, it may be difficult to conclude how much and how certainly a replication has or has not shown the same findings as the original (Stanley & Spence, 2014). One can expect to find a range of results in replications, even under 'ideal conditions' (Stanley & Spence, 2014, p. 309).

If the purpose of the replication study research is to test generalisability, then close, approximate, systematic, and conceptual replications must establish and judge the level of closeness and similarity required between the original study and its replication and the certainty with which claims of similarity and difference can be made. Data analysis, here, can employ a range of statistics and qualitative data analysis techniques in establishing such claims.

Four questions can be addressed concerning data analysis in replication studies:

1 How to conduct the data analysis: which statistics to use in quantitative data analysis and how to conduct a qualitative data analysis?
2 How similar to the findings of the original study must the findings of the replication study be, and in what areas, in order to decide how far the replication has successfully replicated the findings of the original study?
3 How to decide the criteria for similarity and the levels of similarity required?
4 How certain can the replication researcher be of claims made for a successful replication, similarity and difference between the original study and the replication study?

To address these questions, the data analysis must indicate what it is for, what it will do, what it seeks to find out, what tools for data analysis it uses, what it focuses on, and how it is conducted.

Two areas in working on the data analysis

There are two areas in working with the data gathered in the replication study: (a) data analysis and interpretation of the replication study itself, and (b) comparing the findings with those of the original study. This chapter addresses these two areas. The first works with the data collected in the replication study, processing and analysing them in order to judge how successfully the intervention has or has not 'worked'. For example, this might be how much the intervention has improved student performance in the treatment group more than in the control group (in an experimental study), the findings from reworking the original data or very closely matched data (in an exact replication), how much the intervention's 'concept' has 'worked' in improving students' achievements in a different setting, under different conditions, using different samples, tasks, instruments, and treatments, and so on (in a conceptual replication). The data analysis here works on the replication study alone and, like any single study of an intervention, judges how successful the intervention has been in terms of outcomes.

The second area compares the results of the findings with those of the original study and decides how far and where the findings of the two studies are similar and different and what arises from the comparison. In comparing the results of the original and the replication study, the replication researcher has to account for the level of similarity, closeness, and proximity of the results between the original study and the replication study, together with how much certainty and tolerance of difference and uncertainty between and in them respectively is acceptable (Holme, 2019), and where. In quantitative research this can be approached statistically. This chapter indicates which statistics are available and some of the concerns in using them, and it provides examples of these; it also addresses qualitative data analysis.

Tools for data analysis

The researcher should indicate explicitly what is the focus of the data analysis, why and how the analysis addresses these. As in any research study, some of the data for the findings might be numerical, some might be qualitative; indeed, some of the analysis might wish to convert qualitative data into numbers ('quantitising', e.g. in content analysis, Cohen et al., 2018, p. 44). The tools for analysis set out below can be used to identify similarities and differences between groups *within* a single study in Area One (the findings of the replication study) and *between* the results of the original study and its replication in Area Two (comparing the findings of the replication study with those of the original study).

Quantitative data analysis

In analysing numerical data in an exact replication (an internal validation study; a reproducibility replication), Porte and McManus (2019) suggest several ways of working with the data:

- *cross validation*: splitting the original data into two or more groups randomly and then conducting identical analyses on each group to see how similar are the results of each subgroup, thereby identifying if the overall result is replicable or more a matter of 'random variabilities' (p. 66);

- *jackknife analysis*: repeating a test several times, starting with the whole group and removing one subgroup each time, in order to see the similarity of the findings when each removal is conducted; and
- *bootstrapping*: copying the data repeatedly into a large 'mega-file' (p. 67) and then drawing samples from this file and comparing the findings for similarity, thereby using the mega-file as the population and each drawing out of a subgroup to represent the sample.

These require access to the original data, source codes and syntax for running the data analysis software, details and specifications of the system software and the scripts for processing the data, specifications of the models used, and the sequence of analysis (National Academies of Sciences, Engineering, and Medicine, 2019).

Whilst these methods test similarity and difference, they beg the question of how to judge the degree of similarly and difference; here, the researcher can use several statistics, though the final decision on similarity or difference is a matter of informed professional judgement, that is a human rather than formulaic act (Shapin & Schaffer, 1985). There are different ways of judging the success of a replication, with no universally agreed standards for making such judgements (Camerer et al., 2016).

Replication researchers have many possible statistics available to them, for example:

- *Simple descriptive data*, for example: frequencies and distributions (a test of normal distribution is the Kolmogorov-Smirnov statistic), means and confidence intervals, modes, medians, standard deviations, variance, skewness and kurtosis, standard error, z-scores (for standardising scores);
- *Inferential statistics*, for example: difference tests for parametric and non-parametric data (chi-square, t-test, Mann-Whitney test, Analysis of Variance (ANOVA), Wilcoxon test, Kruskal-Wallis test, Friedman test), regression and multiple regression, correlational analysis (Pearson, Spearman), effect sizes.

In working with quantitative data it is important to ensure that the assumptions underpinning the statistic(s) chosen have been met, as set out in Table 6.1 (Cohen et al., 2018).

If parametric data have been collected (interval and ratio data whose distributions conform to a normal curve of distribution), and if the assumptions underpinning them have been met, then inferential statistics available for data analysis include t-test, Analysis of Variance (ANOVA), regression and multiple regression, Pearson correlation, z-scores, effect sizes. If the assumptions underpinning the interval and ratio data have not been met, or if the data are ordinal, then distribution-free, non-parametric tests are available: Mann-Whitney test, Wilcoxon test, Kruskal-Wallis test, Friedman test, chi-square, Spearman correlation. If the data are nominal/categorical, then the research can use frequencies, mode, and the chi-square statistic.

Table 6.1 Assumptions of statistical tests

Test	Assumptions
Mean	Data are normally distributed, with no outliers
Confidence level and confidence interval of the mean	Data are normally distributed, with no outliers
	The variance is independent of the mean
Mode	There are few values and few scores occurring which have a similar frequency
Median	There are many values/points on the scale
Chi-square	Data are categorical (nominal)
	Randomly sampled population
	Independent categories
	Data are discrete (i.e. no decimal places between data points)
	80% of all the cells in a cross-tabulation contain five or more cases
Kolmogorov-Smirnov	The underlying distribution is continuous
	Data are nominal
t-test, Analysis of Variance, effect size	Sample is selected randomly from the population
	Sample is homogeneous
	Parametric data
	Each group is independent of the other
	The groups to be compared are nominal, and the comparison is made using interval and ratio data
	The sets of data to be compared are normally distributed (the bell-shaped Gaussian curve of distribution)
	The sets of scores have approximately equal variances, or the square of the standard deviation is known
	The data are interval or ratio
Wilcoxon	The data are ordinal
	The samples are related
Mann-Whitney and Kruskal-Wallis	The groups to be compared are nominal, and the comparison is made using ordinal data
	The populations from which the samples are drawn have similar distributions
	Samples are drawn randomly
	Samples are independent of each other
Spearman rank order correlation	The data are ordinal
Pearson correlation	The data are interval and ratio

(Continued)

Table 6.1 (Continued)

Test	Assumptions
Regression (simple and multiple)	The data are interval and ratio and derive from a random or probability sample
	Adequate sample size
	The data are interval or ratio (unless ordinal regression is used)
	Avoidance of singularity (where one variable is a combination of independent variables)
	Outliers have been removed
	There is a linear relationship between the independent and dependent variables
	The dependent variable is normally distributed (the bell-shaped Gaussian curve of distribution)
	The residuals for the dependent variable (the differences between calculated and observed scores) are approximately normally and consistently evenly distributed (homoscedasticity: the similarity of scatter across the line of best fit)
	Collinearity is removed (where one independent variable is an exact or very close correlate of another)
	The residuals are not strongly correlated with the independent variables
	Each case is independent of the others

Source: Cohen et al., 2018, pp. 844–845

How, then, can the quantitative replication researcher proceed? How can the degree of similarity and difference be calculated between groups in the replication study, and with what level of certainty? Difference testing can be useful here, discussed below (e.g. statistical significance testing, effect sizes, confidence intervals, range, distributions, standard deviations, skewness, and the direction of the effect). The chapter argues against statistical significance testing, and whilst it advocates using effect sizes, distributions, and confidence intervals, it indicates that these, too, present challenges.

Statistical significance testing

The statistical tests indicated earlier give a result and indicate its level of statistical significance. Statistical significance purports to indicate the probability or likelihood of the findings (e.g. a difference, a correlation) being not simply by chance, given the acceptability of the assumption made of the null hypothesis (which is questionable, e.g. Kline, 2004 and Nassaji, 2012), and with such-and-such a level of confidence. However, statistical significance (null hypothesis significance testing), though widely used, including those inferential statistics indicated earlier, has been called into question on many grounds, to the extent that is has been discredited in many fields of social science (e.g. Carver, 1978; Cohen et al., 2018; Kline, 2004; Morrison, 2021; Worrall, 2007; Ziliak & McCloskey, 2008), for example: the false assumption of the null hypothesis; the limits of randomisation; statistical significance being often taken incorrectly to mean 'given the result, how likely is the null hypothesis' rather than 'given the null hypothesis, how likely is the result'; the influence of sample size on statistical significance (it is often impossible *not* to find statistical significance when a large sample has been used); small samples being prone to a Type II error (false negative); conventional cut-off points in statistical significance (e.g. 0.05, 0.01, 0.001) being somewhat arbitrary and risking leading to false dichotomous thinking, that is, that a finding is or is not statistically significant; statistical significance not telling researchers what they really want or need to know, which is *how big* is a difference or *how strong* is a relationship, or *how strong* is the cause of an effect or the effect of a cause. Statistical significance does not tell researchers 'how much', only *that* such-and-such is the case with such-and-such a level of confidence that it is not by chance. For the *how much* measure we need effect size.

Further, non-statistically significant findings are not necessarily evidence of non-replication in findings, since the null hypothesis may be a false assumption (Anderson & Maxwell, 2016; Ziliak & McCloskey, 2008). The *direction* of statistically significant findings might be more important than their level of significance (Anderson & Maxwell, 2016; Hedges & Schauer, 2019; Moonesinghe et al., 2007).

Effect size

A useful alternative to significance testing is effect size, which purports to measure the size of a difference (something that significance testing cannot do). Effect sizes relate to difference testing; they use average scores and indicate the calculated size of the differences between the means of two groups (e.g. between a control group and a treatment group, between the findings of the original study and the findings of the replication study, between a pre-test and a post-test).

There are several ways of calculating effect sizes (see Cohen et al., 2018; Simonsohn, 2015), for example Cohen's *d*, Glass's delta, Hedges's *g*, eta squared, and partial eta squared. A typical way of calculating the effect size is by subtracting the mean of the control group from the mean of the experimental group and dividing the result by the pooled standard deviation of the two groups (much free software performs this calculation). The effect size can then be considered small, medium, large, very large, and so on. Standardising the means and standard deviations is also useful here, to compare like with like.

Effect sizes can be affected by features of the whole study (Morrison, 2021; Simpson, 2018, 2019, 2020), including: sample size, characteristics, type, homogeneity/heterogeneity; differences in group size; the research design; the intervention and its procedures; context; instrumentation; the range and distribution of scores; the reliability of the measures; the timing of the data collection; statistical power of the study; test construction and characteristics; variances within and between the groups; attrition; who devised the test (e.g. teacher-devised, standardised); and duration of the intervention. Simpson (2018, 2019, 2020) demonstrates that sampling, measures, instruments, and study design influence effect size measurement.

Further, Morrison (2021) notes limitations of what effect size can tell the researcher:

> What does effect size actually tell us? Does it tell us that something 'works'? No. It tells us that if we subtract the mean of one group from the mean of another group and divide it by the pooled standard deviation, we obtain such-and-such a figure in the context of such-and-such a research comparison group and comparison activities, such-and-such a research design, such-and-such a sample size, with such-and-such instrumentation, with such-and-such an amount or duration of intervention, measured at such-and-such a point in time and with such-and-such a power size in a power analysis. It is a measure of an average difference between a given control and treatment group, under multiple conditions, not a measure of 'what works' or the claimed size of the intervention unaffected by design features. 'What works' is a human judgement and it is not possible to simply read [it] off from an effect size. . . . It is a highly limited, highly contingent statistic.
>
> (pp. 165–166)

Effect size works with outcome data alone; it does not take account of what preceded, contextualised, and accompanied the outcome data, and these are the very features that influence effect size.

Anderson and Maxwell (2016) question whether a replication study in fact turns out to be a non-replication if its effect size differs from the original, but there are no clear criteria, foci, cut-off points, and standards for assessing replication 'success', including procedural similarity, levels of precision and accuracy, statistical power, closeness of findings, implementation (see also Camerer et al., 2016; Open Science Collaboration, 2015). If effect sizes differ between the original study and the replication study, it is a matter of human judgement as to how far there is sufficient similarity between the two to count as a successful replication. There are no absolute cut-off points in deciding whether an effect size is small (0.2), medium (0.5), large (0.8) (Cohen, 1988), or weak (0–0.20), modest (0.21–0.50), moderate (0.51–1.00), strong (0.10) (Cohen et al., 2018). Nevertheless, if two effect sizes are in different putative judgement categories, and their margins of standard error are wide and confidence intervals are low, then this suggests that replication is in doubt (see Cohen, 1988; Cohen et al., 2018; Cumming, 2012; Field, 2018).

Caution must be exercised in considering what the effect size can and cannot tell the replication researcher. Rather than being an absolute measure, it is relative to a range of factors that inhere in the replication study design and its components.

Confidence intervals

Confidence intervals can help in judging the degree of similarity or difference between two scores or sets of findings by indicating the boundaries of the highest and lowest values within which the calculated mean can fall, and with how much certainty (e.g. 95 per cent) (Field, 2018). They are a measure of precision, accuracy, and of the probability of the security with which the researcher suggests how close the means found are to the boundaries that have been set (Cohen et al., 2018; Jacob et al., 2019; Nassaji, 2012). The confidence interval, usually expressed as a percentage (often 95 per cent), is an index of how certain the researchers can be (e.g. 95 per cent confident) that the mean lies within a given variation range. Presenting the confidence interval indicates the degree of precision and certainty/uncertainty in the result found.

The level of certainty is often set at 95 per cent, and the range of variation which includes the population is computed statistically, based on the percentage of an area under the normal curve of distribution, for example a 95 per cent confidence level covers 95 per cent of the curve of distribution. The upper and lower limits of variation are calculated automatically in statistical packages (e.g. SPSS). The confidence interval can be set by the researcher or is set automatically, with a default confidence interval setting of 95 per cent. The confidence interval does not indicate that confidence/certainty will occur 95 per cent of the time, only that the researcher can be 95 per cent certain that the result found falls within the two boundaries (upper and lower) (Figure 6.1 provides an example of these).

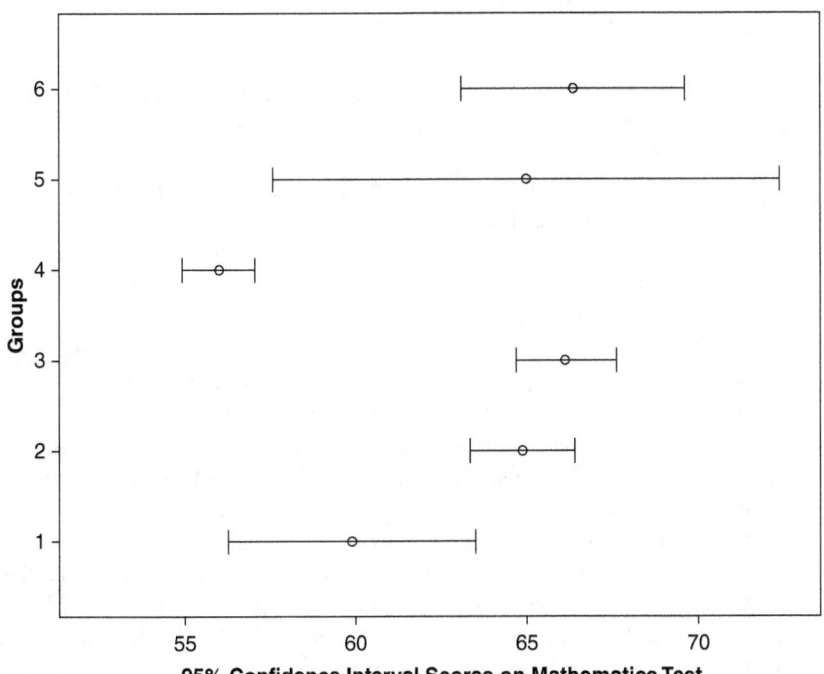

Figure 6.1 Confidence intervals for a mathematics test

In presenting the results of the confidence interval, statistics software packages typically indicate the range of values, bounded above and below the mean of the sample, that are likely to contain the population. The ideal situation for the replication researcher is where the means of groups in the replication study, or in the original study and the replication study, are close to each other, within the specified range boundaries, where the range of variation (upper and lower limits) in both studies is small, and where the distributions of the scores around the means of both studies are similar (see Figure 6.1).

In looking at the means of the original study and the replication study, the replication researcher ascertains how close the two means are to each other, and the degree of variation (upper and lower limits of the range of scores) in the two means, and the similarity of the two distributions (e.g. skewness and kurtosis). The closer the two means are to each other and the smaller the variation is for each mean, and the greater is the similarity of the distributions in the two studies, the greater is the precision and the certainty that there is replication (e.g. Jacob et al., 2019).

Figure 6.1 provides an example of working with confidence intervals (using SPSS). Imagine that these are scores on a mathematics test in a replication study. Here, the scores of six groups of students (the vertical axis) are presented and the scores range from the mid-50s to the mid-70s (horizontal axis). In this example, the confidence interval has been set at the frequently used level of 95 per cent. The means are the circles, and the range – the upper and lower limits – are indicated by the lines either side of the mean.

Several points can be observed in Figure 6.1:

1 Whilst the upper and lower limits of the scores for groups 2, 3, and 4 are small (high precision), those for groups 1, 5, and 6 are large, particularly for group 5 (low precision).
2 Imagine that group 2 was the original study's findings and that group 3 was the replication study's findings. The means are close to each other, the variance (the range) is small, and the distributions of the two scores are almost identical. It is highly unlikely that these are by chance, that is, the replication has confirmed the original study.
3 Imagine that group 1 was the original study's findings and that group 5 was the replication study's findings. The means are some distance from each other, the variance (the range) is high, and the distributions of the two scores differ. There is a higher likelihood than in the second example that these are by chance, that is, the replication has not confirmed with sufficient security the original study.
4 Imagine that group 1 was the original study's findings and that group 3 was the replication study's findings. The means are some distance from each other, the variance in the two groups differs a lot, the range of the upper and lower limits of group 1 has no overlap with that of group 3, and the distributions of the two scores differ. This suggests that the replication has not confirmed the original study.

Data analysis and interpretation 101

5   Imagine that group 3 was the original study's findings and that group 4 was the replication study's findings. The means are a long way from each other, the variance is similar (but that of group 4 is slightly smaller), and the variance of group 3 has no overlap with that of group 4. This suggests that the replication has not confirmed the original study.
6   Imagine that group 2 was the original study's findings and that group 5 was the replication study's findings. Whilst the mean scores of these two groups were almost identical, the low level of precision in group 5 (wide range) compromises claims of replication here, as the likelihood of chance in the means being similar is high. It would be unwise to claim that the replication study has successfully replicated the original study; the results are indeterminate.
7   Imagine that group 3 was the original study's findings and that group 6 was the replication study's findings. Whilst the mean scores of these two groups were almost identical, the low level of precision (wide range) in group 6 compromises a claim of replication here, as the likelihood of chance in the means being similar is reasonably high. It would be unwise to claim with any sense of certainty that the replication study has successfully replicated the original study.
8   Imagine that group 5 was the original study's findings and that group 6 was the replication study's findings. Whilst the means of these two groups were similar, the low level of precision (wide range) in both groups compromises claims of replication here, as the likelihood of chance in the means being similar is high; indeed, it is possible for the mean of group 5 to be outside the lower or upper limit of the scores of group 6. It would be unwise to claim with any sense of certainty that the replication study has successfully replicated the original study; the results are indeterminate.

Figure 6.1 indicates that there are different degrees of replication. The claims made for replication in the second point are much stronger than in the sixth point, and the claims made for non-replication in the fifth point are stronger than for the seventh point.

Let us take another example of working with confidence intervals (Figure 6.2). Imagine that these are scores on a history test in a replication study. Here, the scores of six groups of students are presented (the vertical axis), and the scores range from the upper 40s to the mid-60s (horizontal axis). In this example, the confidence interval has been set at the frequently used level of 95 per cent. The means are the circles, and the range of scores is indicated by the lines either side of the means.

In Figure 6.2, the overall mean has been entered (the vertical line between the score of 54 and 56). Here, the score of group 5 has had a disproportionate effect on the overall mean, lowering it such that all the other groups are above the overall mean. However, the scores of groups 1, 2, and 4 are entirely out of the picture: none of their scores, with the upper and lower limits, contains the overall mean, and the score of group 6 only just contains the overall mean (the lower limit of the score for group six only just overlaps with the mean) (see also Field, 2018).

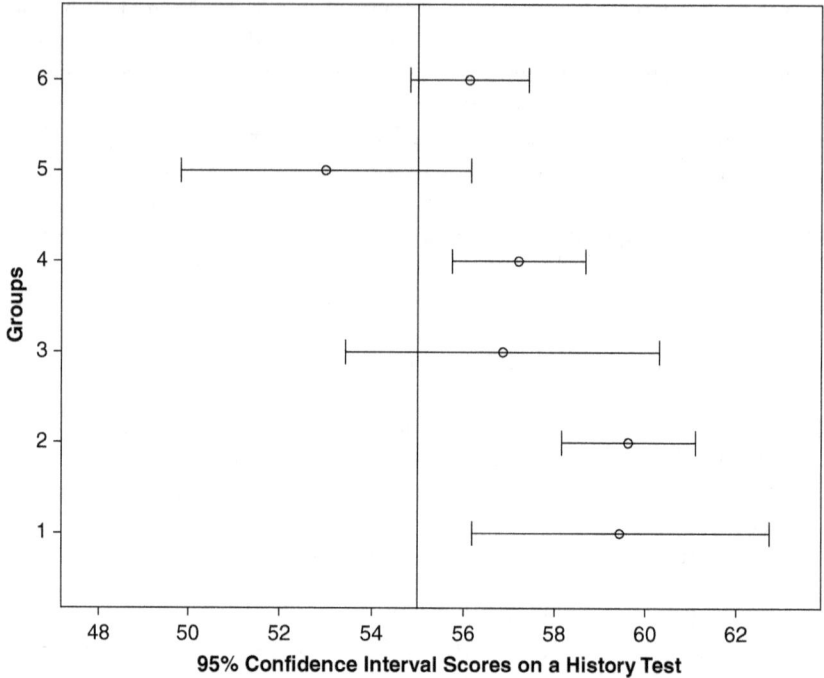

Figure 6.2 Confidence intervals in a history test

This suggests that the groups are not particularly comparable with each other. The challenge facing the researcher here is to render the groups comparable fairly; this can be done by converting the raw scores into standardised scores (z-scores). In Figure 6.3 the scores of the six groups have been standardised to a mean of zero and a standard deviation of 1.00 (a common way of standardising scores), rendering it possible to compare like with like.

Figure 6.3 indicates that, once standardised, groups 1, 3, 4, and 6 contain the overall mean, whilst groups 2 and 5 fall outside the range. The moral of the story is that (a) fair comparison can be made only if the upper and lower limits of each of the means contain the overall mean, and (b) it is preferable to work with standardised scores rather than raw scores, as these enable fair comparisons to be made.

Hedges and Schauer (2019) note the absence of established standards for what constitutes appropriate levels of precision or the width/narrowness of confidence intervals (and standard errors); these are human judgements, informed by the levels of precision and certainty required. Further, if the researcher wishes to have a very high confidence interval (e.g. 99 per cent) then the sample size will be high; if the researcher wants a less stringent confidence interval (e.g. 90 per cent), then the sample size can be smaller. Often a compromise is reached, and the researcher opts for a 95 per cent confidence interval. Some research may require a very stringent confidence interval (e.g. 99 per cent and a very small margin of error, e.g. 1 per cent) to ensure certainty. For example, clinical trials of a new drug cannot

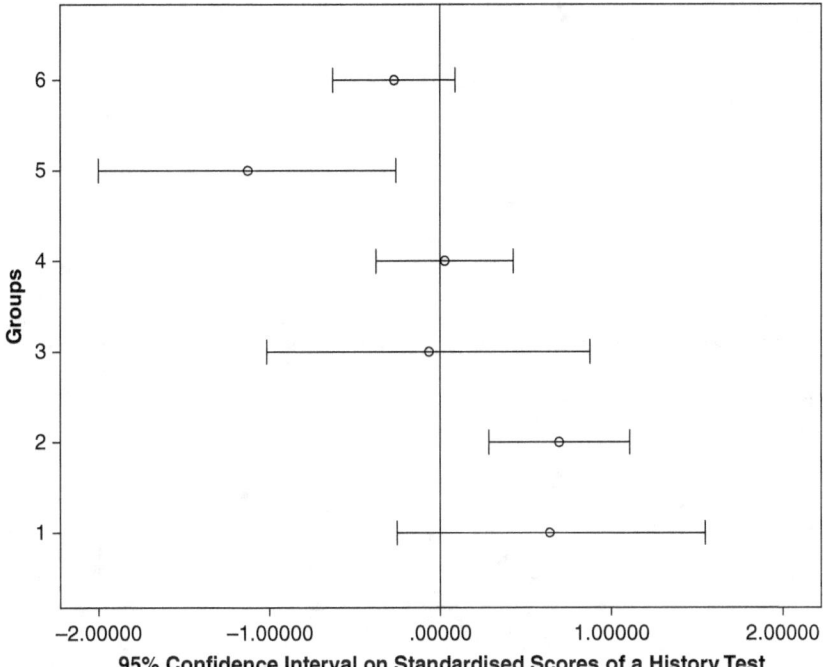

Figure 6.3 Confidence intervals for standardised scores on a history test

tolerate errors or high variation, as an imprecise result could be fatal. Other kinds of research may be content with a less stringent requirement (e.g. 95 per cent confidence interval). For a fuller discussion of confidence intervals, see Cumming (2012), Field (2018), and Jacob et al. (2019), see also the critique of confidence intervals and its claim to indicate precision in Morey et al. (2016).

Standard error

An alternative to confidence intervals is standard error: the standard error of the mean. Like the confidence interval, standard error is a measure of precision: a large standard error (a large distance between the upper and lower limits of a finding: the error margin) indicates limited precision, whilst a small standard error (a small distance between the upper and lower limits: the error margin) indicates greater precision. Standard error bars can extend from one standard deviation below the mean to one standard error above it (Cumming, 2012); this is often a smaller range than that indicated by a confidence interval (a confidence interval can be as much as twice as large as the standard error). For this reason, the confidence interval might be more suitable than the standard error if greater tolerance of uncertainty is acceptable.

Compare, for example, the two graphs in Figure 6.4; using the same data here, the left-hand graph indicates the upper and lower limits of the range using

104 *Data analysis and interpretation*

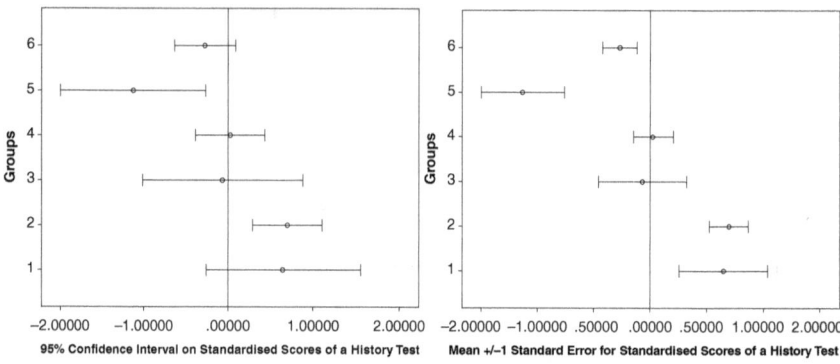

Figure 6.4 Comparing confidence intervals and standard errors

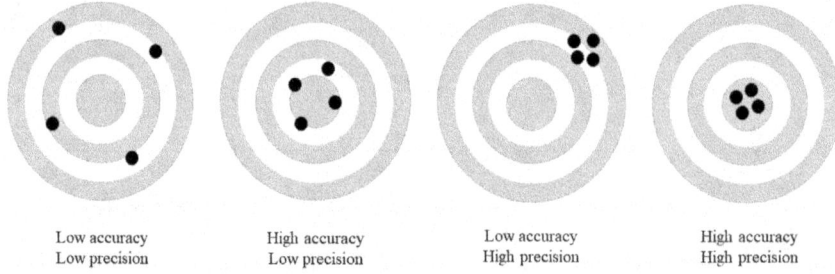

Figure 6.5 Precision and accuracy in measurement

confidence intervals, whilst the right-hand graph indicates the upper and lower limits of the range using standard errors. Here, the confidence interval graph has a wider range of variation around each mean than the standard error. The difference might be important, since the left-hand graph includes groups 1 and 6, but the right-hand graph excludes them (their upper and lower limits respectively do not overlap with the overall mean).

Precision – the degree of closeness in the measurements – is important and has to be complemented by accuracy (see Figure 6.5). Accuracy, the closeness of the results to the 'true' value (the bullseye in the targets), requires keeping to a set standard for 'truth', otherwise there is the potential for bias. Replication on its own does not guarantee accuracy: the original study and the replication study might be identical but identically wrong. Accuracy concerns the validity (e.g. construct validity) of the original and the replication study and the removal of bias and systematic errors. Precision can be measured by using confidence intervals, standard error, standard deviations, and range (the smaller the range, the greater the precision), whilst accuracy can be addressed by ensuring construct validity, by having large samples, by repeated measures, by triangulation of methods, and by employing peer review.

Imagine that a researcher wishes to calculate the level of similarity between the means of two sets of results (e.g. in the original study and the replication study). She conducts a t-test of difference and finds that the average difference in scores between the findings (e.g. of an intervention) of the original study and the replication study is 0.350, with a standard error of the difference being 0.464 (this chapter does not go into how these scores are computed, as this requires knowledge of the t-test). The computer software (SPSS) shows that, with a 95 per cent confidence interval, the mean should lie between −0.579 and +1.278, and this includes the null value (zero). Here, the average difference found (0.350) lies within this range, indicating that the two scores were statistically quite similar, that is, the difference between them was small.

Distributions

The replication researcher can examine two sets of distributions of data (e.g. from the original study and the replication study; from a pre-test and a post-test; from a control group and an experimental group), to ascertain (a) how 'normal' they are (the Gaussian curve of distribution), for example using the Kolmogorov-Smirnov statistic, and (b) how far they depart from the normal distribution by measuring their kurtosis (the steepness of the curve) and their skewness (whether the data are skewed towards one end of the curve, i.e. are asymmetrical). The researcher must exercise judgement in considering how similar and normal are the distributions in the two sets of data, and what level of difference can be tolerated, for example if one data set is positively skewed and the other is negatively skewed, then this suggests that similarity is very slight, as the directions of the skew differ (e.g. Field, 2018).

In using significance testing (inadvisable), effect size, confidence intervals, range, and distributions in the data analysis, the intention is to determine how well the study has 'worked' and with what level of certainty, that is, how well it has achieved its intention and accomplished what it intended to accomplish, and how far, and where, the intervention has been successful. The size of the effect, the breadth and narrowness of the standard error and the confidence intervals, the distributions, the range and standard deviations, the skewness, the statistical power (see Chapter 5) and, if used, the level of statistical significance, can provide statistical clues to the level of success of the intervention. However, how far this constitutes a successful intervention is a human judgement of 'beyond a reasonable doubt', informed by statistical evidence.

Replication studies, like other research studies (e.g. experimental studies), can pre-register the criteria to be used in deciding how far the study has been successful. This includes, for example: indicating the effect size to be reached, the confidence intervals to be used, the standard deviations, distributions, skewness, direction of the findings and, if deemed suitable, the statistical significance level to be found.

In analysing quantitative data, the replication researcher can calculate the following in both the original study and the replication study (Area One) and to compare the two studies (Area Two) (see the earlier discussion of 'Two areas in working on the data analysis'):

- standardised means and standard deviations (to be able to compare means fairly);
- confidence intervals and range of scores (to compare the narrowness of the range of scores and their precision);
- standard deviations (to compare the degrees of variance or dispersal from and around, respectively, their means, which informs judgements of precision);
- effect sizes (to compare the outcomes and impact of the two studies);
- kurtosis (to compare how much the two sets of scores are normal and non-normal distributions);
- skewness (to compare how much the distribution of the two sets of scores are asymmetrical, e.g. skewed to the right or left);
- statistical significance levels (to compare the probability and chance of the level of closeness in their levels of statistical significance);
- statistical power (to compare whether they are underpowered or sufficiently powered to yield secure results);
- direction of their effects (to ensure that they are the same in the two studies);
- sample sizes (to compare their statistical power, accuracy, and avoidance of risks of Type I and Type II errors).

Qualitative data analysis

Chapter 4 addressed the question of whether a replication study could be qualitative, and it argued that this was possible. Qualitative data can feature in a replication study, whether it is qualitative in terms of its paradigmatic nature, or whether it simply contains non-numerical data as well as numbers. Such data might come from, for example:

- interviews (transcribed or not transcribed);
- observations (participant to non-participant);
- field notes and records of events;
- documents, reports, and print materials;
- memos, emails, and diaries;
- audios (e.g. online conversations);
- visual images (e.g. video, photographs);
- websites and website data (e.g. online surveys);
- qualitative survey data (e.g. from questionnaires);
- artifacts.

The most likely types of qualitative data will be written, word-based data, images, and aural data. This chapter does not go into specific details of how to use specific tools of data analysis in education (for this, see, e.g. Cohen et al., 2018), as this is beyond its scope. However, it indicates tools that are available.

In analysing qualitative data for a replication study, the intention is to explore, understand, and make meaning of the data in order to address the purposes of the data analysis in the replication study and to ascertain its success in achieving its intentions. Qualitative data analysis serves the same purposes of the quantitative data analysis: to provide findings which enable the researcher to determine how far the intervention has 'worked', where, for whom, and with what degree of certainty.

The researcher has many ways of proceeding in the organisation, presentation, and analysis of qualitative data (Cohen et al., 2018), for example:

- by people (individual and/or groups);
- by issue or theme;
- by the data collection instrument used in the replication study;
- by case studies;
- by significant events;
- by a narrative account;
- by a time-sequenced account;
- by theoretical perspectives;

The researcher can organise and categorise qualitative data into key findings and key concepts, presenting tables of data or writing a narrative account or summaries of findings, recognising that, with qualitative data, there is an elision of the processing and the analysis of the data (and, indeed, often of the analysis and interpretation of data). This is because decisions on the organisation and presentation of the data involve a degree of analysis of the data, what they are indicating, what are considered to be the key points, what data to select in and select out. The replication researcher using qualitative data has to decide which method of organising and presenting the data is the best fit for purpose, and what that purpose is.

In analysing qualitative data, replication researchers have several tools available to them. They might code the data using codes that have been decided in advance of conducting the data analysis (pre-ordinate codes) and/or those which are generated in response to examining what the data are about and what they indicate (responsive coding). Alternatively, they might avoid coding, and, instead, use their own judgement in determining the key findings from the data and writing a summary of these.

The replication researcher can use tools of grounded theory in analysing qualitative data, including:

- *Coding*: attaching labels to units of text, visual, or aural data, including different types of coding (e.g. open, analytic, axial, selective, theoretical), identifying the levels of generality and specificity of the codes being used and the units of analysis;
- *Identifying the core variable*: 'that variable which accounts for most of the data and to which as much as possible is related. . . . that variable which integrates the greatest number of codes, categories and concepts, and to

which most of them are related and with which they are connected' (Cohen et al., 2018, p. 720);
- *Constant comparison*: features, properties, categories, key concepts, key findings across the data are compared until no more variations or exceptions are found;
- *Saturation*: when no new insights, categories, issues, properties, relationships, codes are produced, even when new data are added (Glaser & Strauss, 1967).

Qualitative data analysis involves data assembly and re-assembly, combining and recombining data in new ways, synthesising and integrating data in order to create a meaningful account and analysis, and for themes and key findings to emerge. Whichever method and tools the replication researcher uses to analyse the qualitative data, the purpose of the analysis is clear: to use the data to judge how far and where, 'beyond a reasonable doubt', the study has been successful in achieving its intended purposes, such as the success of the intervention.

Combining quantitative and qualitative data

Process evaluations are increasingly used in experimental studies in education (Connolly et al., 2018; Joyce, 2019; Morrison, 2021) and mixed-methods research designs, using qualitative and quantitative data. The findings of the quantitative and qualitative data analysis can be compared to determine how far and where they support each other in respect of the main findings of the study, and how well and where the intervention has 'worked', or how far it has failed to achieve its intentions.

Combining quantitative and qualitative data might be, for example, in a study that tests an intervention in a new setting, with new data collection instruments, with a particular population and sample, and so on (e.g. in a conceptual replication). How far the combined, different data types used here can indicate how well the intervention has 'worked' is a human judgement, and the researcher will need to indicate and justify the grounds on which the study can be deemed, on the basis of these data and 'beyond a reasonable doubt', to have 'worked', 'not worked', 'partially worked', or that it is impossible to say ('indeterminate'). Given the nature and strength of the data types, the researcher might need to indicate which data type has the greater persuasive power, and on what grounds. This might be important; for example, if the statistical analysis suggests that the study has 'worked', but the qualitative data are less positive, or if they contradict, qualify, refine, and suggest conditionality to the quantitative findings, which findings should the researcher accept or give preference to, and on what grounds? Indeed, do these two data types focus on the same issue(s)?

The qualitative data may provide information on the contextual and causal conditions and operations in the study, whereas the quantitative data's metrics might suggest the overall 'success' of the intervention; these two data types do different things. The former can qualify, set conditions to, boundaries of, exceptions to, processes of and nuances in, the findings, whereas the latter can give an overall indication of how well, and where the intervention (typically based on average, overall results) has 'worked'.

From a consideration of the tools for data analysis, the chapter moves to the two 'Areas' indicated earlier.

Area one: Data analysis of the replication study

Data analysis in the replication study is as it would be for any single research study. The data might be quantitative, qualitative, or both. There is a need to indicate precisely what the researcher is looking for in the findings, to see how far and where the intervention has been successful, and what are the indicators and evidence of success. Is it to see, for example, how far the intervention has been a partial success, a very limited success, a failure, indeterminate, and, if so, where and why? Or is it to see for whom, under what conditions, and how well the intervention has or has not 'worked'? Which results should the researcher be interrogating, and why? In what level of detail and on what details should the researcher be focusing? 'Findings' might include, for example: the results of a pre-test and a post-test (e.g. in an experimental study) for different groups within the sample; different classroom procedures, processes, and events; specific instruments within the study; different teachers; data after such-and-such controls have been applied, and in comparison to what counterfactuals.

In analysing the data, the researcher can use the statistics introduced earlier and the tools of qualitative data analysis. The decision on how much the replication study has 'worked' is, as indicated earlier, a human judgement, as the researcher has to decide, for example, levels of similarity or difference between groups in an experiment, as the data do not speak for themselves. Difference testing (and the size of the difference, e.g. effect sizes) can be conducted between, for example, two groups in the replication study (control and experimental group), with or without applying controls on the data.

Area two: Data comparison between the original study and the replication study

Here, the replication researcher compares the replication study with the original study. This is challenging. Even if the researcher can ensure that the focus of the comparison is the same, the instruments used for the data collection and data analysis in the two studies might differ. Indeed, one of the purposes of the replication study might be to vary the instrumentation and other aspects of the original study (e.g. in a conceptual replication). The question is raised, then, of how fair any comparison might be. This returns the researcher to the issues of sameness in Chapter 2.

The instruments of the original study and the replication study, their scaling and scoring, might differ. How, then, can they be compared fairly, even if the instruments used have passed checks for validity and reliability? What if one study used ordinal data and the other used ratio data? What if the distributions of the scores are different or if their means differ? One answer, if a statistical approach is used, is to insist that the scores of the original study and the replication study are standardised (z-scores) to have the same mean and standard deviation, in order to compare like with like. This assumes that it can actually be done. For example, the researcher may not have access to the raw scores and data in the original study. However, this is only part of the difficulty with scores. Added to these are issues of what happens if there is inequality of variance between the two sets of scores or the ranges of scores differ widely, or if they have different degrees of homoscedasticity, or differences in the confidence intervals, or if the residuals differ, or if the distributions are differently skewed?

There are further challenges. For example, setting the confidence interval at 95 per cent does not necessarily ease the issue of comparability between the original study and the replication study, as, for example, a poor quality or small-scale original study risks having a replication study which, because of the wide range of the scores included in the confidence interval, might easily confirm the findings of the original study. This is a problem, for example in meta-analysis, as poor quality studies find their way into meta-analyses (Morrison, 2021). Such variance yields little of value to the researcher or the user of the research, even if statistical significance or large effect sizes are found. If confidence intervals are wide, then replication might be confirmed easily (e.g. in the *Reproducibility Project: Psychology*, Gelman & Loken, 2014). Similar results might be found between an original study and its replication study, but this will have little meaning, utility, or indication of the real effect if one or both studies have large confidence intervals (Patil et al., 2016).

Another problem exists if the replication study finds similar results to those of the original study but the replication study and/or the original study is underpowered. This might have limited utility, and the often suggested solution to this, such as increasing the size of the samples in order to increase statistical power, might be expensive, impractical, or impossible (Anderson & Maxwell, 2016).

Further, though Patil et al. (2016) argue that a study can be deemed to replicate successfully if the data in the replication study have the same distribution as in the original study, this is only part, not the whole, of the story. Comparing the two studies is an inexact art rather than a science. It requires the exercise of informed professional judgement, transparently disclosed and based on clear criteria and evidence.

An exact replication, working with the original data, might be the most straightforward to conduct here, for example to determine whether the analysis has succeeded in validating the original study (by reworking the original data and looking for the same result). However, this offers little solace to the replication researcher in education, as such a type of replication is almost impossible and is very rare (but see the re-analysis of the original data in the celebrated case of *Teaching Styles and Pupil Progress*, Bennett, 1976, undertaken by Aitken et al., 1981). Rather, the conceptual studies bring a myriad of issues in determining how far the replication has confirmed or can confirm the original study, or, if it can, then only in terms of the 'concept' in a particular context (Chapter 3). Or take the issue raised in Chapter 4, of whether qualitative data are admissible in a replication study, as qualitative studies might distil the features of the unique, non-replicable identity of the replication study (e.g. Peels, 2019).

The replication researcher, then, in comparing the replication study with the original study, is faced with serious challenges, to the extent that there is no unequivocal judgement of how far a replication confirms, disconfirms the original study, or is indeterminate. What if the findings of the replication study are dissimilar to those of the original study? Which one is correct, or are they both correct and simply different, and, if so, what can the researcher take from this? How much uncertainty is tolerable?

In comparing the findings of the original study and the replication study, Table 6.2 suggests several questions that can be addressed.

The questions in Table 6.2 are designed to encourage the replication researcher to probe deeply into the comparability of the original study and the replication

Table 6.2 Questions in comparing the original study and the replication study

---

Questions in comparing the original study and the replication study can include the following:

- What were the main purposes of the replication study?
- What similarities and differences of purpose are there between the original and replication study, and with what effects?
- How effectively has the replication study served its declared purposes, and on what grounds and criteria?
- What has the replication kept the same as in the original study, why and with what effects and impact?
- What answers to the research questions are provided in the replication study, and how are these similar to/different from those in the original study, and why?
- What are the main findings from the replication study?
- How significant and important are the similarities and differences in the findings of the replication study and the original study?
- What has the replication study changed/amended/added with regard to the original study, why, and with what results, effects, and impact (e.g. research design; sampling and population; independent and dependent variables included; controls and counterfactuals; data types; data collection points; areas of focus in the data analysis; data analysis techniques, statistics, and procedures; fidelity to the assumptions of the statistical tests, coding of qualitative data, and interpretation of data)?
- How (dis)similar to the original study is the replication in terms of research design, research questions, ontology, epistemology, methodology, and instrumentation, and why?
- How have changes between the original study and the replication study affected reliability and validity, and in what respects?
- How comparable, and where, is and is not the replication study comparable to the original study, and with what effects?
- How to present, discuss, and explain similarities and differences between the original and the replication study?
- What and where have similarities and differences been found in the conduct and the results of the original and replication studies, and how to explain and account for these?

(Continued)

Table 6.2 (Continued)

- What findings are consistent with, and different from, those in the original study, what is confirmed and refuted, what is a moot point, what cannot be confirmed or refuted (and why/not), and how can these be explained/accounted for?
- What are the 'cut-off' points and criteria in deciding how far the findings of the replication study confirm, qualify, refute, or render indeterminate those of the original study (e.g. using significance levels, effect sizes, confidence intervals, means and standard deviations, statistical power, reliability indices, standardised scores in the original study and the replication)?
- What are the criteria, indicators, and evidence need to judge how far, and where, the original study and the replication study are very similar, moderately similar, a little similar, indeterminate, a little dissimilar, moderately dissimilar, very dissimilar, and in respect of what (e.g. the research questions; the research design and methodology; the intervention contents, procedures, tasks, conduct, settings; the data collection instruments and measures; the data analysis; the findings)?
- What additional, new/adjusted data have been collected and analysed in the replication study, and with what effects and significance, and why?
- What data types, analyses and presentation in the original study have been dropped in the replication study, and with what effects and significance, and why?
- What similarities and differences in causality have been found between the original and replication study, and with what effects?
- What conclusions can be drawn from the replication study, about what, and how comparable to/similar to/different from the original study are these, why, and what implications can be drawn from this?
- What limitations are there to the replication study and the original study?
- What further research is suggested, implied, or required that stems from the replication study?

study, the findings of each of these, and what can be taken from those findings, in terms of how far they confirm or disconfirm the findings of the original study (or, indeed, find indeterminate results), and with how much certainty. This does not preclude the replication study from confirming or disconfirming an original study which had found statistically non-significant results of an intervention.

In interpreting the findings of a replication study, researchers are faced with deciding what constitutes a 'success' or a 'failure' of replication, or what is indeterminate (and why). Brandt et al. (2014) note that there is a lack of consensus on this matter, indeed on what a replication should keep the same as that in the original study, for example the design, methodology, procedures, and findings. How similar must the findings of the replication study and the original study be, and with what level of certainty, probability, and tolerance of uncertainty, in order to decide how far, and where the replication study is successful (and whether it has successfully achieved its intentions, e.g. to validate the original study, to generalise beyond the original study)? This returns us to the question of the meaning of a 'successful' replication (Chapters 2 and 5). Does it require finding sufficiently similar results to those in the original study, or does it mean following the same methodological requirements and protocols as the original research, regardless of the findings?

In comparing the original study and the replication study, the researcher can use several tools to see where there are similarities and differences, and to judge the importance, weight, and consequences of these, and with which overall and subgroup elements of the two studies, thus:

- means and standard deviations (standardised and non-standardised), and difference tests, if the assumptions of the null hypothesis are secure; standardised scores enable fairer comparisons to be made;
- their confidence intervals, ranges, standard errors, and standard deviations, to compare the breadth or narrowness – the precision – of the two sets of scores, their range, and the limits on what can be taken from wide confidence intervals and large standard deviations, (i.e. dispersal around their means);
- their effect sizes and the directions of these, to compare the results and impact of the two studies;
- their kurtosis and skewness, to judge whether the two sets of scores have normal and non-normal distributions, to see if they have similar directions of skewness and whether they can be fairly compared;
- their statistical significance levels, to compare the levels of statistical significances found (e.g. in correlations and difference testing);
- the results of difference testing, to look at the sizes of difference between the two sets of scores and any subsets of interest (effect sizes);
- their statistical power and sample sizes, to see if the studies are underpowered, which can affect the trustworthiness and reliability of the conclusions drawn concerning similarity, effect sizes, and avoidance of Type I and Type II errors.

In judging how far, and where, the replication study has 'worked', for quantitative data these include the following considerations, many of which can feature in pre-registration of replication studies and/or in judging similarity, difference, indeterminacy, confirmation, disconfirmation of successes, and failure to replicate (e.g. National Academies of Sciences, Engineering, and Medicine, 2019):

- Set, specify, and justify the similarity, magnitude, thresholds, and boundaries (amount of variability to be tolerated both within and between the two studies) of means/medians/modes and effect sizes required in the original study and the replication study, and indicate for which findings (i.e. focusing on which aspects of the original study and the replication study), for confirming how far and where the original study has been successfully replicated, and with what degrees of (un)certainty. Note that effect sizes of large-sample studies with high statistical power might be lower than those of small-sample studies with low statistical power. If statistical significance testing is used (not advised), then avoid slavish adherence to fixed statistical significance levels (e.g. intolerance of a significance level of 0.053 if the p value is set at 0.05). Set, specify, and justify the required direction of the effects in the original study and the replication study.

- Set, specify, and justify the similarity, magnitude, thresholds, and boundaries (amount of variability to be tolerated both within and between the two studies) of similarities, closeness, and (un)certainty required in comparing the two studies, including, for each study, their data types and instruments, distributions and range, kurtosis and skewness of distributions, standard deviations, standard error, confidence intervals, sample size and statistical power, precision and accuracy, and statistics used in the two studies.
- Indicate what judgements of replication can be made if both studies meet threshold requirements, but one is markedly different from the other (e.g. if the original study found an effect size of 0.46 and the replication study found an effect size of 0.81, and if the original study found a statistical significance level of 0.03 and the replication study found a statistical significance level of 0.001).
- Set, specify, and justify the controls, counterfactuals (where appropriate) operating in the two data sets, and the steps taken in both studies to reduce the risk of Type I errors (false positives) and Type II errors (false negatives).
- Ensure that there is symmetry in judgements made about the replication (i.e. the findings of the original study are replicated in the replication study *and* the findings of the replication study are replicated in the original study), in order to avoid contradictions.
- Given the levels of (un)certainty, closeness, and similarity set, indicate and justify the levels of divergence of results, in what and where, for the replication study to be judged to be a non-replication. This can require a high threshold of similarity for determining replication, a low threshold of similarity for determining non-replication, and an intermediate zone that is between the two thresholds for stating that the results are 'indeterminate' in considering whether there is or is not replication. Studies with wide confidence intervals and low power might lead to findings and judgements that are classed as 'indeterminate'.
- Identify the possible effects on the findings of outliers (e.g. they may contribute to replication or non-replication) and indicate how the presence of outliers has been handled in the two studies, and what justifications – and their defensibility – have been made for removing outliers.
- Indicate whether there is sufficient information, detail, precision, and accuracy in the original study and the replication study for a safe judgement to be made of replication, non-replication, or whether the results are 'indeterminate'.
- Ensure that sources of bias have been sufficiently reduced (Jadad & Enkin, 2007; Meinert, 2011) in the original study and the replication study, for fair comparisons and judgements to be made.
- Indicate differences in the features and components of the two studies, and what possible effects these might have on the results.

The argument here is for great transparency, trustworthiness, and detail in the criteria, indicators, and measures used in judging replication, non-replication and the category of 'indeterminate'. This includes clear and full descriptions of all aspects of the research and the data analysis, the limits and constraints on what can be concluded from the research, and an indication of what is uncertain.

In setting the requirements for replication in quantitative research, the following example is simply illustrative rather than prescriptive or normative:

- The standardised means of the two studies must be no more than half a standardised standard deviation apart from each other.
- The confidence intervals of the two studies must be no wider than 95 per cent.
- The range of scores of the replication study must be no greater than that of the original study, with an excess tolerance of 5 per cent.
- The standardised standard deviations of each of the two studies must be no greater than 0.5.
- The effect size of the replication study must be no lower than 0.2 of that of the original study for a positive replication and must be lower by more than 0.2 of the original study for a non-replication (using Cohen's d).
- The statistical significance level of the two studies must be 0.05, plus or minus 0.005.
- The statistical power of the replication study must be no less than 0.80.
- The direction of the effects of the two studies must be the same.
- The kurtosis of the two studies must be within the range of normality and must not differ by more than 0.5.
- The skewness of the two studies must be within the range of normality and must not differ by more than 0.5.
- The sample size of the replication study must be no smaller than that of the original study.

Any deviation from these requirements should go to the researcher to judge how far it constitutes a replication, a non-replication, or an indeterminate replication. The researcher should take account of the *relative* importance of similarities and differences: in what areas and sub-areas the two studies differ and are similar. As with other statistical processes, human judgement rather than purely statistically determined judgements is the order of the day; making judgements from statistics is an art as well as a science; as in a court of law, the judgement must be 'beyond a reasonable doubt'.

The researcher must decide and indicate how much tolerance of uncertainty, similarity, and difference is acceptable or required in coming to a judgement on replication. Here, the more rigorous, demanding, and secure the replication results seek to be, the narrower are the margins of difference between the original study and the replication study in, for example, means, standard deviations, range, kurtosis and skewness, confidence intervals, standard errors, and minimum effect sizes. At the same time, the larger is the sample size, the greater is the likelihood of statistical power, and more demanding the statistical significance level must be.

In comparing the findings of original and replication studies that are based on qualitative data, the task is complicated by the inherent nature of the research itself. For example, qualitative studies which purportedly focus on unique situations and the agentic interactions of participants may not be seeking to 'prove' or to test a hypothesis. They may not, in principle, be replicable or seek to be replicable. However, not all qualitative studies are in this mould, and the researcher can use a qualitative study to replicate an original study. In this, the intention is to determine the signal that arises from the contextual noise (if, indeed, that is possible or desirable in a qualitative study), and this can be approached by using the tools outlined earlier, for example coding, thematisation, constant comparison, and theoretical saturation.

Judging the qualitative evidence concerns its plausibility, credibility, defensibility, coverage of the phenomenon, dependability and trustworthiness, authenticity and honesty, richness, significance, consistency across parties, fairness to the phenomenon and the context, triangulation (e.g. of data types and sources, researchers, time and space), transferability, accuracy, and fidelity to the natural context and its specificity (Cohen et al., 2018). In comparing qualitative original and replication studies, issues to be addressed include:

- Set, specify, and justify the nature and content of the similarities and/or differences between the two studies, their importance, and the boundaries of the findings of the two studies, indicating the focus/foci of the original study and the replication study for confirming how far and where the original study has been successfully replicated, with how much (un)certainty, and based on what evidence, criteria, and indicators. What are important similarities and differences between the two studies with regard to judgements of replication, non-replication, or indeterminate replication? On what issues are the two studies similar and different, and what is the relative importance of these?
- Set, specify, and justify decisions on what matters the two studies must be identical, very similar and/or similar, and on what matters differences can be tolerated, and on what grounds.
- Set, specify, and justify on what matters the differences must be no more than slight, and on what matters greater differences between the two studies can be tolerated, and on what grounds.
- Set, specify and justify what judgements of replication can be made if both studies meet stipulated criteria of similarity and difference, but one has additional marked differences from the other, and what this implies. Identify and justify the boundaries of tolerance for differences and variability between the two studies: where and why.
- Given the nature and importance of (un)certainty, closeness, and similarity, specify and justify any divergence of results, where and how, for the replication study to be judged to be a non-replication. What must be similar and what must not be markedly different in order to qualify as a replication or a non-replication? What must be unclear and varied in order to qualify as being an 'indeterminate' replication?
- Identify the possible effects on the findings, of critical and/or negative incidents and events, participants, features, and components of the two studies,

and what possible effects these might have on the results (e.g. they may constitute non-replication) and indicate how the presence of these has been handled in the two studies.
- Indicate whether there is sufficient information and detail in the original study and the replication study for a safe judgement to be made of replication, non-replication, or whether the results are 'indeterminate'.
- Ensure that sources of bias have been sufficiently reduced in the original study and the replication study, for fair comparisons and judgements to be made.

Again, the argument here is for great transparency, trustworthiness, disclosure, and detail in the criteria, indicators, and evidence used in judging replication, non-replication, and an 'indeterminate' decision. The qualitative replication researcher must focus on the original study and identify: the standard, quality, and range of evidence provided; the judgements and conclusions drawn; how securely the conclusions follow from the evidence provided; the credibility and plausibility of evidence; the extent to which the signal of the main findings rises above the noise of the context; the richness and scope of the data; whether the data streams have a sufficiently wide embrace; whether the data have been blind-analysed by a third party; and how far the priorities and key points identified by the researcher are defensible. Having done this for the original study, the same deliberative judgement is applied to the replication study, and, having conducted this similar analysis of the replication study, the researcher is then in a position to judge:

- where, and on what, there are similarities and differences between the two studies;
- how significant to the replication study's findings are the similarities and differences between the original and the replication study;
- how context-dependent is the signal in the replication study and the original study;
- what alternative explanations can be provided for the similarities and differences, and which of these explanations is the most plausible and acceptable;
- on what grounds, criteria, evidence, and warrants the judgement can be made of replication, non-replication, or indeterminate replication;
- what are the key contributors to the outcomes of the original study and the replication, and how similar are the key causal and contextual factors at work in the two studies;
- how similar are the *effects* of the key causal and contextual factors at work in the two studies;
- how successful have the two studies been in achieving the goal of the intervention, based on what criteria and evidence, and with what level of trustworthiness;
- what is insufficiently clear and data-rich for a secure judgement to be made about replication or non-replication (i.e. where the results are indeterminate, and why).

The researcher has to decide what the safest decision is, for example: how far and where the original study has been replicated successfully or is a non-replication; whether some parts are replicated and others not, and which these are; whether the study is insufficiently detailed for anything but a judgement of 'indeterminate' to be given. The researcher's judgement must be transparent, defensible, and 'beyond a reasonable doubt'.

In quantitative and qualitative studies, the task is to identify the level, quality, and trustworthiness of the evidence required in order to come to a judgement as to how much, where, in what respects, and with what significance (not in the statistical sense) the replication study must have similar findings to those of the original study.

Interpreting replication results

Interpreting replication results is challenging in establishing replication, as confounding factors can create alternative explanations for results (Hunter & Schmidt, 2004; Stanley & Spence, 2014). As introduced earlier, contexts, times, cultures, samples, and history vary, and variability exists within large samples, such that the likelihood of a research claim being insecure might be greater than it is of being secure (valid, accurate, and reliable) (Ioannidis, 2005; See, 2020). Indeed, researchers vary in their interpretation of, and inferences from, the same data (Moonesinghe et al., 2007; Science News, 2019).

Suppose that replication findings confirm those of the original study. Does this indicate that the original study's findings are valid and reliable? Not necessarily, as chance/coincidence might still obtain (even with statistical significance testing), and biases or weaknesses in the original study might have been retained in the replication, or different conditions, circumstances, and factors present may have contributed to, or caused, the similar findings, rather than the intervention's contents themselves, that is, not the signal but the noise, as mentioned in Chapter 3. There are many possible causes and 'causal cakes' (Cartwright & Hardie, 2012, p. 61) at work in a replication study, and these influence its findings. The replication researcher should consider, indeed report, causal factors, conditions, contexts, settings, and operations, as these are key issues (Matthews et al., 2018). Further, as indicated in Chapter 3, a conceptual replication whose findings differ from those in the original study may or may not call into question the original 'concept'; we simply don't know.

Let us say that a replication study has different findings from those of the original study; does this show whether it was the original study or the replication study that was perhaps flawed or lacks credibility (Makel & Plucker, 2015)? Again, we don't know; the original and/or the replication findings might or might not stand. The results simply suggest that something happened that caused the difference found; the challenge here is to find the causal factors at work. The point here is that the replication researcher should consider possible reasons for similarities and differences between the findings of the original study and the replication study.

Indeed, disconfirming the findings of the original study result can be as important as confirming it, as this serves the interests of a self-correcting science (Kim, 2019).

If the findings of the replication study differ from those of the original study, what can the researcher take from this? Maybe it was because the procedures of the original study were not followed sufficiently closely in the replication study. Maybe the conditions, settings, contexts, samples, sample size, scope of the study, natural variation within factors and/or other factors differed between the original study and the replication study, and these reduced the level of certainty that such-and-such an effect was caused by such-and-such a cause, either singly or, more likely, in combination with other causes, since, as discussed earlier, changing one cause, variable, or condition has knock-on effects on other causes, variables, and conditions.

The National Academies of Sciences, Engineering, and Medicine (2019) indicates several possible reasons for non-replication, and many of these apply strongly to replication studies in education:

- the complexity of the phenomenon being investigated and the interactions of many variables in the original and replication studies (the greater the complexity, the greater is the risk of non-replication);
- the number of the variables in the system or factor under investigation, and their relationships;
- the (in)ability to exercise controls in the original and replication studies (exercising controls may be limited or even impossible in the complex, emergent, recursive, agentic world of education);
- the amount and degree of noise present in the system in the original and replication studies, and the ratio of signal to noise;
- a mismatch between the scale of the phenomenon under investigation and the scale at which the phenomenon under investigation can be measured (i.e. the limitations of the instruments in fairly matching the scope and size of the phenomenon in question in the original and replication studies);
- the stability of the underlying principles of the phenomenon across contexts (temporal and spatial) of the original and replication studies;
- the appropriateness of the measures being used for the phenomenon/construct in question (e.g. direct or indirect measures; indirect measures risk non-replication of the studies in question);
- the prior plausibility and probability level of the hypothesis being tested;
- the susceptibility of the phenomenon in question to being measured accurately;
- the inherent levels of uncertainty in the phenomenon in question;
- the poor research design in the original and/or the replication study;
- the possible bias in the original study and/or the replication study.

Replication studies might tell us how far, and where, the original study and the replication study have similar, different, or indeterminate findings, but they do not tell us how far the findings of the original study and/or the replication study are, *per se*, valid and safe to use. What they can tell us is that, given this intervention under such-and-such a set of conditions and contexts, the findings are such-and-such.

Morrison (2019) raises five questions and answers for consideration when comparing the findings of a replication study with those of the original study:

- Do different findings in the replication study undermine the original study? Not necessarily, as the original and/or the replication study may be at fault or simply different because of many factors operating at the time.
- Does a replication study which finds similar results to the original study confirm the original study? Not necessarily, as other factors may have been contributing to the similar findings.
- If an original study and a replication study find different results, which result should one accept, and on what basis?
- How to find whether the findings of the original study or the replication study, or both, yield a false positive or a false negative when the studies agree?
- How to find whether the findings of the original study or the replication study yield a false positive or a false negative when the studies disagree?

(p. 428)

Finding similarity between the findings of the original study and the replication study is no guarantee of the reliability, credibility, and validity of the original study, the replication study, or, indeed, both of them. For these to be more certain, as Chapter 2 indicated (Yong, 2012), the original study should be duplicated, not changed, that is, the replication researcher conducts as near to an exact replication as is possible; in education, this is difficult.

Replication of findings, Morrison (2019) argues, is not a *necessary* condition for reliability and validity. Both the original study and the replication study might be completely reliable and valid but yield different results, for many reasons. For example, in a conceptual replication, finding similar or different results might depend on how the concept is framed, its constituent elements, their operation and relative weightings, their implementation, settings, contexts, conditions, causal operations, and so on. Further, it might depend on how closely the replication study has conformed to the original study's procedures. Cartwright and Hardie (2012) add to this the impossibility of changing only one variable and no others in the replication study, as to change one variable sets up a whole new 'causal cake'.

The challenges in comparing the finding of the original study and the replication study, and drawing conclusions from such comparisons, do not end there. For example, just because we might find a similarity of findings between the original study and its replication study, can we legitimately and safely conclude from this that the findings are secure and generalisable? No; both studies might be mistaken (i.e. the replication perpetuates a fallacy) (Ioannidis, 2012).

Data analysis and interpretation

Table 6.3 provides an illustration of challenges in interpreting the findings of an original study and its replication study. By way of example, it works with 'true positives', 'false positives', 'true negatives', and 'false negatives' in the statistical sense. It takes these and provides four possible sets of permutations in considering agreement and disagreement between an original study's and a replication study's findings. Here, the location/source of the 'true' and 'false' positives and negatives (in the original or replication study) may be impossible to detect, and, indeed, the inability to identify the location frustrates attempts to identify unequivocally what and which to believe (and, thereby, to trace causality). Table 6.3 indicates that the similarity or difference between the findings of the original study and the replication study might be for one of 40 initial reasons, such that it might be impossible to identify, from the findings alone, which study/studies is/are valid and

Table 6.3 Agreement and disagreement between original and replication study

		Permutation 1	Permutation 2	Permutation 3	Permutation 4	Status of each permutation
1.	Original study	True positive	False positive	True negative	False negative	Original and replication study agree
	Replication study	True positive	False positive	True negative	False negative	
2.	Original study	True positive	False positive	True negative	False negative	Original and replication study disagree
	Replication study	False positive	True positive	False negative	True negative	
3.	Original study	False positive	True positive	False negative	True negative	Original and replication study disagree
	Replication study	True positive	False positive	True negative	False negative	
4.	Original study	True positive	False positive	True negative	False negative	Original and replication study disagree
	Replication study	No true positive found	No false positive found	No false positive found	No true negative found	
5.	Original study	No true positive found	No false positive found	No false positive found	No true negative found	Original and replication study disagree
	Replication study	True positive	False positive	True negative	False negative	

Source: Morrison, 2019, p. 429

reliable. Table 6.3 includes four categories (using 'true' and 'false' in a statistical sense): 'true', 'not true', 'false', and 'not false'. Simply because a study has not found something to be 'true' does not mean that, therefore, it is 'false', and just because it has not found something to be 'false' does not mean that, therefore, it is 'true' (Morrison, 2019).

For Table 6.3, Morrison (2019) argues that, in considering the relations between findings of the original study and the replication study, it is important to consider 'true positives', 'false positives', 'true negatives', and 'false negatives' in both the original study and the replication study, along with 'true replications', 'false replications', 'true non-replications', and 'false non-replications'. 'False non-replications' might be a rarity (Ioannidis, 2012), and this suggests that the researcher cannot take for granted the correctness of refutation stemming from a replication study, not least as this may be partly due to the replication study having low statistical power and/or high bias.

Judging the level of similarity and difference between the original study and the replication study depends, in part, on the criteria used and how the burden of proof is defined. Hedges and Schauer (2019) show that the burden of proof rests on showing non-replication if the null hypothesis is that the findings and procedures *do* replicate, but the burden of proof shifts to finding similarity (replication) if the null hypothesis is that the findings and procedures are *not* similar, in which case the burden of proof might be greater.

A replication study might have *similar* findings to those of the original study, for many reasons (Morrison, 2019), for example: (a) both studies had secure, valid, and reliable results; (b) changes made in the replication study had no real or significant effects on the replication study or its findings; (c) new factors were present in the replication study, which were absent in the original study, and these caused the results found; (d) the original study's results were over-determined by uncontrolled endogenous and exogenous factors, and some of these were present in the replication study. In the variable-dense, context-rich, causally complex world of education, these are significant issues.

Suppose that, in a conceptual replication, the replication study has *similar* findings to those of the original study. Does this mean that the original study's 'concept' is confirmed in the conceptual replication study? Not necessarily; a range of factors could have caused the similarity of findings (see also Chapter 3). For example, teachers in either study or both of the studies might have worked hard on the intervention in question, intensively and incessantly, and it was this that made the results of the intervention in the replication study similar to those of the original study. Or the causal factors in the original study and the replication study might have differed, and the replication would not have found similar results to those in the original study *but for* such-and-such a factor in the replication study which was not present in the original study. A false positive or a false negative might have existed in the original study and/or the replication study, and/or contextual factors might have contributed to the difference. The findings might be the same, and the 'concept' might be present in both studies in a conceptual replication, but this might be of limited utility, given the operation of other factors in the situation.

Caution, therefore, is needed in judging a replication study's worth and utility simply by its findings.

On the other hand, if the replication study has *different* findings from those of the original study (e.g. in a conceptual replication), this might be for many reasons: (a) the original study and/or the replication study was/were flawed; (b) in both studies, the original 'concept' was correct, but it was affected by endogenous or exogenous factors in either study or both studies. This is an inherent difficulty for a conceptual replication, as it strives to show that, regardless of changes in several components, for example settings, research design, methodology, instrumentation, sampling, tasks, procedures, and regardless of contextual factors, the original study's 'concept' holds true, but this might have held true in the replication study *but for* the presence of other factors in the replication study. In the original study, if such-and-such a set of conditions was present (or, indeed, absent) in the replication study, then the replication study would have 'worked', 'not worked', 'partially worked', or 'indeterminately 'worked', but which of those absent or present conditions affected the results is unclear. The key point here is that a conceptual replication tests the *application* of a concept, an idea, a set of practices, but it leaves the actual concept and its utility unquestioned.

What starts out as a seemingly straightforward matter of comparing the findings of the original and the replication study in order to determine where, on the continuum of 'very strongly confirm' to 'very strongly disconfirm', with a putative midpoint of being 'indeterminate, the replication study stands with relation to the original study, turns out to be a hornet's nest of challenges and difficulties.

Added to these is the frequently observed risk of bias and 'confirmation bias' in interpreting findings from replication studies (Barshay, 2019; Ioannidis, 2015; Slavin, 2016). Here, researchers select out and select in certain data according to what they want to find ('cherry-picking'). To address calls for blinding in replication studies, together with using complete data sets (the whole truth) (Begley, 2013), to avoid selection bias in reporting, ('"pseudo" replication') (Moonesinghe et al., 2007, p. 1220), to consider pre-registration of replication studies, to provide open access to data, and, indeed, for the researcher in the replication study to be unrelated to the original study.

Conclusion

This chapter has focused on two areas in data analysis: evaluating the replication study *per se* and comparing the findings of the replication study with those of the original study. Here, the chapter argued that the replication study must ascertain how well it has achieved its intended purpose, and that the evidence for this must be valid, secure, and trustworthy. In comparing the original study and the replication study, there are two important considerations to be addressed: (a) the issue of similarity and difference between the two studies (and the criteria to be used in judging these), and (b) the level of certainty in judging how far and where the findings of the replication study are similar to and/or different from those of the original study, or whether the results are indeterminate. These issues pose challenges for replication researchers, as certainty not only is a statistical matter but also concerns the potentially confounding factors present in the original study and its replication study.

The chapter argued for attention to the rigour of both studies, ensuring:

- sufficient statistical power in the replication study;
- sufficient precision in the focus of the study and the analysis;
- selecting appropriate measures, of effect size and direction, confidence intervals, distributions and range, skewness;
- adherence to the assumptions underpinning particular statistics;
- clarification, disclosure, and justification of the criteria and evidence for judging how far, and where, the replication's findings are valid, reliable, and sufficiently similar to those of the original study;
- the independence of researchers, transparency, disclosure, and pre-registration.

The chapter indicated challenges in using null hypothesis significance testing, suggested avoiding this statistic, and indicating why. The chapter indicated challenges that face difference testing, effect size calculation, and the use of confidence intervals and distributions, whilst advocating their use. The chapter made a case for using qualitative data in data analysis, and it cautioned the researcher to be clear in what qualitative data can and cannot do.

Whilst an exact replication is useful for validating the original study, the opportunity to conduct this in education is limited, even impossible. In comparing the original study and the replication study in a conceptual replication, the chapter advocated focusing on findings, indicating that the specific focus of these must be clear, and that the role of context must be clarified. The chapter pointed to the need not only for rigorous data analysis but also for the exercise of professional judgement and transparency in deciding and disclosing the criteria and evidence used in judging the extent to which the original study was replicated successfully, not replicated, partially replicated, or whether there is insufficient evidence to judge the replication to be anything but 'indeterminate', based on the principle of 'beyond reasonable doubt'. The chapter set out questions and considerations that could be addressed in comparing the findings of the original study and the replication study. It set out challenges in comparing the original study and the replication study, and it provided examples of limitations on what could be taken from such comparisons, including in terms of how far, and where, the replication study confirmed or disconfirmed the original study, how well the original and/or the replication study was validated and successful, or whether the findings were 'indeterminate'.

In comparing the original study and the replication study, the judgement concerns how far both studies have 'worked', whether one of the studies has 'worked' and the other 'has not', whether both studies have failed to 'work', whether there was a partial replication and, if so, in what respects, or whether we simply do not have enough evidence to come to a safe decision (an indeterminate replication). Judgements on replication, here, should be transparent, deliberative, and evidence-informed; they are not derived automatically or mechanistically.

7 Reporting a replication study in education

Overview

This chapter sets out key points in writing up a replication study. It recognises that two main purposes need to be served: writing up the replication study itself and comparing it to the original study, to indicate their similarities and differences and to judge how much and where the replication study has confirmed the original study. In doing so, it addresses several key points:

- areas to address in the report;
- research purposes and research questions;
- the details of the intervention;
- research design, methodology, and conduct;
- data analysis;
- the findings of the replication study;
- discussion and conclusion;
- organising and presenting the report;
- checking the replication report.

The chapter provides a template for writing up the report and it gives examples of how to organise the report. The report of the research should examine and compare the findings of the original study and the replication study, to see how much and where the replication confirmed, partially confirmed, refuted, neither confirmed nor disconfirmed (i.e. was indeterminate), qualified, extended, applied, and generalised from the original study. In short, it should identify whether the replication study has achieved its purposes, how well it has 'worked', what, if any, are moot points about confirmation, and what the replication study has shown when comparing it to the original study (e.g. what issues and areas need further investigation). The chapter closes with a summary list of 'safety checks' in ensuring that the report is sufficiently comprehensive, inclusive, detailed, and conclusive.

Purposes of the replication study report

Reporting a replication study in education has a twofold purpose: to write up the replication study itself and to write up the comparison between the original study and the replication study. The former follows a familiar sequence and layout that can be found in published research articles, and this chapter indicates what that is. The latter involves reporting what has been kept the same between the original study and the replication study, what has been changed, and, for both of these, the reasons why, and with what effects. This should happen throughout the write-up, addressing the issue of sameness that was first raised in Chapter 2. This is likely to increase the length and level of detail of the replication report, as full reporting is necessary for the reader to be able to see where the original study and the replication study are similar and different.

A replication study report may be considerably more detailed than the original study (e.g. Melhuish, 2018), and/or, in the interests of conciseness, it may focus largely on those parts of the original study that were changed in the replication (e.g. Coyne et al., 2016). In order to reduce the overall size of the report, supplementary data and details may be made available in a different repository, be it open access or by registration.

The write-up of the replication study should be sufficiently detailed and complete for the reader to understand how the reported results have been reached (National Academies of Sciences, Engineering, and Medicine, 2019). This involves details of, for example:

- the methods, instruments, tasks, materials, metrics and measurements, procedures, and the other variables that were involved in the replication study, with sufficient detail, clarity, and transparency for the results to be checked and, if deemed appropriate, replicated;
- how the intervention was conducted and any choices made;
- the conditions and settings of the intervention;
- research design, methodology, sampling, and population;
- how the data were analysed, and why they were analysed in that way;
- why data were excluded or included in the analysis;
- decisions that were taken concerning the data analysis;
- the expected limits and constraints on the generalisability of the study, (e.g. if there were any methodological items that varied from those of the original study, and why, and what variables were not changed, i.e. remained constant between the two studies, and why);
- the statistical power and precision of the study (e.g. sample size, confidence intervals, range, standard deviations, and error margins);
- the levels of certainty and uncertainty from the measurements used;
- the findings and any inferences made from the replication study;
- the correctness and fitness for purpose of the statistical analysis.

The purpose(s) and significance of, and reasons for, the changes made to the original study will need to be made clear. For example, were they of a relatively minor nature (e.g. slight improvements to the original instruments for data collection or adjustments to the confidence intervals to increase precision) or of a more major nature (e.g. change of methodology, radical changes to data collection instruments, changes of population and sampling, changes to the implementation of the intervention) in order to generalise to a different context.

Maybe the replication researcher did not have access to the same population and sample as in the original study, or maybe she or he deliberately wanted a different population and sample in order to test for generalisability of the concept in the conceptual replication. Maybe the researcher chose a very different research design from that of the original study, again to test for the generalisability of the concept in the conceptual replication, that is, to ensure that the strength, security, transferability, generalisability, and correctness of the concept were not simply an artifact of the research design and methodology, and that the concept was independent of the context and setting that gave rise to it.

At issue here is the need for the researcher to make explicit what has been retained from the original study without adjustment, what has been changed and why, and the effects of these changes on the replication study. This reinforces the point that writing up a replication study must refer to the original study.

Areas to address in writing up the report

Writing up the replication includes many areas, for example:

- justification for the replication study;
- statement of need, statement of the problem;
- purposes of the research;
- what the research will do and 'deliver';
- significance of the research and its findings, and to what to draw attention;
- literature review;
- research questions;
- research design and type of replication;
    - methodology of the research;
    - statistical power of the study (where relevant);
    - contents and tasks of the intervention;
    - procedures and conduct of the intervention;
    - population and sampling;
    - setting of the replication;
    - instrumentation and measures used in the research, and their reliability and validity;
    - data types used in the replication, and their credibility, dependability, and meaningfulness of the data types;
    - confidence intervals used;
    - range and standard deviations;
    - effect size(s) used;
    - levels of certainty and probability used, and levels of uncertainty tolerated;
    - levels of precision in the findings and their interpretation;

- fidelity to the original study;
- ethics of the research;
- data analysis in the research;
- findings and key findings;
- discussion;
- limitations;
- generalisability;
- conclusions;
- implications;
- what the comparisons of the findings between the original and the replication study show;
- suggestions and recommendations for future research.

The key findings and conclusions will refer to comparison with the original study, for example what the replication study confirms, refutes, extends, refines, qualifies, adds to, generalises to, validates. The later part of the chapter sets out a possible sequence for writing up the report. This chapter follows a sequence of writing up the report (see below).

Research purposes

The replication study's purposes may not be identical to those of the original study unless an exact replication is being conducted (which, as already mentioned, is unlikely in education). The purpose of the replication may be, for example, to confirm, modify, refute, generalise from the claims made from the original study, hence, it is fundamentally different in purpose from that of the original study. However, separate from the purpose of comparison is the purpose of the replication study *per se*, as if it were a self-standing study, and this purpose might have some similarity to the purposes of the original study.

With regard to the replication study as a self-standing study, its purposes should refer to the study as if it were independent of the original study, so that its design, conduct, data analysis, evaluation, and so on are made with reference to the replication study itself, and not to the original study, that is, so that the replication study is treated as if it were any other single research study. Here, the purposes of the replication study might be to see how well the intervention 'works', why and under what conditions, contexts, and settings, with what qualifiers and limitations, and so on.

With regard to the purpose of comparing the findings of the original study to those of the replication study, the replication study may focus on one or more aspects of the original study instead of the entire study, or make improvements to the original study, or extend the scope of the original study, or seek to generalise from the original study, or make the features of the original study more precise, or operationalise the original study differently. The point here is that the report of the replication study should refer to the original study's aims and purposes, indicating what those were and comparing them to those of the replication study, so that the reader can see what changes have been made, and why, where there are similarities and differences, how significant the changes and the constants are, and how the replication study works with and on the original study.

Changes made to the purposes of the study might affect the research design and methodology, instrumentation, and so on, and the replication study report should indicate what these effects were anticipated to be, how these were addressed, and how they might or might not have influenced the findings, that is, their importance.

Research questions

In presenting the research questions for the replication study, Porte and McManus (2019) suggest that it is useful to include those of the original study in the same section of the report on research questions, so that the reader can compare the two sets of research questions in order to see what has been kept the same and what has been altered, adjusted, added to, removed, and so on, and why. The report should indicate what the original research questions were and the context in which they were set, what has changed and what has remained the same in the replication study.

For example, the researcher might have changed the research questions from those of the original study, perhaps adding to them or modifying the original questions. If this is the case, then the researcher should indicate which research questions have been changed from those in the original study, and the reasons and justifications for this. The changes could have been, for example, to make the research questions more precise and focused, or to change their focus. The researcher can comment, also, on how similar to, or different from, the original research questions are those in the replication study, where those similarities and differences lie, and the reasons for such changes.

The details of the intervention

The reporting of the research must provide the reader with sufficient detail and transparency to understand the intervention and to be able to compare it to the original study. These include:

- the purposes of the intervention;
- key features of the intervention;
- the contents and tasks of the intervention;
- the procedures and conduct of the intervention;
- the frequency, duration, and number and duration of sessions per week and in total of the intervention;
- the pacing, sequence, and operations of the intervention – how the intervention was conducted;
- the ethics of the intervention;
- what happened in the intervention.

At issue here is the need for the reader to be able to understand what happened in the intervention and to see how far and where this was similar to, and different from, the intervention in the original study. The report should make it clear which features of the intervention in the original study were kept the same in the replication study, which were altered, and why.

Research design, methodology, and conduct

Depending in part on the purpose and type of replication study will be its methodology, which, in turn affects the conduct of the research. For example, an exact replication will strive to keep to the identical methodology of the original study, working on the same data or as close as possible to identical new data, or it might address the data analysis differently. In contrast, a conceptual replication might deliberately change the methodology, for example from a randomised controlled trial to a quasi-experiment, or from an experimental methodology to a series of case studies or action research, in order to see how independent of the research methodology the concept really is, and to see how much the concept is confirmed, regardless of changes to methodology.

The replication study design and methodology can include:

- the type of research study (its nature and type);
- the population and sample: the sampling strategy, type, size, scope, features, access and recruitment, and who is included and excluded;
- the training, development, and preparation of those who carry out the intervention;
- the contents of, and tasks, procedures, and instructions for the intervention: what happened in the intervention and how it was organised and conducted;
- the duration of the intervention, and its frequency, intensity, amount, timing, and strength;
- the settings, contexts, conditions, contingencies, limits on, and location of the intervention;
- the controls, counterfactuals, independent and dependent variables;
- the scope, limitations, and boundaries of the research;
- the data collection instruments, data types, contents and tasks, procedures, number, reliability and validity, methods and measures, timing and frequency of tasks and data collection;
- the ethics of the study;
- the data analysis types, methods, controls, and procedures.

For these, the replication report should indicate what remains the same as in the original study and why, and what has been changed, added to, or removed from the original study, why, and with what effects on the study and its findings. These include: addressing what are the connections with, similarities to, differences between, and modifications to the original study, for what purposes and with what justifications; where are the similarities and differences between the original study and the replication study, and why; and what assumptions have been made in the original study and the replication study. Changes could be to the context and setting of the study, the sample, and the way in which the intervention was conducted. These might be in order to address the generalisability of the replication study, to test the validity of the findings by reworking the data analysis of the original study (an exact replication), to clarify the independent and dependent variables, to change dichotomous questions (e.g. 'yes/no') to questions of degree (e.g. 'to what extent', 'how much', 'how frequently'), and so on.

Changes to one or more of the previous items are likely to have effects on the others, and this should be discussed. For example, changing the research design is likely to influence the sampling, the instruments for data collection and, hence, the data analysis. Changing the sample, for example from older children to younger children, may affect the nature and contents of the instrumentation for data collection, the procedures for, and conduct of, the intervention, and the tasks in the intervention. Changing the setting of the intervention may affect: the training, development, and preparation of the participants; the data collection procedures; the conduct of the intervention; and so on. Hence, it is important not only for changes to be reported, including where those changes have been made, and why, but also to compare and evaluate the size, importance, and consequences of these in the original study and its replication study.

One consequence of focusing on these items and their similarity to, and differences from, the original study is that the replication report will likely be more detailed and longer than typical journal articles, as it has to include material not only on the replication study itself, but also on the original study, together with a comparison between them. The considerable level of detail serves transparency, and it is essential that the reader can evaluate the replication study not only as a self-standing study but also as a replication, that is, to compare it exactly and minutely with the original study, in order to judge how far the replication can confirm or refute the findings of the original study, the original concept, and with what level of security in the judgements made.

Data analysis

The reporting of the replication study, like other research studies, should indicate how the data analysis was undertaken, why that method was used, how it was fit for purpose, how valid and reliable it was, what level of precision was addressed, and how useful were the findings. The report should be sufficiently detailed, transparent, and clear for the reader to understand exactly what was happening in the data analysis and how and where comparisons could be made between the original study and the replication study.

In reporting the data analysis, the replication research has the dual task of reporting the replication study *per se* and reporting its comparison with the original study. The former will report the methods and tools for the data analysis in the replication study, together with their justification. The latter will include, for example: where, on what, there were no changes, and why;

where changes were made, and to what exactly, and why, how major or minor were these changes, and how similar to, and different from, the original study these were; and what was the effect and impact of these changes on the findings of the study and the conclusions drawn when comparing the findings of the replication study with those of the original study. The data analysis should also indicate what analyses have been removed from, or added to, those used in the original study, and why.

In comparing the data analyses of the original study and the replication study, the replication researcher has to account for no change, similarities and differences between the original study and the replication study, and to indicate how comparisons were made between the two studies. All of this should be included in the report, so that the reader can identify the level of sameness and judge whether, or how far, the two studies are really comparable and how far such comparability extends and with what limits, as this affects judgements of how far the replication study fairly confirms or refutes the findings of the original study. The report should indicate and justify claims for comparability, sameness, similarity and difference, and it should indicate the limits of the data analysis and what can be taken from it.

Because making changes to the replication study can affect the level and extent of comparability, the significance of such changes needs to be made clear in the report. For example, if the study purported to be an exact replication, then making changes may violate the essence of the replication. By contrast, in conceptual replications the door is open to making changes in the replication study, indeed can be advocated, as long as the concept itself is left untouched, as this tests the generalisability (and its limits) of the concept in question, however defined (see Chapter 3).

For a statistically based replication study, the researcher should report and justify using the same statistics as in the original study, and changes made to the statistics used in the replication study (see Chapter 6). This includes indicating how the statistics in the replication study were more fit for purpose than those in the original study or were an improvement on those used in the original study (e.g. increasing the level of precision and the ability to avoid a Type I or Type II error, extending the scope of the data analysis). Indeed, if it is possible, the researcher might choose to analyse the data of the replication study using the same statistics as those in the original study as well as any new statistics, and comparing and reporting the results. The report should indicate confidence intervals and precision, and what the levels of (un)certainty are.

For a qualitative replication study, the researcher should report and justify using the same methods and tools for qualitative data analysis as in the original study, and changes made to these in the replication study (see Chapter 6, e.g. coding, thematic analysis, constant comparison, identification of the core variable, saturation). The new data analysis method and tools should indicate how they are more fit for purpose than those in the original study, for example making more precise distinctions between participants and issues, indicating the causal sequences operating in the intervention, clarifying the significance of contextual matters and conditions in the intervention, comparing findings in different contexts and settings. If it is possible, the researcher might wish to analyse the data of the replication study using the same codes, thematic analyses, core variables as those in the original study as well as new codes, and comparing and reporting the results.

In a statistical approach, the report should indicate how the statistics used in the data analysis were faithful to the assumptions underpinning those statistics (see Chapter 6), what controls were used in analysing the data and why, what statistical modelling (if any) was undertaken, and what account was taken of exogenous and endogenous variables. In a qualitative data analysis, the researcher should indicate the assumptions made in the methods used, for example: the credibility, authenticity, and legitimacy of the data; the emergent and evolutionary nature of the intervention; the attempts made to ensure theoretical saturation; if appropriate, respondent validation (e.g. of the interpretation placed on the data); triangulation of methods of analysis, perspectives, researchers, data types, times; and the concurrent validity of the findings.

The findings of the replication study

As with the preceding issues in this chapter, the replication researcher should report: (a) the findings and their evaluation of the replication study *per se*, that is, as one would report and discuss the findings of any research study; (b) the outcomes of the comparison between the findings of the original study and the replication study.

For (a), the replication study researcher reports the findings and makes warrantable claims for what they show and what are the limits to what they show. This includes checking that the claims drawn from the findings really follow from the data analysis and its outcomes, and that the claims are fair, not understated, overstated, or unfair. For (b), the researcher reports the comparison of the findings of the two studies and makes a case for how far the replication has 'worked' (and what that actually means), how far it confirms or refutes the findings of the original study, based on what criteria and evidence, and with what reservations, limits, or conditions. This is not straightforward, since, as indicated in Chapter 6, even the term 'findings' is, itself, ambiguous; hence, the replication researcher should report exactly which findings, and findings about what, are being addressed.

The issue here is to report the findings and what they show clearly, fully, and fairly, be they of the replication study on its own or of the comparison between the findings of the replication study and the original study, and what can be taken from these.

A re-analysis of the original data in an exact replication should expect to find identical results, whereas an approximate or conceptual replication may not have identical results to those of the original study, but it is important to make clear what any differences indicate. For example, as Chapter 3 mentions, replication study findings that differ from those of the original study cannot falsify those of the original study.

With regard to the findings of the comparison between the original study and the replication study, the report should write these up point by point, indicating on what particular finding the two studies are similar or different, possibly setting them out on a continuum from very similar to very dissimilar (see the framework of questions in Chapter 6). In this respect, Porte and McManus (2019) suggest that, wherever possible, it is useful to follow the presentation structure and sequence of the original study, as this enables a direct comparison to be made between the two studies on specific points. The authors note that this might not always be possible, as the nature of the replication study and how much it has changed the variables may prevent or obstruct this.

Depending on the nature of the original study and the replication study, for example an experimental study with similar features (such as a pre-test and a post-test), Table 7.1 sets out a tabular approach that might be possible for presenting some findings of the comparison between the original study and the replication study. Such a table requires a commentary in order to indicate main points of similarity and difference and what these suggest, how important they are, and what can be concluded from them with regard to how far the findings of the replication study confirm, partially confirm, or refute those of the original study, or whether the findings are indeterminate. Where the two studies do not lend themselves to tabular presentation of findings, the report can use a narrative text that provides a summary of the findings and what they show in comparison to each other.

Table 7.1 Comparing the findings of the original study and the replication study

	Sample size	Pre-test			Post-test			Effect size	Significance level (if used)	Confidence interval (95%)		Statistical power	Range	Kurtosis	Skewness (with the direction of the skew)
		Mean	Standard deviation	Standard error	Mean	Standard deviation	Standard error			Lower level	Upper level				
Original study															
Replication study															

Discussion and conclusion

The discussion of, and conclusions from, the findings operate in the replication study on its own, and in the comparison between the original study and the replication study. With regard to the former, these can follow the kinds of discussions and statements of conclusions in standard research studies, addressing: what the study found and what might be the explanation(s) and reasons for the findings; how effectively the study addressed the research questions and purposes of the research; how and how well the study addressed the theoretical warrants and issues raised in the literature review; what was found that confirmed, qualified, refined, questioned, extended, contradicted the literature review; what were the limits, limitations, strengths and weaknesses of the study; what were important and less important findings, why and based on what grounds; what were the main findings; what unexpected findings there were, and how these could be explained; how strong are the claims that can be made from the study, and on what grounds; what needs further investigation and why; what implications can be drawn from the study, and on what grounds.

With regard to comparing the original study with the replication study, the discussion and conclusion can address: what the replication study sought to do, accomplish, and 'deliver'; key similarities and differences found between the two studies, and explanations for these; how far and where the two studies agree and disagree, and why this might be. The comparison can also include: the significance of the different contexts of the studies (and the discussion can remind the reader of the context and key features of the original study, its design and conduct); the main findings from the comparison; how far and where the replication study confirmed, partially confirmed, and refuted the findings of the original study, and how strong was the confirmation/refutation; what is a moot point (e.g. indeterminate) in judging the success of the replication study, and why. The discussion and conclusion should also include how similar, dissimilar, and contrasted are the findings, in what respects and based on what criteria and evidence, and what are the possible explanations for this. The report should state how well the generalisability of the original study has been demonstrated (in a close, approximate, systematic, or conceptual replication), and how securely the validity of the original study has been confirmed (in an exact replication).

Organising and presenting the report

In writing the report, the researcher must make crystal clear what is being reported, and how. This requires attention to: the organisation and layout of the report; the use of tables, figures, charts, and graphics and what they show (i.e. a commentary on these, to include what they show); the text, its tone and register; the sequence of the report; the use of sections and subtitles; the benefits of an executive summary; the main findings and conclusions; the discussion of the findings; the limitations, boundaries, and critique of the study; the implications of the study and its findings;

recommendations for action and further research, and so on. As mentioned earlier, Porte and McManus (2019) suggest that, wherever possible and appropriate, it is useful to follow the presentation structure and sequence of the original study, as this enables the original study and the replication study to compare specific points clearly. Earlier it was suggested that, rather than having a section that reports the areas in which no changes and some changes have been made between to the original study and the replication study, it is preferable to indicate these where they occur in the specific areas of the study, for example the sampling, instrumentation, research design, the intervention's contents and procedures, data analysis.

Throughout this chapter, reference has been made to the twofold nature of reporting: reporting on the replication study alone and reporting on the comparison between the original study and the replication study. Whilst the chapter has recommended interleaving the comparison between the original study and the replication study wherever relevant and possible, in respect of specific aspects of the replication study, there is also a benefit in having a clear statement, probably towards the end of the report, on how far, if at all, the replication study has successfully replicated the original study and if so, in what terms and respects, and what this shows.

Guidance on writing up research reports can be found in, for example, the EQUATOR network (equator-network.org), the CONSORT and PRISMA guidelines in clinical research, the *Reporting Guide for Study Authors* by the U.S. Department of Education (2018) and the *Reporting Template* by the Education Endowment Foundation (2019). Further, the journal *Nature* (2016) contains a checklist for articles on life sciences, many of whose requirements can apply to social sciences. Similarly, the *Companion Guidelines on Replication and Reproducibility in Education Research* from the National Science Foundation and Institute of Education Sciences (2018) provides introductory guidance on transparency. For replication as reproducibility, the Center for Open Science's (2015) *Guidelines for Transparency and Openness Promotion (TOP) in Journal Policies and Practices* indicates steps that can be taken here, and include references to citation, data transparency, analytic methods (code) transparency, research materials transparency, design and analysis transparency, preregistration of studies, preregistration of analysis plans, and replication. Each of these has three levels of transparency.

In writing up the report, a suggested sequence of headings and subheadings is provided in Table 7.2. Whilst the contents of Table 7.2 might appear to be somewhat formidable, it strives to ensure that key points are included, for example judging the quality of the replication study in itself and comparing the original study and the replication study. In Table 7.2, the term 'replication study' means the specific research study conducted, whilst the term 'replication exercise' refers to the entire exercise of conducting the research study and comparing it with the original study and what can be drawn from and concluded from the comparison, for example: how far and where the original study and its findings are confirmed, refuted, or indeterminate; how far the original study has been successfully validated (e.g. in an exact replication) and successfully generalised (e.g. in a conceptual replication); and where the replication has 'worked' (been a success) and based on what grounds, criteria, and evidence. Whilst Table 7.2 is intentionally exhaustive, the amount of attention given to specific items may vary.

Table 7.2 A template for writing up the replication study

A template for organising and presenting the report can include, in sequence:
- need for the replication study;
  - statement of need for the replication study;
  - justification for the replication study;
  - statement of the problem (if appropriate);
- purposes of the replication study;
  - overall purpose of replication;
  - what the replication study will do and 'deliver' in itself;
  - purpose of the replication study with regard to the original study;
  - significance of the replication study and its findings;
- literature review;
- method of the replication;
  - research questions (of the original study and the replication study);
  - research design (of the original study and the replication study);
  - type of replication study and the justification for this;
  - methodology of the original study and the replication study;
  - statistical power (where relevant) of the original study and the replication study;
  - contents and tasks of the intervention in the original study and the replication study;
  - procedures and conduct of the intervention in the original study and the replication study;
  - population and sampling in the original study and the replication study;
  - context and setting of the original study and the replication study;
  - instrumentation and measures used in the original study and the replication study, and their reliability and validity;
  - data types used the original study and the replication study, and their credibility, dependability, and meaningfulness;
  - ethics of the research in the original study and the replication study;
- data analysis of the original study and the replication study;
  - type of data analyses;
  - metrics and statistics;
  - tools for qualitative data analysis;
- findings and key findings of the original study and the replication study;
- discussion of the original study and the replication study;
- limitations of the original study and the replication study;
  - limitations of the replication exercise;
- conclusions of the original study and the replication study;
  - conclusions from the entire exercise;
- implications of the replication study and the replication exercise;
  - overall statement of the key findings of the original and the replication study and the conclusions drawn from comparing them;
  - how far the replication has confirmed, partially confirmed, refuted, qualified, extended, applied, generalised from the original study;
  - what has the replication study confirmed, partially confirmed, refuted, and what is a moot point ('indeterminate');
  - how well has the replication study 'worked' (fulfilled its intention, e.g. to validate, improve on, extend the original; to generalise the 'concept');
- what the replication exercise has shown;
- suggestions and recommendations for future research.

For an exact replication Brown (2012, pp. 175–176) suggests the following structure of the report:

Introduction

- introduction to the problem;
- importance of the problem;
- relevant scholarship;
- statement of the purpose;

Method

- participants;
- materials;
- procedures;

Results

Discussion

Conclusion

- limitations;
- implications;
- suggestions for future research.

Eckerth (2012) uses the following structure in reporting an approximate replication study, making reference to the original study wherever relevant throughout the report:

Introduction

- literature review;
- need for the replication;
- goal of the replication study;
- focus;
- additions in the replication study;
- similarities and differences between the original study and the replication study.

The original research study

- purpose;
- focus;
- method.

The replication study

- areas of closeness to the original study;
- participants;
- setting;
- tasks;
- data collection;
- transcription and coding (i.e. data processing and analysis).

Results

Discussion

- comparison with findings of the original study.

Conclusion

It can be seen that, however the report is organised, it addresses the twin purposes in reporting: to judge the replication study in itself and to compare the replication study and the original study.

Safety checks for the replication report

In reviewing the replication report, questions can be asked as 'safety checks'. These enable replication researchers to ensure that key elements of the replication have been addressed and included in the report. The following questions draw from the preceding chapters and address the different areas of the replication study. Answers to these can be included in the report of the replication study. For each of these, the replication researcher can ask where these have been addressed and what justifications have been provided for the answers given.

Initial questions in the replication study

- Does the original study need to be replicated and, if so, on what grounds?
- What are the reasons for the replication?
- What is the purpose of the replication?
- What is the exact focus of the replication?
- Is the replication feasible and practicable?
- What type of replication is being conducted, and how is it fit for purpose?

Planning the replication study

- How close/distant is the replication study from the original study, why, and in what terms?

- How similar to and different from the original study is the replication study, why, and in what terms?
- What does the replication keep the same as those in the original study, and why?
- What does the replication change from those in the original study, and why?
- What might be the effects of making changes to the original study, and effects on what?
- What are the success criteria for judging the replication study?
- What are the 'cut-off' points for judging how far the replication study confirms, partially confirms, successfully applies, disconfirms, extends, and so on the original study, or yields indeterminate results?
- What level of certainty is required in judging how far the original study has been replicated successfully?
- What levels of uncertainty and probability will be tolerated in judging whether the original study has been successfully replicated?
- What is the research design of the replication study, all its features and components, and where and why do these depart from those in the original study?
- What are the research questions, how are they operationalised in the replication study, how similar are they to those of the original study, and why?
- What measures of success are being used in the replication study?
- What steps have been taken to ensure the reliability, validity, credibility, and correctness of the replication?
- Have the replication study and its success criteria been pre-registered?
- What is meant by a fair replication here?
- What steps have been taken to ensure that the replication study is a fair test of the original study?
- How fully and unambiguously is the statement of the 'concept' (in a conceptual replication)?
- What are the confidence levels, statistical power, sample size, and level of precision in the replication study?

Data analysis
- What statistics are used in the data analysis?
- What key statistics are used to judge how much the replication study confirms the findings of the original study?
- What informed professional judgements are being made in interpreting the findings of the replication study and comparing them with those of the original study?
- What informed professional judgements of replication are being made in the case of qualitative data?
- What steps have been taken in the replication study to address Type I (false positive) and Type II (false negative) errors?
- What controls are included in the replication study?

Data interpretation and conclusion

- How clearly stated are the conclusions from the replication study, and concerning what?
- What are the limits of what can be drawn and concluded from the replication study, and why?
- How and how much has account been taken of the possible effects of the context, settings, conditions, constraints, situation on the replication study's results?
- Have sufficient comparisons been made between the findings of the original study and those of the replication study, and what has been concluded from them?
- What might have affected the findings of the replication study, and the implications of these on what can be taken from the replication study and its comparison with the original study?
- What confidence can be placed in the conclusions from the replication study, and on what grounds and what evidence?
- How well does the replication study meet its own stated purposes, and based on what criteria?
- How successfully and completely does the replication study compare its findings, interpretations, and conclusions to those of the original study?

Overall

- How comprehensive, inclusive, transparent, detailed, precise, focused, and complete is the report on the replication study?
- How sufficiently does the replication study indicate its limitations, confounders and constraints, and the effects of these on what can be drawn from the results?
- How significant are the replication study and its findings, for what and why?
- What, if any, further replications and/or investigations are needed, and if so, why and to focus on what?

At issue here is the need for transparency, detail and clarity in all the components of the replication study's report.

With regard to publishing the report, until such time as journals are persuaded to publish replication studies, other outlets are available (Frank & Saxe, 2012; Hartshorne & Schachner, 2012; Hildebrandt, 2016; Holcombe & Pashler, 2012), for example https://www.openingscience.org/tag/psychfiledrawer/ and openscienceframework.org report; these further the openness of data and methods for replications of analyses.

Conclusion

Writing a replication report must write up the replication study and compare it to the original study so that the reader can detect their similarities and differences, and judge how far the replication study is sufficiently similar to constitute a fair replication (the issue of sameness), and judge how far the findings of the original study are confirmed, partially confirmed, or refuted, and where. Here, the chapter has suggested that ongoing comparisons should be made between each element of the original study and the replication study, and that a later part of the report should indicate how far the replication study has confirmed the original study, and based on what grounds, indicators, and evidence. The chapter has suggested that the organisation of the original study's report might be a useful guide in organising the write-up, and it has indicated what the contents of the write-up should contain; it has provided a possible template for this, indicating that the author's judgement should guide which parts to emphasise.

The replication report is designed to enable the reader to understand the necessary details of the original study and the replication study, where they are similar and different. This is so that an informed judgement can be made not only of how well the replication study has achieved its own declared purposes but also how far, and where, it has confirmed the findings of the original study. The report can state clearly how well the findings of an exact replication stand up to a rigorous re-examination and how far the 'concept' in a conceptual replication has generalised and held fast in different contexts, settings, research design features, and so on, that is, whether the signal has succeeded in rising above the noise. To make such comparisons, the chapter provided a list of 'safety checks' for ensuring that the report has met sufficiently the significant features of the replication study and its comparisons with the original study. This, in turn, can lend credibility, reliability, trustworthiness, and validity to the conclusions drawn in the report.

8 Training for replication research

Overview

The chapter makes the case for providing training and development on conducting replication research, and it identifies skills on which to focus and how to develop them. Whilst previous chapters have identified areas of substantive *knowledge* that replication researchers in education should have, this chapter sets out a range of *skills* needed: in higher order thinking; personal, social, and interpersonal; management; and decision making. Underpinning the skills needed are two areas of focus: (a) working on the replication study as if it were a stand-alone study, with all the requisites for planning, conducting, and reporting a research study in itself; and (b) comparing the replication study with the original study.

To address these twin concerns, the chapter identifies skills needed at each stage of replication research:

- choosing a study for replication;
- deciding the feasibility and utility of the replication;
- planning the replication study;
- conducting the intervention in the replication study;
- data analysis, interpretation, and conclusions in the replication study;
- reporting the replication study.

This raises ongoing challenges of identifying sameness and closeness, and of conducting a replication study in the complex, variable-dense, and context-rich world of education.

Having set out key skills required, the chapter indicates how they can be developed. In doing so, it advocates practical learning-by-doing rather than by second-hand learning. This includes, for example, working with a supervised group or individually on planning, conducting, and reporting a replication from a given or self-chosen original study and, where relevant, publishing this study or placing it in a registry or other repository of replication studies. Here, the replication study of a published original study can be publishable, that is, the learning is real rather than being simply an exercise, thereby making a meaningful, real, and useful contribution to the field of education in which it is operating.

DOI: 10.4324/9781003204237-9

Skill sets for a replication researcher

To conduct a replication study requires the routine research skills that one would expect of the educational researcher conducting an original study, drawing on them in a different way in conducting a replication study, and using additional skills. Calls for replication research training are appearing in several disciplines, including education (e.g. National Academies of Sciences, Engineering, and Medicine, 2019; National Science Foundation and Institute of Education Sciences, 2018), as the skill set that one needs for replication work is substantial. We cannot simply assume that researchers will have the knowledge and skills needed for replication research.

Conducting a replication study is not the same as conducting an original study, and this may require researchers to receive training and development in skills for doing replication studies. These skills range from selecting an appropriate study for replication, to assessing replicability, to planning and conducting a re-analysis of original data or an entirely new study, to comparing results of two studies, to reporting the replication study and comparisons made between the two studies. Further, with the rise of big data and data streams that combine data from many sources, the training in using bespoke or widely used open source and proprietary software and data analysis increases. Further, identifying the level of replication is a matter of informed professional judgement, and it is unwise simply to crank out a judgement based on a few sets of numbers alone.

There is an increasing need for training in correct statistical analysis and in what can be drawn from it, in working with data from an original study, and in addressing 'computational reproducibility' (National Academies of Sciences, Engineering, and Medicine, 2019, p. 126). Educational institutions should provide training in methods and tools of computation in order to strengthen the quality of the data analysis and in using codes needed for producing research that is reproducible; this should extend to collaborating with experts if the resident level of training is insufficient to meet specific requirements of the research. Training should be undertaken in order to ensure that replication researchers have the skills, knowledge, and tools needed to conduct research and to review published work with regard to its replicability (ibid.).

Skills are needed at each main stage of conducting a replication study. These are indicated in sequence, from identifying the original study to be replicated, to planning and conducting the replication, analysing the data and drawing conclusions from the analysis, both *per se* and in comparing them to those of the original study. The chapter also indicates what can be done to address the training and development of these skills.

Choosing a study for replication

Chapter 1 presented a set of criteria for choosing an original study to replicate and for justifying the choice. Here, skills involved address:

- identifying original studies that would benefit from replication, making and justifying a choice;

- interrogating and critiquing original studies, identifying what needs to be replicated and addressed in the replication and how, and what the replication should do;
- deciding whether the original study contains sufficient detail, clarity, and transparency for it to be able to be replicated (e.g. as a direct replication, an approximate replication, or a conceptual replication), that is, to judge whether the replication study can actually be conducted, whether it is practicable.

Whilst it is commonplace for research training to involve critiquing original studies *per se*, critiquing them with an eye to conducting a possible replication adds another layer to this. For choosing an original study to replicate, in sequence, firstly the researcher applies the criteria set out in Chapter 1 in order to find possible contenders for replication, looking to see if the study or studies have met one or more of the criteria selected in Chapter 1, that is, if they are suitable for replication. Then the researcher critiques the study to find exactly what would benefit from replication, the reasons for this, what the purposes of the replication would be, and what type of possible replication is necessary or desirable. Then the researcher examines the original study to see if it provides sufficient detail, clarity, and transparency to enable the replication study to be conducted. The sequence is set out in Figure 8.1, in three stages.

At Stage 1, skills required include the ability to select the study based on the application of one or more of the criteria in Chapter 1, which of those criteria to apply, and why, and how and how well the possible studies fit the criteria, together with their relevance for the replication researcher's purposes, their fitness for purpose, and what those purposes are. More than one study might be a contender at this stage. Researchers must be able to read studies critically in order to judge which can be considered for a possible replication (e.g. Abbhul, 2012; Porte & McManus, 2019).

At Stage 2, skills include the ability to identify strengths and weaknesses in the original study or studies, how they might suggest the need for replication of one or more elements, and what those elements are. In turn, this requires the researcher to identify and justify the purposes of the replication, which, in turn, affect the kind of replication chosen. This might whittle down the number of eligible original

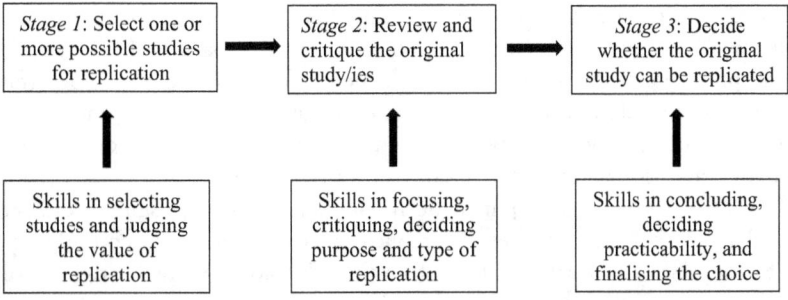

Figure 8.1 Deciding the original study for replication

studies selected at Stage 1. At this stage, researchers must be able to read studies critically, for example to identify flaws, biases, areas that need clarification, refinement, and/or further investigation. The review and critique of the original studies can include, for each study, the quality, acceptability, sufficiency, correctness, clarity, transparency, and detail of:

- the background to the study;
- the statement of the problem or question;
- the purposes of the study;
- the research questions/hypotheses and their derivation from the literature review;
- the setting, context, and conditions in the study;
- the research design;
- the details of the population and sampling;
- the details of the contents, tasks, procedures, timing, duration, and key components, methods, and materials of the intervention;
- the details of the instruments for data collection and their reliability and validity;
- the measures being used;
- the independent and dependent variables in the study;
- the pre-test and post-test;
- data analysis and the correctness of the (statistical) tests use;
- confounds in the study;
- the findings of the original study and the claims made from the findings.

At Stage 3, there are two main tasks. Task one requires the researcher to review the chosen possible studies to see if they include sufficient detail (and on what) for a replication to be conducted, winnowing out those studies which do not meet this requirement. A key issue here is for the replication researcher to judge the original study not only on its own merits, but also to see if sufficient clarity, transparency, and detail are provided for a replication actually to be able to be conducted. For example, if the replication researcher has identified a possible problem in the original study, such that re-analysis of the original data is required (the reproducibility issue in an exact replication), is there sufficient access to those original data, their coding, the details of statistical treatments and processes that were used, the software that was used and how it was used, for the replication, in reality, to be conducted? If the replication researcher has identified an original study that has a useful 'concept' for a conceptual replication to be conducted, is there sufficient detail, clarity, and transparency with regard to the information on the operationalisation and conduct of the original research for the replication researcher to know what to hold constant, what to change, and why, and how to conduct the replication research?

Task two in this stage requires the researcher to judge feasibility and practicability (see below): whether the replication can actually be carried out by the researcher(s). In turn, this leads to a final decision on which original study to select and which part(s) of it to replicate, for what purposes, what type of replication study to conduct, and what the replication study will do, focus on, and seek to demonstrate.

These three stages might run sequentially or (partially) simultaneously and might involve several iterations and ongoing modifications; they are likely to be mutually informing.

Deciding the feasibility and utility of the replication

If, in the judgement of the replication researcher, the original study can be replicated, and is worthwhile replicating, can the replication study actually be conducted? For example, does the replication researcher have access to the following for the replication research to be a realistic option: original data and their coding for an exact replication; participants for the replication research; equipment, materials, and resources for the replication research to be a realistic option? Can the replication study be sufficiently faithful to the original study for it to be valid and reliable? This includes the level of detail and transparency on key areas of the original study. The replication researcher is faced with the following questions and decisions that have similarities to those asked of an original study:

- Is it feasible and practicable to conduct the replication research?
- Is the potential benefit worth the cost, and to whom and to what?

In short, can the replication research actually be done, and is it worth doing? This involves critical, analytical, evaluative, and judgemental skills such as in:

- conducting a cost-benefit analysis;
- identifying and judging the possible short-term, medium-term, and long-term benefits of the replication study;
- conducting a needs analysis (e.g. of staff training required to be able to conduct the replication research, and whether the cost in terms of meeting training needs is worth the benefit); what resources (and of different types) are required;
- conducting a resource analysis of what currently exists and what is required (e.g. human, material, administrative, computational, financial, temporal, locational), and whether it is possible to have or obtain them;
- conducting a risk analysis;
- conducting a situational analysis;
- conducting a feasibility analysis;
- conducting an expertise analysis (is there sufficient resident expertise to conduct the replication study, and what access is there to other expertise, e.g. people, consultation, and information);
- identifying whether there is access to participants for the study;
- identifying and working with criteria for making judgements, and success criteria, indicators, and evidence needed for reaching an answer to the previous two questions.

This involves examining and evaluating how these features were addressed in the original study and then comparing them to what is possible in the replication study. Further, it requires coming to a judgement on whether the replication study will be sufficiently similar to the original study for it to qualify as a genuine replication (restating the importance of decisions concerning sameness).

Planning the replication study

In planning the replication study, replication researchers must have 'standard' skills in planning research, with attention to detail and transparency (e.g. Morrison, 2021; National Academies of Sciences, Engineering, and Medicine, 2019; National Science Foundation and Institute of Education Sciences, 2018). In addition to these, replication researchers must take cognizance of the original study, planning the replication with the original study centrally in mind, as the replication study seeks to judge its own findings and conclusions in relation to those of the original study. Given this, additional requirements for a replication study include:

- planning a replication study and its relationship to the original study;
- identifying, setting out, and justifying the purposes and type of replication to be conducted and ensuring that is fit for the purpose of replication;
- identifying and justifying the exact focus and contents of the replication study and how these relate to the original study;
- indicating exactly what the replication study seeks to replicate and why;
- indicating what the replication study will alter from that/those of the original study, why, and with what possible effects on claims for replication;
- writing research questions for a replication study (i.e. in relating them to the original study);
- stating and justifying what confidence levels and degree of uncertainty and certainty will be tolerated and required, respectively, for the replication to be judged as successful (this should be decided in advance of the study and possibly pre-registered, i.e. before findings are obtained, in order to avoid possible bias, data dredging, cherry-picking, p-hacking, and the 'file drawer problem');
- identifying and justifying (and pre-registering) the criteria for judging how far the replication study successfully replicates the original;
- trialling the replication study (if possible or deemed necessary).

This list is designed to enable the replication researcher to (a) judge the closeness of the relationships between the original study and the proposed replication study, and (b) identify which parts of the original study remain the same as, or are different from, those of the original study, thereby enabling the researcher to judge how genuine and credible the replication study will be. In turn, this raises the issue of rendering transparent the criteria being used to judge with sufficient certainty that the replication is fair and to state the levels of certainty and uncertainty in judging the results of the replication.

Conducting the intervention in the replication study

The replication study requires not only the skills that one would associate with conducting a self-standing piece of research but, additionally, skills in ensuring that the conduct of the replication research is as sufficiently close to the original study as it was intended to be, and that it keeps 'on track' of its plans. In the world of education, these constitute a major issue. Tilley (1993) comments that social contexts frustrate 'strict' replications whilst, simultaneously, being essential and key drivers in replication research. Strict replication is impossible in trials, as participants change, protocols and methods differ, schedules differ, and even intervention contents differ (Meinert, 2011). Indeed, Morrison (2021), writing on randomised controlled trials in education, notes that classrooms are highly complex, variable-dense, causally dense, contingency-rich, conditions-saturated, multi-dimensional, multi-layered, and multi-factorial (p. 7), and that

> teachers rarely leave interventions or prescribed practices untouched; they do something with them, they use their informed professional judgement and experience in deciding 'what works' for them or the persons in their charge.
> (p. 56)

> as professionals, people 'do something' with standard procedures, modifying them for the situation in hand. It is impossible, even undesirable or unethical, to expect standard, uniform procedures for an RCT [randomised controlled trial] in education to be followed slavishly in differing contexts, with different participants.
> (p. 125)

The replication researcher is faced with the challenge of ensuring sufficient fidelity to both the original study and the planned replication study. The former raises questions of fairness of comparability to the original study; the latter raises questions of what can be concluded from the results of the replication, in its own terms and in comparison to those of the original study. The replication researcher needs skills and abilities to:

- judge fidelity to the original study as the replication study is running;
- judge fidelity to the planned replication study as the replication study is running: to determine how well and how closely what is intended to happen is actually happening in the intervention (i.e. how close is the match between the intended and transacted intervention, and how to keep it 'on track');
- keep the intended components of the replication study 'on track';
- judge when divergence from the intended replication plan is necessary (e.g. due to the exigencies of a particular emergent situation) and the effect(s) of this on the replication and the judgements of what the replication study shows (Nutley et al., 2007);
- work with different people involved in the replication study;
- work with those involved in the original study (if appropriate).

Such skills concern not only the contents and management of the intervention itself but also sophisticated and well-developed interpersonal skills in working with people. In relation to conducting a study, issues of access, to, for example, schools and students, are not always straightforward, and a process of negotiation might be required before and during the replication study concerning what can be done in the replication setting, and who decides. Here, Morrison (2006) notes that compromises may have to be reached between what the researcher in education would like to do and what is possible, particularly when schools and teachers hold the whip hand. He notes that it often comes to a choice between compromising, that is, following the teachers' wishes and decisions, or abandoning the study.

Further, if an exact replication seeks access to the original data, this may be difficult if the author of the original study is unable, or reluctant, to release data or coding of data that might lead to challenging the original findings (Morrison, 2019), or, indeed, the researcher himself or herself, or if there is a proprietary ban or moratorium on releasing data (National Academies of Sciences, Engineering, and Medicine, 2019). This may occur in exact, reproducibility replications, though there is increasing advocacy of lodging suitably anonymised data in a central, open, and secure repository, and many journals in education request authors to provide such access.

Data analysis, interpretation, and conclusions in the replication study

A replication study requires not only 'standard' skills of data analysis and interpretation but also the development of additional skills. For example, if the replication study uses the original data, and/or the codes for statistical analysis, and/or the software and procedures that were used in the original analysis (e.g. how the statistics were computed), and/or new technologies and software, then this might involve issues of access and expertise. The National Academies of Sciences, Engineering, and Medicine (2019) puts this as a major issue in reproducibility research/exact replications.

The data analysis in a replication study is not confined to the replication study alone; it includes making comparisons with the findings of the original study. This brings additional skills in analysing data that are specific to a replication study, including:

- deciding and justifying whether or not to use the same methods of analysis as in the original study (including codes used in the original study);
- identifying and justifying what elements, procedures, and kinds of data analysis are the same and/or different between the studies;
- knowing and justifying how to compare the original study and the replication study;
- judging and justifying how far the replication confirms, disconfirms, partially confirms, indeterminately confirms the original study and, in the case

of approximate and conceptual replications, generalises beyond the original study;
- identifying, knowing, applying, and justifying what to look for, what criteria to use in judging replication success or otherwise, and how to judge findings;
- setting and justifying cut-off points to adopt in judging 'successful' replication;
- how to compare the original study and the replication study if they have different degrees of precision, accuracy, variance in means, range, distributions, standard distributions, skewness, standard errors, confidence intervals;
- identifying and justifying the levels of certainty that are required in comparing the results of the original study with those of the replication study;
- judging and justifying the level of uncertainty that can be tolerated in coming to a decision on whether the replication study confirms the findings of the original study;
- exercising and justifying professional expertise in coming to judgements about the 'success' of replication, deriving from the data used;
- higher order thinking and analytical skills in making judgements from the analysis, interpreting and explaining findings, and linking findings to research questions;
- drawing and justifying conclusions not only from the replication study *per se* but also in relation to the original study, to indicate how far the replication confirms, disconfirms, qualifies, partially or indeterminately confirms, extends, and so on, the original study.

The skills needed here involve those of making informed judgements and their justification. Judgements cannot simply be read off or cranked out by looking at figures; figures on their own are not self-explanatory. Rather, informed judgement is required, to judge 'beyond a reasonable doubt'; whilst some of this is often a function of experience over time, training replication researchers in such skills can expedite this.

Reporting the replication study

Whilst Chapter 7 provided guidelines on what to include in a replication report and how to organise the report, there are additional skills to those typically required in compiling a report on a replication study. They concern making comparisons between the original and the replication study, in particular:

- indicating, justifying, and taking account of changes the replication study made to the original study, and the implications of these;
- identifying, justifying, and taking account of differences in the features of the original study and the replication study, and their impact (if any) on the results;
- indicating, justifying, and interpreting any new analyses conducted in the replication study, and their impact (if any) on the results;

- reporting how much and where the findings of the replication study confirm and/or disconfirm those of the original study;
- indicating, discussing, and interpreting the limits of what can be taken from the replication study in judging how far the findings of the replication study confirm, disconfirm, qualify, partially confirm, indeterminately confirm, extend, and so on, the original study;
- indicating, discussing, and interpreting the similarities and differences between the original study and the replication study, and their significance;
- indicating, discussing, and justifying how much, and where, the replication has been successful, and based on what criteria and evidence;
- in the case of findings in the replication study that do not confirm those of the original study, indicating, discussing, and justifying what can and cannot be said about the original study;
- organising the report and its subsections (see Chapter 7) (e.g. presenting the points of the original study followed by those of the replication, and then drawing out, discussing, and concluding from, their similarities and differences);
- comparing, contrasting, discussing, and explaining the results of the original study and the replication study;
- avoiding personal affront to the author(s) of the original study if the replication study's findings differ from those of the original study (Brown, 2012);
- setting out and summarising the key messages of the replication study;
- indicating implications for further research.

The skills needed here, as earlier in this chapter, concern higher order thinking: focusing, critiquing, comparing, contrasting, synthesising, interpreting, summarising, explaining, discussing, evaluating, justifying, organising, and presenting.

Developing the skills required

The skills required here reside in many fields: higher order thinking; personal, social, and interpersonal; management; judgement and decision making. Whilst some of these come with experience over time, this does not preclude training and development in replication research. Whilst specific knowledge, for example of computation and statistics, requires its own training (National Academies of Sciences, Engineering, and Medicine, 2019), and whilst some skills are learned by doing replication studies in the field and then reflecting on them, at issue here is how skill development in conducting replication studies can be provided. Abbhul (2012), Fitzpatrick (2012), and Porte and McManus (2019) provide examples from applied linguistics; Benson and Borrego (2015) provide examples from engineering education; Frank and Saxe (2012) provide examples from psychology; their examples are transferable to education, as indicated below.

Skill training includes doing and reviewing replication studies on (graduate) research training programmes, by planning, conducting, and working through a replication study (Plucker & Makel, 2021). This includes critical reading of original studies and replication studies, as this can aid the selection of an original study for subsequent replication, identifying what needs to be done in the replication study and what to focus on specifically. Such critical reading engages interrogating, reviewing, and evaluating published original studies to find those that are suitable for replication and have replication potential, choosing an original study for replication, and justifying the choice (using criteria set out in Chapter 1). It also involves identifying the focus of the replication, what it should do, and how it should be conducted. This moves from the original study to the replication study, identifying what improvements to make to the original study, what follows from the original study, what can be kept the same in the replication study and what should change, and why.

Abbhul (2012) provides an example of using a fictional original study that deliberately has several flaws, so that replication research students can sharpen up their analytical, critical, and evaluative skills in identifying how to improve the original study in a replication study. Learning about replication study skills can also come from studying examples of replication study reports and write-ups, to see how effectively, clearly, and comprehensively they report, including judgements of 'success' in the replication, and making comparisons with those of the original study, deciding how far and where the findings of the original study are confirmed by the replication, and with how much (un)certainty. This helps students to learn about replication research: how to compare original and replication studies; how to write up the comparisons and their results; how to write implications of the findings of the replication study; how to critique the replication study; and how to make suggestions for future research arising from the replication. This can involve working with given examples.

Training and development can also focus on doing in-class replications. Frank and Saxe (2012) advocate having students perform a replication study as part of their course work. Here, students focus on replicating cutting-edge research. The authors suggest conducting direct replications of recently published experiments, as: (a) the recency of the study increases students' interest in, and motivation to work on, the study; (b) the original authors have already devised the research question(s) and the design of the original experiment, so that some of the 'hard work' (p. 601) has already been done for novice replication researchers; and (c) because the original study is new and needs validating, the scientific community needs a replication to be conducted in order to see how reliable the results of the original study are, that is, the replication has a useful purpose and contribution to make.

Here, the students and their teacher work through original studies to identify those which might be suitable for replication, and then they construct a proposal for a direct replication, including, as the authors note, attention to statistical power and changes to the original study that will be made in the replication study, the reasons for these, the potential threats to a genuine replication and its findings that stem from making such changes. Frank and Saxe (2012) advocate using the same materials as those used by the authors of the original study. The replication study learners and their teacher conduct the replication research together (an apprentice model), analyse and interpret the data together and, if it is deemed important and suitable, publish results or submit them to a repository or registry of replication studies. The intention here is to design, conduct, and report a 'real' replication study, suitably supervised, so that a valid, reliable, and rigorous replication has been conducted.

Frank and Saxe (2012) suggest that student-led, student-decided, and student-planned in-class replications of original studies can be conducted, and that working on these can contribute to the overall grading of the students' performance. Not only are these inexpensive, but also their practicability is assured. Further, they are 'real' experiments in which students, working in groups, 'own' their own study. As the authors note, this is motivating for students, as they know that they are conducting experiments not simply as an exercise in building skills but to make a useful contribution to knowledge. Guidance from the instructor is needed in order to avoid novice replication students being overambitious in choosing and planning a study whose complexities are beyond their abilities, and in order to match the demand of the proposed replication study to the different abilities of the students, that is, the instructor provides scaffolding for the students.

Here, the opportunity to publish or submit a replication to a repository is high. The students work through all the components of the original study and the planning, conduct, analysis, and reporting of the replication study, that is, the whole process from start to finish. The genuine uncertainty of the results of the replication is a stimulus to conducting it and a motivator for the students, as the exercise is 'real' and significant (ibid.). Further, having students read, discuss, and critique the replication studies and reports of their class members can benefit everyone involved, helping them to identify and appreciate high quality studies and weaknesses in studies, to tolerate frustration in planning and conducting a replication, and to give and receive advice, learning the value of sharing, which is, itself, an increasing feature of doing research in education.

Frank and Saxe (2012) note that having students of replication research working on replication studies of a published original study is preferable to having them devise their own original studies, as the demands of setting up and conducting an original study might be too great for many novices, and might be impractical. Conducting direct replications on given original studies can be a useful 'jump start' (p. 603) to replication research and original research. Having in-class replication studies has students addressing issues of closeness and sameness between the original study and its replication. The time available is likely to lead to easier, rather than more complex, studies being replicated, which is fitting for novice replication researchers and students.

At issue here is the need for skill development for learning about and conducting replication studies to be realistic, real-world, and comprehensive. It involves specific skill development and training on design and planning issues, methodology, instrumentation, sampling and settings, instructions and procedures, interventions, conducting the replication, analysing original and new data, discussing findings, drawing conclusions, identifying limitations, making comparisons, reporting, and so on. The pedagogical implications of this suggest the benefits of workshop-based instruction and hands-on practical learning, working on given, real-life examples, and on creating and conducting replications of provided or chosen original studies. This can be in-class or outside class; the point here is that it is learning-by-doing rather than learning by listening, reading, or watching, that is, by first-hand learning rather than second-hand learning.

For the replication researcher working alone, for example a member of an institution of higher education who is not part of a research team, or who is a doctorate student, whilst one might expect that member to have research skills, the need for ongoing development might hinge, in part, on discussions with colleagues, submissions of replications for peer-reviewed publication, open source publication and feedback, self-learning, and the common channels for self-improvement that are part of being a member of a higher education institution.

Conclusion

Considering and conducting replication studies in education brings its own skill set that may be new to those who are already versed in conducting stand-alone research studies or non-replication-type studies. Such skills include comparing and contrasting an original study and its replication study at each stage of the replication and for each of its components, with close-grained analysis and critique, and in drawing conclusions from such analysis.

The gamut of these skills is wide, and they draw on higher order thinking at all stages of the replication, from conception to reporting, together with personal, social, and interpersonal, management and decision-making skills. The inherent uncertainty of replication findings, and the unavoidable absence of absolute standards for judging sameness, closeness, and 'success' in a replication, place a premium on skills of informed decision making and defensible judgement on what a replication actually and credibly shows.

Whilst some of these skills mature with experience in doing replication research, there is significant benefit from training and development provision. The chapter has argued for practical, hands-on, supervised experiential learning here, learning-by-doing, preferably in groups. The interchange of critiques, ideas, issues, and shared planning, conduct, analysis, and reporting constitutes a powerful method of learning. The chapter has argued that these should be combined with the motivational, meaningful, and professional contribution potential of working on, publishing, and/or reporting of real-world replication studies of given or self-chosen original studies. In doing so, this transforms a mere learning exercise into a real and useful contribution to the field of education in which it is operating.

9 Conclusions and the future of replication studies in education

Replication studies at work

This book has made a claim for replication studies in education on many grounds. Some claims appeal to the exceptionless, self-correcting, cumulative, objective nature of science and the generalisability and stability of its findings, accompanied by the hallmarks of rigorous testing. However, these claims are contested in principle as well as practice, as the complexity of education, classrooms, teaching, and learning confounds easy attempts to identify 'what works' in either the original study or its replication and, indeed, challenges the feasibility and utility of replication studies, for validity and generalisability. Chapter 3 showed how this occurred in special education, though it applies much more widely in education. Indeed, the question was raised of whether the enterprise of replication is fundamentally ill-judged and misguided, rehearsing the question of how far education is or is not a science, given the uncontrollability of significant variables and of the human, agentic, hermeneutic nature of education, and, if it is not a science, then how much is it an art?

The book has suggested avoiding simplistic dichotomous thinking – education as a scientific or a humanistic, hermeneutic matter – by arguing not only that education is, in part, a science but also that this does not mean that it might not be suitable to use methods from the sciences carefully. In this spirit, the book has argued that replication studies are worth doing, provided that, and only provided that, the contingencies, conditions, uncertainties of planning, conducting and drawing conclusions from, and potentially significant limitations of replication studies, are acknowledged and factored into human judgements concerning replication, what they show and what can be taken from them.

Absolute certainty in replication studies is a chimera, an illusion. Replication deals in degrees of success and failure, certainty and uncertainty, probability and likelihood, even in a putative exact replication. Given this, the book has argued that the exercise of judgement is essential at all stages of a replication study, from deciding what, whether, how, and why to conduct a replication, and what the purpose of the replication study is (given that replication studies can serve different purposes), to deciding what the replication study shows and what can be drawn from it 'beyond a reasonable doubt', not only in its own terms but also in

DOI: 10.4324/9781003204237-10

comparison to the original study that gave rise to the replication in the first place. Such decisions should extend to consideration not only of original studies with large effect sizes or high statistical significance but also of replicating an original study whose findings might have small effect sizes and non-statistically significant findings, as the original study might contain important or interesting implications. In other words, judgements have to be made on which criteria (see Chapters 1 and 5) are more or less important than others in judging whether an original study should be replicated.

Choosing an original study to replicate is not straightforward, easy, or arbitrary. Judgement is needed in deciding whether an original study is not only worth replicating, but whether, even if it is desirable, it is possible. Needs analysis is a necessary but insufficient condition for conducting a replication; the replication study must be feasible and practicable. Judgement is required on whether the original study provides sufficient detail, clarity, and transparency for the replication study to be able to work on it at all, and this applies to both the original study and the replication study. For the former, this is to enable the would-be replication researcher to see if a replication study is possible, and for the latter, for reviewers of replication studies to judge how valid and reliable the replication study is and how much confidence can be placed in its findings and conclusions. Detail, clarity, transparency, and trustworthiness are requisites for each component of the replication study; these have been a *leitmotiv* running through the book.

Deciding whether to conduct a replication study requires different analyses to be conducted on practicability in the field, for example access: to participants; to computational requirements; to cost-benefit and risk analysis; to situational analysis; to human, temporal, material, administrative, locational and financial resources. These practical matters can frustrate or modify attempts to conduct a close replication. In the world of education, these are powerful considerations, not least as teachers, applying their professional judgement, necessarily adjust what happens in their classrooms to the exigencies of the students and classrooms in which replications studies might be conducted.

Whether a replication study can exert sufficient controls on the multi-factorial, causally complex, variable-dense, setting-sensitive, humanistic, agentic, emergent, and contingency-rich world of the classrooms is an open question. Clearly, not all factors can be controlled or controlled out. Is that good enough for replication in education? The uncertainty factor is potentially huge, and, indeed, researchers might be uncertain as to how (un)certain the (un)certainty is. As Chapter 6 indicates, there are many reasons why a replication study might or might not replicate the original study, such that replication and non-replication are complex matters. How much does this compromise or frustrate the replication? This is particularly important when the replication study is being compared with the original study, and the argument throughout this book is that such comparisons are essential at every stage and with regard to every component of both studies.

The level of certainty required, or uncertainty tolerated, features when deciding on the type of replication to be conducted, for example an exact, an approximate, or a conceptual replication. These are only three points on a continuum of closeness to the original study, and issues of sameness and closeness suffuse and permeate the entire book. Variation extends to deciding what, actually, a replication is, and, for a conceptual replication, what, exactly, the 'concept' is. The book indicated that replication *qua* reproducibility, re-analysing data from the first study or conducting an exact replication of the original study, whilst it might be attractive and feasible in some disciplines, is both unlikely and rare in the world of education. One alternative, an approximate replication, whilst abiding by the definitions of replication advanced in the opening chapter of the book, opens the door to uncertainty as to how far the replication really is fair and how far whatever it shows can comment fairly or usefully on the original study; the reduction of sameness exacts a high price in what can be taken from a putative replication study. In this context, Chapter 3 introduced several features of a fair test of replication.

The problem of sameness is exacerbated when one moves to a conceptual replication, since, provided that it keeps constant the 'concept' of the original study in the replication study, a host of changes can be made between the original study and its replication. The payback for risking replication here is that, by changing the name of the game and its rules, from replication to generalisability, open season is declared on what can be changed in the replication study. Defining replication as generalisability, whilst being definitionally suspect (a category switch), licenses the replication researcher to make many changes in the replication study. However, the effects of this are to disable the replication study from commenting safely on the internal validity, confirmability, correctness, quality, and reliability of the original study and its findings. As Chapter 3 remarked, conceptual replications are constitutionally unable to falsify an original study, and, indeed, they might only trivially verify or validate the findings of an original study. Making changes, even if they are minor, calls into question how different the replication study can be from the original study.

However, abandoning features of the original study offers rich rewards, for example in testing the generalisability of the signal of the concept alone, uncontaminated by the noise of context and research methods. Is this an unacceptable distortion of, and departure from, the original purpose and notion of replication, or a useful redefinition and realignment of a replication study to test for generalisability? A fair replication or a loose, flabby, all-accepting, all-permitting study? A Faustian pact or a useful service? This reasserts the need for human judgement to intervene. Further, Chapter 3 indicated that conceptual replications risk overlooking the significance of under-determination and over-determination in accounting for the findings of the replication study.

The attractions of generalisability in a conceptual replication should not trump the need to test the validity of the original study, however mundane and pedestrian this might be. Whilst conceptual replications might serve external validity, this should not come at the expense of internal validity. The book has argued that this suggests conducting initial replication studies that adhere as far as possible to the original study.

Sameness touches all aspects and stages of the study. The book argued that some features of the original study – paradigmatic, ontological, epistemological – should

Conclusions 159

be retained in the replication study, and that to alter these is to commit a category error which render the original and replication studies unable to be fairly compared, akin to comparing oil and water. Some components of the original study might be changed in a conceptual replication (e.g. population and sampling, metrics and measures, instrumentation, settings, implementation of the intervention, tasks in the intervention, data analysis), but this comes at the price of distancing the replication study from the original study. How far this matters in a conceptual replication involves human judgement, though the argument was made that it *does* matter, as it limits what can be drawn and concluded from the replication study in relation to the original study.

The book argued that a requirement of replication is its attention to detail, clarity, transparency, precision, and accuracy (validity) in both the original study and its replication study. These, it was argued, enable the replication researcher to judge whether the original study contains sufficient information for a fair replication to be conducted. It also helps in identifying what should be the exact focus of the replication study, and this enables valid operationalisability of the replication study to be addressed.

Whilst detail, clarity, transparency, precision, and accuracy are laudable, the point was raised that, if the replication study makes changes to the original study, then the levels of precision and accuracy of the original study and the replication study are likely to differ, calling into question the comparability of the two studies. In turn, there is a need to identify, state, and justify the grounds, criteria, evidence, indicators, and measures to be used in judging how much sameness, similarity, and closeness are present for the replication to be judged a success, that is, to judge how far the findings of the replication study confirm, partially confirm, extend, disconfirm, or call into question the findings of the original study, or, indeed to reserve judgement and require further investigation (indeterminacy). Replication research must indicate and justify: what levels of precision are required; what levels of certainty of the findings are required; what levels of uncertainty are tolerable (and much statistical analysis is premised on probability); how much variance, error, and range are tolerable; and how close, and concerning what items, the results of the original study and the replication study must be for the replication to be judged a 'success' beyond reasonable doubt.

The book has argued that the very notion of 'success' in a replication study is unclear. It can mean that the results of the replication study and the original study concur sufficiently. However, if one adopts a wider perspective, then, if a replication study yields findings that disconfirm the original study, or render the results indeterminate, then this, too, is successful but in a different sense: here, it has successfully limited the boundaries of a conceptual replication, or it has called into question the original findings. It is akin to many findings in the social sciences: if you find agreement, then this is important but, if you find no agreement, then this is important as well.

In handling issues of success and precision, some of the tools available to the replication researcher include standardised means and standard deviations, effect size, statistical significance testing (though the book questions this), confidence intervals, distributions, skewness, error margins, range, and statistical power. Each of these has its own limitations, assumptions, and conditions as well as affordances, and in the end it is the researcher who *judges* how close and sufficiently certain are the findings of the original study and the replication study for the replication to be judged as having 'worked'. It is a human judgement.

Whilst 'cut-off' levels of closeness, certainty, and uncertainty can be set in advance in a statistical world (and pre-registration of a replication study is advocated in order to avoid data dredging, *p*-hacking, and cherry-picking), the world is more than a set of statistics; statistics inform, but they do not make decisions. Human judgement is required in judging how much the replication study confirms the findings of the original study, that is: decides 'beyond a reasonable doubt'. Chapter 4 indicated that deciding how much a replication study has been successful is a matter of degree and judgement, and these call for detail, trustworthiness, disclosure, and transparency in criteria, indicators, evidence, and judgements, all of which are evaluated and judged by the replication researcher (and, subsequently, by readers and reviewers, if the report is published). One cannot crank out from a set of calculations a definitive judgement on how far the replication study has or has not sufficiently confirmed the findings of the original study; the final judgement is a human act. The grounds, criteria, and evidence for judging the findings of the replication and comparing it with the original study must be justified, defensible, trustworthy, transparent, and detailed.

The book argued that the requirements of a replication study, for detail; clarity; transparency; precision; comparison with the original study; reporting and justifying changes to the original study; statements of and justifications for criteria, grounds, evidence, indicators, success criteria; and conclusions in judging a replication, are likely to lead to a replication study report that exceeds the normal length of an article in an academic journal. This is because the replication study not only has to fulfil the requirements of reporting the replication research study itself, but also, all along the way, has to compare the replication study with the original study, that is, it has more than one main purpose. It has to report key features of the original study as well as those of the replication study. It is likely that there will be several subsections of the report, for clarity and a clear structure and sequence, addressing the components of the original study and those of the replication study. It was suggested that the report should follow the layout and sequence of the original study, where possible and suitable, for ease of comparison. It also noted that it is important to conduct 'safety checks' to ensure that the replication study report has addressed key areas of the comparison between the original study and the replication study, and the conclusions drawn from the exercise.

What starts off, then, as an apparently straightforward exercise of replicating an original study turns out to be problematic at every step. Even though we might have an 'intuitive sense' (Bollen et al., 2015, p. 5) of what it means for findings to replicate the original study, the closer we look, the less clear this becomes. In order to understand the challenges of replication and to come to reliable and valid judgements in the face of meanings of results that might be less than clear, the book has argued for skills training in the conduct of the replication research study

Conclusions 161

itself, in making comparisons with the original study and then concluding from these about what the replication study has and has not shown.

Such skills do not reside solely in matters of planning the research, data analysis, and reporting; rather, they concern social and interpersonal matters, management and decision making, evaluation and judgement. These come into play at every stage of the replication study. In developing these skills, the book argued for reflective practice, learning-by-planning and learning-by-doing replications, by evaluating replications, by conducting a detailed analysis and critique of original studies in order to identify what to replicate, and reflecting on the results of replication studies. These skills, the book argues, are learned usefully in groups, with expert supervisors. To counter the unattractiveness of replication studies in many quarters (e.g. to editors and publishers, to career-minded academics), the book suggested that graduate training programmes can include planning, registering, conducting, publishing, and reporting real-life replication studies of published original studies, though how realistic these are depends in part on the level of demand of the original study (e.g. complexity, practicability, difficulty, access, resources).

Limitations of the book

This book has focused on research that involved interventions. Whilst other types of research are possible, the decision to focus on interventions is because they concern the 'what happens if. . . . ?' type of research in education. This brings with it ethical concerns that are attached to experimental and other types of research (e.g. quasi-experiments, case studies), and, whilst these have been mentioned, a further volume could go into greater detail on these others.

Education has very many dimensions and spheres. The book is generic in nature; it has deliberately not differentiated between different aspects of education, for example age groups, primary and secondary schools, higher education, nurseries and kindergartens, special education, adult learning groups, further education. Nor has it raised curricular and subject-specific issues. Rather, it has raised and addressed issues that apply to replication research studies in general.

Further, the book has not differentiated between small-scale and large-scale replication research. Whilst small-scale replication research might be possible, nevertheless, given the complexity of many original studies and their preparation and conduct by teams of researchers, large-scale replication studies can provide both statistical power and insights that are not available to smaller-scale students (e.g. the Open Science Collaboration, 2015, found that small-scale studies risk inflating effect sizes; Cheung & Slavin, 2016; Lortie-Forges & Inglis, 2019; Malouf & Taymans, 2016; Slavin, 2018). However, small-scale replication studies, the province of small teams or individuals, are also valuable (e.g. Coyne et al., 2013; Melhuish, 2018; Melhuish & Thanheiser, 2018; Therrien et al., 2016). The issues raised in this book apply from small-scale to large-scale replication studies.

The issue of 'cut-off' points in deciding how far a replication study successfully replicates the original study emphasised the significance of human judgement in such decisions. Such judgement must be educated and informed, not least as important policy decisions and/or educational practice might hang on it. How such informed human judgement can be improved and used was suggested in Chapters 6 and 8, but this is a matter for further investigation and development.

As with much research evidence, getting the results of replication studies into the wider domain of education and educational practice is challenging (Gorard, 2020; Nutley et al., 2007). The present book has taken the topic of replication studies *per se*, rather than their subsequent outcomes, uses, uptake, and impact, and these would benefit from further investigation and a different kind of publication, broadening the scope beyond that of the present volume.

Some parts of the book have adopted a healthy scepticism to replication studies in principle and practice, their desirability, worthwhileness, practicability, utility, view of the nature of education, and the susceptibility of education to trials which attempt to control the uncontrollable (Biesta, 2020; Morrison, 2021). On the other hand, the book has been at pains to stress that replication studies, when they are planned, implemented, and reported with meticulous care and self-awareness of their scope, trustworthiness, limits, and claims from their findings, can make a positive contribution to educational research. The debate on whether, or how far, replication studies serve particular values and ideologies in education is contentious (e.g. Biesta, 2020, notes that the 'what works' agenda risks overlooking the 'what for' agenda), and further debate on this is required. Teaching and learning concern values and require more than applied technicism, though this does not obviate the need for securing research findings.

Looking to the future

Replication studies are important in educational research. Their current presence in educational research is slight. It must increase. For replication studies in education to take a stronger foothold in educational research requires making them more attractive to researchers to undertake (Ioannidis, 2012) and journal editors to publish (Alm, 2010; Artino, 2013; Cai et al., 2018; Makel et al., 2016; Pashler & Wagenmakers, 2012; Warne, 2014), together with a change of mind-set that moves from thinking that single studies, regardless of their size, are sufficient for policy and practice.

Frank and Saxe (2012) note that, whilst there is widespread agreement on the importance of replication studies, there is currently 'no clear consensus' (p. 600) on how to encourage them. Many stakeholders should be involved in promoting replication studies: government organisations, professional societies and associations, journal editors, funders, academic institutions (holding more positive attitudes to replication studies for promotion and career development), researchers and researcher training providers. This is accompanied by opening up repositories of data from original studies and replication studies. Incentives to promote replication studies, from publishers, journal editors, funders, academic institutions, and so on, can be offered here, with awards, prizes, certification of open practice, sponsorship of pre-publication checking, pre-registration (National Academies of Sciences, Engineering, and Medicine, 2019; Nosek et al., 2018). It can also include publishing findings that are negative and setting and publishing standards for reproducibility and replication. This can extend to reviewing articles that have their results removed, in order to separate the findings of the replication study from the evaluation of the significance and importance of the research questions themselves, and focusing on the quality of the research design, methodology, and conduct of the research (National Academies of Sciences, Engineering, and Medicine, 2019), in order to judge whether an important question has been tested rigorously, regardless of the findings. Support for replication studies can be increased by more training and development initiatives in replication research (e.g. by funders and academic institutions) and by persuading funding agencies to fund replication studies.

Future replication research faces an important and considerable agenda (e.g. Vealé, 2019). This includes examining how to conceptualise and define replication and its constitution, boundaries, limitations, and criteria; how to validate replication studies and ensure their reliability; how to understand and interrogate their findings; how many replication studies are required (when 'enough is enough', who decides, and on what basis); how to draw secure, trustworthy conclusions from the replication studies and what they really show, both *per se* and in comparison to the original study; how to move from findings to their implications for, and impact on, educational research, policy, outcomes, and practices; how to decide how far, and where, a replication study is successful (and what 'success' means); how to decide how far, and where, the replication study confirms, disconfirms, partially confirms, extends, and so on the original study; how to take account of multiple causality, variable-dense conditionality, rich contextuality, evolutionary, agentic, and dynamic situations in classrooms; and how to take account of exogenous and endogenous factors present in the original study and the replication study.

Truth emerges only slowly and unsteadily (Meinert, 2011), and there is no final supreme arbiter to decide whether the replication study has 'worked' and what can be taken from it. Even if all the requirements for a replication study are secure, how its findings translate into policy making, educational research, and practice creates another set of challenges. That is for another publication. Replication studies promise much in the evidence-informed and 'what works' agendas in education. However, just as 'what works' is vastly unclear, so replication studies are not straightforward to plan, conduct and report, and judge. Nor should they be. They are demanding, just like education.

References

Abbhul, R. (2012). Practical methods for teaching replication to applied linguistics students. In G. Porte (Ed.), *Replication research in applied linguistics* (pp. 135–150). Cambridge University Press.

Aguilar, M. S. (2020). Replication studies in mathematics education: What kind of questions would be productive to explore? *International Journal of Science and Mathematics Education, 18*(1), S37–S50. https://doi.org/10.1007/s10763-020-10069-7

Aitken, M., Bennett, S. N., & Hesketh, J. (1981). Teaching styles and pupil progress: A reanalysis. *British Journal of Educational Psychology, 51*, 170–186. https://doi.org/10.1111/j.2044-8279.1981.tb02472.x

Alm, J. (2010). A call for replication studies. *Public Finance Review, 38*(3), 275–281. https://doi.org/10.1177/1091142110374569

American Political Science Association. (2012). *A guide to professional ethics in political science* (2nd ed.). American Political Science Association.

Anderson, S. F., & Maxwell, S. E. (2016). There's more than one way to conduct a replication study: Beyond statistical significance. *Psychological Methods, 21*(1), 1–12. https://doi.org/10.1037/met0000051

Artino, A. R. Jr. (2013). Why don't we conduct replication studies in medical education? *Medical Education, 47*(7), 745–747. https://doi.org/10.1111/medu.12204

Bakker, M., van Dijk, A., & Wicherts, J. M. (2012). The rules of the game called Psychological Science. *Perspectives on Psychological Science, 7*(6), 543–554. https://doi.org/10.1177/1745691612459060

Barshay, J. (2019). The dark side of education research: Widespread bias. *The Hechinger Report.* https://hechingerreport.org/the-dark-side-if-education-research-widespread-bias/

Begley, C. G. (2013). Six red flags for suspect work. *Nature, 497*(7450), 433–434. https://doi.org/10.1038/497433a

Bennett, S. N. (1976). *Teaching styles and pupil progress*. Open Books.

Benson, L., & Borrego, M. (2015). The role of replication in engineering education research. *Journal of Engineering Education, 104*(4), 388–392. https://doi.org/10.1002/jee.20082

Bienefeld, M., Böhm-Kasper, O., & Demmer, C. (2020). Highly recommended and yet neglected: The rarity of replication studies in educational science. *Journal for Educational Research Online (Journal für Bildungsforschung Online), 12*(3), S3–S22. www.waxmann.com/index.php?eID=download&id_artikel=ART104306&uid=frei

Biesta, G. (2020). *Educational research: An unorthodox introduction.* Bloomsbury.

Block, J., & Kuckertz, A. (2018). Seven principles of effective replication studies: Strengthening the evidence base of management research. *Management Review Quarterly, 68*(4), 355–359. https://doi.org/10.1007/s11301-018-0139-3

Bollen, K., Cacioppe, J. T., Kaplan, R. M., Krosnjick, J. A., & Olds, J. L. (2015). *Social, behavioural, and economic sciences perspectives on robust and reliable science* (Report of the Subcommittee on Replicability in Science Advisory Committee to the National Science Foundation Directorate for Social, Behavioral, and Economic Sciences). National Science Foundation.

Brandt, M. J., Ijzerman, H., Dijksterhuis, A., Farach, F. J., Geller, J., Giner-Sorolla, R., . . . van't Veer, A. (2014). The replication recipe: What makes for a convincing replication? *Journal of Experimental Social Psychology*, 50, 217–224. https://doi.org/10.1016/j.jesp.2013.10.005

British Educational Research Association. (2018). *Ethical guidelines for educational research* (4th ed.). www.bera.ac.uk/researchers-resources/publications/ethical-guidelines-for-educational-research-2018

Brown, A. N. (2021). Personal communication.

Brown, A. N., & Wood, B. D. K. (2014). When is an error not an error? *Guest Post on World Bank . . . Blogs*. https://blogs.worldbank.org/impactevaluations/when-error-not-error-guest-post-annette-n-brown-and-benjamin-d-k-wood

Brown, A. N., & Wood, B. D. K. (2018). Which tests not witch hunts: A diagnostic approach for replication research. *Economics: The Open Access, Open-Assessment E-Journal*, 12(2018-53), 1–26. http://dx.doi.org/10.5018/economics-ejournal.ja.2018-53

Brown, A. N., & Wood, B. D. K. (2019). Replication studies of development impact evaluations. *The Journal of Development Studies*, 55(5), 917–925. https://doi.org/10.1080/00220388.2018.1506582

Brown, J. D. (2012). Writing up a replication report. In G. Porte (Ed.), *Replication research in applied linguistics* (pp. 173–197). Cambridge University Press.

Cai, J., Morris, A., Hohensee, C., Hwang, S., Robison, V., & Hiebert, J. (2018). The role of replication studies in educational research. *Journal for Research in Mathematics Education*, 49(1), 2–8. https://doi.org/10.5951/jresematheduc.49.1.0002

Camerer, C. F., Dreber, A., Forsell, E., Ho, T.-H., Huber, J., Johannesson, M., . . . Wu, H. (2016). Evaluating replicability of laboratory experiments in economics. *Science*, 351(6280), 1433–1436. https://doi.org/10.1126/science.aaf0918

Cartwright, N. (2019). What is meant by 'rigour' in evidence-based educational policy and what's so good about it? *Educational Research and Evaluation*, 25(1–2), 63–80. https://doi.org/10.1080/13803611.2019.1617990

Cartwright, N., & Hardie, J. (2012). *Evidence-based policy: A practical guide to doing it better*. Oxford University Press.

Carver, R. P. (1978). The case against significance testing. *Harvard Educational Review*, 48(3), 378–399. www.jstor.org/stable/20152382

Center for Open Science. (2015). *Guidelines for transparency and openness promotion (TOP) in journal policies and practices*. Center for Open Science. https://osf.io/ud578/

Cheung, A. C. K., & Slavin, R. E. (2016). How methodological features affect effect sizes in education. *Educational Researcher*, 45(5), 282–292. https://doi.org/10.3102/0013189X6656615

Chhin, C. S., Taylor, K. A., & Wei, W. S. (2018). Supporting a culture of replication: An examination of education and special education research grants funded by the Institute of Education Sciences. *Educational Researcher*, 47(9), 594–605. https://doi.org/10.3102/0013189X18788047

Cohen, J. (1988). *Statistical power analysis for the behavioral sciences*. Erlbaum.

Cohen, L., Manion, L., & Morrison, K. R. B. (2018). *Research methods in education* (8th ed.). Routledge.

Collins, H. M. (1985). *Changing order: Replication and induction in scientific practice*. Sage.

Connolly, P., Keenan, C., & Urbanska, K. (2018). The trials of evidence-based practice in education: A systematic review of randomised controlled trials in education research 1980–2016. *Educational Research*, 60(3), 276–291. https://doi.org/10.1080/00131881.2018.1493353

Coyne, M. D., Cook, B. G., & Therrien, W. J. (2016). Recommendations for replication research in special education: A framework of systematic, conceptual replications. *Remedial and Special Education*, 37(4), 244–253. https://doi.org/10.1177/0741932516648463

Coyne, M. D., Little, M., Rawlinson, D., Simmons, D., Kwok, O., Kim, M., . . . Civetelli, C. (2013). Replicating the impact of a supplemental beginning reading intervention: The role of instructional context. *Journal of Research on Educational Effectiveness*, 6(1), 1–23. https://doi.org/10.1080/19345747.2012.706694

Cumming, G. (2012). *Understanding the new statistics: Effect sizes, confidence intervals and meta-analysis*. Routledge.

Deaton, A., & Cartwright, N. (2018). Understanding and misunderstanding randomized controlled trials. *Social Science & Medicine*, 210, 2–21. https://doi.org/10.1016/j.socscimed.2017.12.005

Dennis, A. R., & Valacich, J. S. (2014). A replication manifesto. *AIS Transactions on Replication Research*, 1, Article 1. https://doi.org/10.17705/1atrr.00001

Dickersin, K. (2005). Publication bias: Recognizing the problem, understanding its origins and scope, and preventing harm. In H. R. Rothstein, A. J. Sutton, & M. Borenstein (Eds.), *Publication bias in meta-analysis: Prevention, assessment, and adjustments* (pp. 11–33). Wiley.

Earp, B. D., & Trafimow, D. (2015). Replication, falsification, and the crisis of confidence in social psychology. *Frontiers in Psychology*, 6, Article 621. https://doi.org/10.3389/fpsyg.2015.00621

Eckerth, J. (2012). Negotiated interaction in the L2 classroom: An approximate replication. In G. Porte (Ed.), *Replication research in applied linguistics* (pp. 198–227). Cambridge University Press.

Eden, D. (2002). Replication, meta-analysis, scientific progress and AMJ's publication policy. *The Academy of Management Journal*, 45(5), 841–846. https://doi.org/10.5465/amj.2002.7718946

Education Endowment Foundation. (2019). *Impact evaluation report template*. https://educationendowmentfoundation.org.uk/public/files/Evaluation/Writing_a_Research_Report/EEF_evaluation_report_template_2019.docx

Ellis, P. D. (2010). *The essential guide to effect sizes*. Cambridge University Press.

Fabry, G., & Fischer, M. R. (2015). Replication – the ugly duckling of science. *GMS Zeitschrift für Medizinische Ausbildung*, 32(5), 1–7. https://doi.org/10.3205/zma000999

Farrimond, H. (2013). *Doing ethical research*. Palgrave Macmillan.

Field, A. (2018). *Discovering statistics using IBM SPSS Statistics* (5th ed.). Sage.

Fitzpatrick, T. (2012). Conducting replication studies: Lessons from a graduate program. In G. Porte (Ed.), *Replication research in applied linguistics* (pp. 151–170). Cambridge University Press.

Flyvberg, B. (2011). *Making social science matter: Why social inquiry fails and how it can succeed again*. Cambridge University Press.

Frank, M. C., & Saxe, R. (2012). Teaching replication. *Perspectives on Psychological Science*, 7(6), 600–604. https://doi.org/10.1177/1745691612460686

Gelman, A. (2018). Don't characterize replications as successes or failures. *The Behavioral and Brain Sciences*, 41, e128–e120. https://doi.org/10.1017/S0140525X18000638

Gelman, A., & Loken, E. (2014). The statistical crisis in science. *American Scientist, 102*(6), 460–465. https://doi.org/10.1511/2014.111.460

Gersten, R., Rolfhus, E., Clarke, B., Decker, L. E., Wilkins, C., & Dimino, J. (2015). Intervention for first graders with limited number knowledge: Large-scale replication of a randomized controlled trial. *American Educational Research Journal, 52*(3), 516–546. https://doi.org/10.3102/0002831214565787

Glaser, B. G., & Strauss, A. L. (1967). *The Discovery of Grounded Theory*. Aldane.

Glazerman, S., Levy, D. M., & Myers, D. (2002). *Nonexperimental replications of social experiments: A systematic review*. www.mathematica.org/our-publications-and-findings/publications/nonexperimental-replications-of-social-experiments-a-systematic-review-interim-reportdiscussion-paper

Goldacre, B. (2013). *Building evidence into education*. Department for Education.

Gómez, O. S., Juristo, N., & Vegas, S. (2010). Replications types in experimental disciplines. In *ESEM'10: Proceedings of the 2010 ACM-IEEE international symposium on empirical software engineering and measurement* (Article No. 3, pp. 1–10). Association for Computing Machinery. https://doi.org/10.1145/1852786.1852790

Gorard, S. (Ed.). (2020). *Getting evidence into education: Evaluating the routes to policy and practice*. Routledge.

Gorard, S., & Gorard, J. (2016). What to do instead of significance testing? Calculating the number of counterfactual cases needed to disturb a finding, *International Journal of Social Research Methodology, 19*(4), 481–490. https://doi.org/10.1080/13645579.2015.1091235

Guba, E. G., & Lincoln, Y. S. (1991). What is the constructivist paradigm? In D. S. Anderson & B. J. Biddle (Eds.), *Knowledge for policy: Improving education through research* (pp. 158–170). Falmer Press.

Hammersley, M. (2014). *The limits of social science: Causal explanation and value relevance*. Sage.

Hammersley, M., & Traianou, A. (2012). *Ethics in qualitative research: Controversies and contexts*. Sage.

Hao, N. (2015, April 3). What can educational researchers do to make their studies replicable? *AACE Review*. www.aace.org/review/the-effort-educational-researchers-should-try-to-make-their-studies-replicable/

Hao, Q., Smith, D. H. IV, Iriumi, N., Tsikerdekis, M., & Ko, A. J. (2019). A systematic investigation of replications in computing education research. *ACM Transactions on Computing Education, 19*(4), Article 42. https://doi.org/10.1145/3345328

Hartshorne, J., & Schachner, A. (2012). Tracking replicability as a method of post-publication open evaluation. *Frontiers in Computational Neuroscience, 6*, Article 8. https://doi.org/10.3389/fncom.2012.00008

Hawe, P., Bond, L., Ghali, L. M., Perry, R., Davison, C. M., Casey, D. M., . . . Scholz, B. (2015). Replication of a whole school ethos-changing intervention: Different context, similar effects, additional insights. *BMC Public Health, 15*(265). https://doi.org/10.1186/s12889-015-1538-3

Hedges, L. V., & Schauer, J. M. (2019). More than one replication study is needed for unambiguous tests of replication. *Journal of Educational and Behavioral Statistics, 44*(5), 543–570. https://doi.org/10.3102/1076998619852953

Hendrick, C. (1991). Replications, strict replications, and conceptual replications: Are they important? In J. W. Neuliep (Ed.), *Replication research in the social sciences* (pp. 41–49). Sage.

Hildebrandt, F. (2016). *Reporting checklist for life sciences articles*. Nature Publishing Group. https://media.nature.com/original/nature-assets/ng/journal/v49/n10/extref/ng.3933-S2.pdf

Holcombe, A. O., & Pashler, H. (2012). Making it quick and easy to report replications. *The Psychologist*, 25(5), 355–356.

Holme, T. A. (2019). Reproducibility, replication, and generalization in research about teaching innovation. *Journal of Chemical Education*, 96(11), 2359–2360. https://doi.org/10.1021/acs.jchemed.9b00982

Hüffmeier, J., Mazei, J., & Schultze, T. (2016). Reconceptualizing replication as a sequence of different studies: A replication typology. *Journal of Experimental Social Psychology*, 66, 81–92. https://doi.org/10.1016/j.jesp.2015.09.009

Hunter, J. E., & Schmidt, F. L. (2004). *Methods of meta-analysis: Correcting error and bias in research findings* (2nd ed.). Sage.

Ioannidis, J. P. A. (2005). Why most published research findings are false. *PLoS Medicine*, 2(8), Article e124, 0696–0701. https://doi.org/10.1371/journal.pmed.0020124

Ioannidis, J. P. A. (2012). Why science is not necessarily self-correcting. *Perspectives on Psychological Science*, 7(6), 645–654. https://doi.org/10.1177/1745691612464056

Ioannidis, J. P. A. (2015, November–December). Failure to replicate: Sound the alarm. *Cerebrum*, cer-12a-15. www.ncbi.nlm.nih.gov/pmc/articles/PMC4938249/

Irvine, E. (2021). The role of replication studies in theory building. *Perspectives on Psychological Science*, 9(1), 59–71. https://doi.org/10.1177/1745691620970558

Jacob, R. T., Doolittle, F., Kemple, J., & Somers, M. A. (2019). A framework for learning from null results. *Educational Researcher*, 48(9), 580–589. https://doi.org/10.3102/0013189X19891955

Jacobson, E., & Simpson, A. (2019). Prospective elementary teachers' conceptions of multidigit number: Exemplifying a replication framework for mathematics education. *Mathematics Education Research Journal*, 31(1), 67–88. https://doi.org/10.1007/s13394-018-0242-x

Jadad, A. R., & Enkin, M. W. (2007). *Randomized controlled trials* (2nd ed.). Blackwell Publishing.

Johnston, J. M., & Pennypacker, H. S. (2009). *Strategies and tactics of behavioral research* (3rd ed.). Routledge.

Jones, K. S., Derby, P. L., & Schmidlin, E. A. (2010). An investigation of the prevalence of replication research in human factors. *Human Factors*, 52(5), 586–595. https://doi.org/10.1177/0018720810384394

Jones, R. R. (1978). A review of *Single-case experimental designs: Strategies for studying behavior change* by Michel Hersen and David H. Barlow. *Journal of Applied Behavior Analysis*, 11(2), 309–313. https://doi.org/10.1901/jaba.1978.11-309

Joyce, K. E. (2019). The key role of representativeness in evidence-based education. *Educational Research and Evaluation*, 25(1–2), 43–62. https://doi.org/10.1080/13803611.2019.1617989

Kane, E. J. (1984). Why journal editors should encourage the replication of applied econometric research. *Quarterly Journal of Business and Economics*, 23(1), 3–8. www.jstor.org/stable/23526567

Kelly, C. D. (2006). Replicating empirical research in behavioral ecology: How and why it should be done but rarely ever is. *Quarterly Review of Biology*, 81(3), 221–236. https://doi.org/10.1086/506236

Kerlinger, F. N. (1970). *Foundations of behavioral research*. Holt, Rinehart and Winston.

Kettley, N. (2012). *Theory building in educational research*. Continuum Books.

Kim, J. S. (2019). Making every study count: Learning from replication failure to improve intervention research. *Educational Researcher*, 48(9), 599–607. https://doi.org/10.3102/0013189X19891428

King, G. (1995). Replication, replication. *Political Science and Politics*, 28(3), 444–452. https://doi.org/10.2307/420301

Kline, R. B. (2004). *Beyond significance testing: Reforming data analysis methods in behavioral research*. American Psychological Association.

Kuhn, T. S. (1962). *The structure of scientific revolutions*. University of Chicago Press.

Kvernbekk, T. (2016). *Evidence-based practice in education*. Routledge.

Lehr, R. (1992). Sixteen S-squared over D-squared: A relation for crude sample size estimates. *Statistics in Medicine*, 11(8), 1099–1102. https://doi.org/10.1002/sim.4780110811

Lemons, C. J., King, S. A., Davidson, K. A., Berryessa, T. L., Gajjar, S. A., & Sacks, L. H. (2016). An inadvertent concurrent replication: Same roadmap, different journey. *Remedial and Special Education*, 37(4), 213–222. https://doi.org/10.1177/0741932516631116

Leppink, J. (2017). Revisiting the quantitative-qualitative-mixed methods labels: Research questions, developments, and the need for replication. *Journal of Taibah University Medical Sciences*, 12(2), 97–101. https://doi.org/10.1016/j.jtumed.2016.11.008

Lindsay, R. M., & Ehrenberg, A. S. C. (1993). The design of replicated studies. *The American Statistician*, 47(3), 217–228. https://doi.org/10.2307/2684982

Lortie-Forgues, H., & Inglis, M. (2019). Rigorous large-scale educational RCTs are often uninformative: Should we be concerned? *Educational Researcher*, 48(3), 158–166. https://doi.org/10.3102/0013189X19832850

Lucas, J. W., Morrell, K., & Posard, M. (2013). Considerations on the 'replication problem' in sociology. *The American Sociologist*, 44(2), 217–232. https://doi.org/10.1007/s12108-013-9176-7

Lykken, D. T. (1968). Statistical significance in psychological research. *Psychological Bulletin*, 70(3, Pt. 1), 151–159. https://doi.org/10.1037/h0026141

Mackey, A., & Gass, S. M. (2005). *Second language research: Methodology and design*. Lawrence Erlbaum Associates.

Mahoney, J., & Goertz, G. (2006). A tale of two cultures: Contrasting quantitative and qualitative research. *Political Analysis*, 14(3), 227–249. https://doi.org/10.1093/pan/mpj017

Major, L. E., & Higgins, S. (2019). *What works? Research and evidence for successful teaching*. Bloomsbury Education.

Makel, M. C., & Plucker, J. A. (2014). Facts are more important than novelty: Replication in the education sciences. *Educational Researcher*, 43(6), 304–316. https://doi.org/10.1037/a0035811

Makel, M. C., & Plucker, J. A. (2015). An introduction to replication research in gifted education: Shiny and new is not the same as useful. *Gifted Child Quarterly*, 59(3), 157–164. https://doi.org/10.1177/0016986215578747

Makel, M. C., Plucker, J. A., Freeman, J., Lombardi, A., Simonsen, B., & Coyne, M. (2016). Replication of special education research: Necessary but far too rare. *Remedial and Special Education*, 37(4), 205–212. https://doi.org/10.1177/0741932516646083

Makel, M. C., Plucker, J. A., & Hegarty, B. (2012). Replications in psychology research: How often do they really occur? *Perspectives on Psychological Science*, 7(6), 537–542. https://doi.org/10.1177/1745691612460688

Malouf, D. B., & Taymans, J. M. (2016). Anatomy of an evidence base. *Educational Researcher*, 45(8), 454–459. https://doi.org/10.3102/0013189X16678417

Manzi, J. (2012). *Uncontrolled: The surprising payoff of trial-and-error for business, politics, and society*. Basic Books.

Margolis, E., & Laurence, S. (2019). Concepts. In *Stanford encyclopedia of philosophy*. https://plato.stanford.edu/entries/concepts

Markee, N. (2017). Are replication studies possible in qualitative second/foreign language classroom research? A call for comparative re-production research. *Language Teaching*, 50(3), 367–383. https://doi.org/10.1017/s0261444815000099

Matthews, H. M., Hirsch, S. E., & Therrien, W. J. (2018). Becoming critical consumers of research: Understanding replication. *Intervention in School and Clinic*, 53(5), 267–275. https://doi.org/10.1177/1053451217736863

Meinert, C. L. (2011). *An insider's guide to clinical trials*. Oxford University Press.

Melhuish, K. (2018). Three conceptual replication studies in group theory. *Journal for Research in Mathematics Education*, 49(1), 9–38. https://doi.org/10.5951/jresematheduc.49.1.0009

Melhuish, K., & Thanheiser, E. (2018). Research commentary: A rejoinder: Reframing replication studies as studies of generalizability: A response to critiques of the nature and necessity of replication. *Journal for Research in Mathematics Education*, 49(1), 104–110. https://doi.org/10.5951/jresematheduc.49.1.0104

Merton, R. K. (1967). *On theoretical sociology: Five essays old and new*. The Free Press.

Miles, M. B., & Huberman, M. A. (1984). *Qualitative data analysis*. Sage.

Miles, M. B., & Huberman, A. M. (1994). *Qualitative data analysis: An expanded sourcebook* (2nd ed.). Sage.

Mingers, J. (2004). Paradigm wars: Ceasefire announced who will set up the new administration? *Journal of Information Technology*, 19(3), 165–171. https://doi.org/10.1057/palgrave.jit.2000021

Moonesinghe, R., Khoury, M. J., & Janssens, C. J. W. (2007). Most published research findings are false – but a little replication goes a long way. *PLoS Medicine*, 4(2), Article e28, 0218–0221. https://doi.org/10.1371/journal.pmed.0040028

Morey, R. D., Hoeksrea, R., Rouder, J. N., Lee, M. D., & Wagenmakers, E. J. (2016). The fallacy of placing confidence in confidence intervals. *Psychonomic Bulletin & Review*, 23(1), 103–123. https://doi.org: 10.3758/s13423-015-0947-8

Morrison, K. R. B. (1998). *Management theories for educational change*. Sage & Paul Chapman Publishing.

Morrison, K. R. B. (2006). Sensitive educational research in small states and territories: The case of Macau. *Compare*, 36(2), 249–264. https://doi.org/10.1080/03057920600741297

Morrison, K. R. B. (2009). *Causation in educational research*. Routledge.

Morrison, K. R. B. (2019). Realizing the promises of replication studies in education. *Educational Research and Evaluation*, 25(7–8), 412–441. https://doi.org/10.1080/13803611.2020.1838300

Morrison, K. R. B. (2021). *Taming randomized controlled trials in education: Exploring key claims, issues and debates*. Routledge.

Morrison, R., Matuszek, T., & Self, D. (2010). Preparing a replication or update study in the business disciplines. *European Journal of Scientific Research*, 47(2), 278–287. www.eurojournals.com/ejsr.htm

Nassaji, H. (2012). Statistical significance test and result generalizability: Issues, misconception, and a case for replication. In G. Porte (Ed.), *Replication research in applied linguistics* (pp. 92–115). Cambridge University Press.

National Academies of Sciences, Engineering, and Medicine. (2019). *Reproducibility and replicability in science*. National Academies Press.

National Science Foundation and Institute of Education Sciences. (2018). *Companion guidelines on replication & reproducibility in education research*. www.nsf.gov/pubs/2019/nsf19022/nsf19022.pdf

Nosek, B. A., Ebersole, C. R., DeHaven, A. C., & Mellor, D. T. (2018). The preregistration revolution. *Proceedings of the National Academy of Sciences of the United States of America*, 115(11), 2600–2606. https://doi.org/10.10773/pnas.1708274114

Nutley, S. M., Walter, I., & Davies, H. T. O. (2007). *Using evidence: How research can inform public services.* Policy Press.
O'Leary, M., & Chia, R. (2007). Epistemes and structures of sensemaking in organizational life. *Journal of Management Inquiry, 16*(4), 392–406. https://doi.org/10.1177/1056492607310976
Open Science Collaboration. (2015). Estimating the reproducibility of psychological science. *Science, 349*(6251), aac4716–aac4716. https://doi.org/10.1126/science.aac4716
Pashler, H., & Harris, C. R. (2012). Is the replicability crisis overblown? Three arguments examined. *Perspectives on Psychological Science, 7*(6), 531–536. https://doi.org/10.1177/1745691612363401
Pashler, H., & Wagenmakers, E. J. (2012). Editors' introduction to the special section on replicability in psychological science: A crisis of confidence? *Perspectives on Psychological Science, 7*(6), 528–530. https://doi.org/10.1177/1745691612465253
Paterson, T. A., Harms, P. D., Streel, P., & Credé, M. (2016). An assessment the magnitude of effect sizes: Evidence from 30 years of meta-analysis in management. *Journal of Leadership & Organizational Studies, 23*(1), 66–81. https://doi.org/10.1177/1548051815614321
Patil, P., Peng, R. D., & Leek, J. T. (2016). What should researchers expect when they replicate studies? A statistical view of replicability in psychological science. *Perspectives on Psychological Science, 11*(4), 539–544. https://doi.org/10.1177/1745691616646366
Peels, R. (2019). Replicability and replication in the humanities. *Research Integrity and Peer Review, 4*(2), 1–12. https://doi.org/10.1186/s41073-018-0060-4
Peels, R., & Boulter, L. (2018). Replication drive for humanities. *Nature, 7710*(558), 372. https://doi.org/10.1038/d41586-018-05454-w
Pigott, T. D., Valentine, J. C., Polanin, J. R., Williams, R. T., & Canada, D. D. (2013). Outcome-reporting bias in education research. *Educational Researcher, 42*(8), 424–432. https://doi.org/10.3102/0013189X13507104
Plonsky, L. (2012). Replication, meta-analysis, and generalizability. In G. Porte (Ed.), *Replication research in applied linguistics* (pp. 116–132). Cambridge University Press.
Plucker, J. A., & Makel, M. C. (2021). Replication is important for educational psychology: Recent developments and key issues. *Educational Psychologist.* https://doi.org/10.1080/00461520.2021.1895796
Popper, K. R. (1959). *The logic of scientific discovery.* Hutchinson & Co.
Popper, K. R. (1962). *Conjectures and refutations.* Basic Books.
Porte, G. (Ed.). (2012). *Replication research in applied linguistics.* Cambridge University Press.
Porte, G., & McManus, K. (2019). *Doing replication research in applied linguistics.* Routledge.
Raloff, J. (2015, September 11). When a study can't be replicated. *Science News for Students.* www.sciencenewsforstudents.org/article/when-study-cant-be-replicated
Reed, I. (2008). Justifying sociological knowledge: From realism to interpretation. *Sociological Theory, 26*(2), 101–129. https://doi.org/10.1111/j.1467-9558.2008.00321.x
Roediger, H. L. III. (2012, January 31). Psychology's woes and a partial cure: The value of replication. *Academic Observer.* www.psychologicalscience.org/observer/psychologyswoes-and-a-partial-cure-the-value-of-replication
Rosenthal, R. (1979). The 'file drawer problem' and tolerance for null results. *Psychological Bulletin, 86*(3), 638–641. https://doi.org/10.1037/0033-2909.86.3.638
Rosenthal, R. (1991). Replication in behavioral research. In J. W. Neuliep (Ed.), *Replication research in the social sciences* (pp. 1–30). Sage.
Royal Netherlands Academy of Arts and Sciences. (2018). *Replication studies: Improving reproducibility in the empirical sciences.* Royal Netherlands Academy of Arts and Sciences. www.knaw.nl/shared/resources/actueel/publicaties/pdf/20180115-replication-studies-web
Sacks, P. (1999). *Standardized minds.* Perseus Books.

Schmidt, S. (2009). Shall we do it again? The powerful concept of replication is neglected in the social sciences. *Review of General Psychology, 13*(2), 90–100. https://doi.org/10.1037/a0015108

Schoenfeld, A. (2018). On replications. *Journal for Research in Mathematics Education, 49*(1), 91–97. https://doi.org/10.5951/jresematheduc.49.1.0091

Science News. (2019, October). Beyond the 'replication crisis', does research face an 'inference crisis'? *Science Daily.* www.sciencedaily.com/releases/2019/10/191010161540.htm

See, B. H. (2018). Evaluating the evidence in evidence-based policy and practice: Examples from systematic reviews of literature. *Research in Education, 102*(1), 37–61. https://doi.org/10.1177/0034523717741915

See, B. H. (2020). Why is it difficult to get evidence into use? In S. Gorard (Ed.), *Getting evidence into use* (pp. 84–99). Routledge.

Shanahan, T. (2017). Reading research: The importance of replication. *Reading Teacher, 70*(4), 507–510. https://doi.org/10.1002/trtr.1520

Shapin, S., & Schaffer, S. (1985). *Leviathan and the air-pump: Hobbes, Boyle, and the experimental life.* Princeton University Press.

Silver, N. (2012). *The signal and the noise.* The Penguin Press.

Simonsohn, U. (2015). Small telescopes: Detectability and the evaluation of replication results. *Psychological Science, 26*(5), 559–569. https://doi.org/10.1177/0956797614567341

Simpson, A. (2018). Princesses are bigger than elephants: Effect size as a category error in evidence-based education. *British Educational Research Journal, 44*(5), 897–913. https://doi.org/10.1002/berj.3474

Simpson, A. (2019). Separating arguments from conclusions: The mistaken role of effect size in educational policy research. *Educational Research and Evaluation, 25*(1–2), 99–109. https://doi.org/10.1080/13803611.2019.1617170

Simpson, A. (2020). On the misinterpretation of effect size. *Educational Studies in Mathematics, 103*(1), 125–133. https://doi.org/10.1007/s10649-019-09924-4

Slavin, R. E. (2016, December 8). Education policy in the age of unproven school and classroom approaches. *Robert Slavin's Blog.* https://robertslavinsblog.wordpress.com/2016/12/08/education-policy-in-the-age-of-proven-school-and-classroom-approaches/

Slavin, R. E. (2018, February 28). What kinds of studies are likely to replicate? *Robert Slavin's Blog.* https://robertslavinsblog.wordpress.com/2018/02/28/what-kinds-of-studies-are-likely-to-replicate/

Spector, J. M., Johnson, T. E., & Young, P. A. (2015). An editorial on replication studies and scaling up effects. *Educational Technology Research and Development, 63*(1), 1–4. https://doi.org/10.1007/s11423-014-9364-3

Stanley, D. J., & Spence, J. R. (2014). Expectations for replications: Are yours realistic? *Perspectives on Psychological Science, 9*(3), 305–318. https://doi.org/10.1177/1745691614528518

Sternberg, R. J. (1995). Theory and measurement of tacit knowledge as a part of practical intelligence. *Zeitschrift für Psychologie, 203*(4), 319–334.

Stout, D. E., & Heck, J. L. (1995, Fall). The need for replications and extensions in financial education research: An editorial comment. *Journal of Financial Education, 21*, 19–21.

Sundie, J. M., Beal, D. J., Neuberg, S. L., & Kenrick, D. T. (2019). Moving beyond unwise replication practices: The case of romantic motivation. *Journal of Experimental Psychology: General, 148*(4), e1–e11. http://dx.doi.org/10.1037/xge0000527

Therrien, W. J., Mathews, H. M., Hirsch, S. E., & Solis, M. (2016). Progeny review: An alternative approach for examining the replication of intervention studies in special education. *Remedial and Special Education, 37*(4), 235–243. https://doi.org/10.1177/0741932516646081

Thomas, G. (2010). Doing case study: Abduction, not induction, phronesis not theory. *Qualitative Inquiry*, 16(7), 575–582. https://doi.org/10.1177/1077800410372601

Thomas, G. (2012). Changing our landscape of inquiry for a new science of education. *Harvard Educational Review*, 82(1), 26–51. https://doi.org/10.17763/haer.82.1.6t2r0891715x3377

Thomas, G. (2016). After the gold rush: Questioning the 'Gold Standard' and reappraising the status of experiment and randomized controlled trials in education. *Harvard Educational Review*, 86(3), 390–411. https://doi.org/10.17763/1943-5045-86.3.390

Tilley, N. (1993). *After Kirkholt: Theory, methods and results of replication evaluation*. Home Office Police Department, Police Research Group.

Tincani, M., & Travers, J. (2019). Replication research, publication bias, and applied behaviour analysis. *Perspectives on Behavior Science*, 42(1), 59–75. https://doi.org/10.1007/s40614-019-00191-5

Torgerson, C. J., & Torgerson, D. J. (2008). *Designing randomised trials in health, education and the social sciences*. Palgrave Macmillan.

Travers, J. C., Cook, B. G., Therrien, W. J., & Coyne, M. D. (2016). Replication research and special education. *Remedial and Special Education*, 37(4), 195–204. https://doi.org/10.1177/0741932516648462

Tsang, E., & Kwan, K. M. (1999). Replication and theory development in organizational science: A critical realist perspective. *The Academy of Management Review*, 24(4), 759–780. https://doi.org/10.5465/amr.1999.2553252

Tyson, C. (2014, August 14). Failure to replicate. *Inside Higher Education*. www.insidehighered.com/news/2014/08/14/almost-no-education-research-replicated-new-article-shows

Van der Zee, T., & Reich, J. (2018). Open education science. *AERA Open*, 4(3), 1–15. https://doi.org/10.1177/2332858418787466

Vealé, B. L. (2019). Future research and replication studies. *Radiologic Technology*, 90(4), 425–416.

Warne, R. W. (2014). Two additional suggested reforms to encourage replication studies in educational research. *Educational Researcher*, 43(9), 465–465. https://doi.org/10.3102/0013189X14562294

What Works Clearinghouse. (2018). *Reporting guide for study authors: Group design studies*. Institute of Education Sciences.

Worrall, J. (2007). Why there's no cause to randomize. *The British Journal for the Philosophy of Science*, 55(3), 451–488. https://doi.org/10.1093/bjps/axm024

Wrigley, T. (2018). The power of 'evidence': Reliable science of a set of blunt tools? *British Educational Research Journal*, 4(3), 359–376. https://doi.org/10.1002/berj.3338

Yaffe, J. (2019). From the Editor – Do we have a replication crisis in social work research? *Journal of Social Work Education*, 55(1), 1–4. https://doi.org/10.1080/10437797.2019.1594399

Yin, R. K. (2018). *Case study research and applications: Design and methods* (6th ed.). Sage.

Yong, E. (2012). Bad copy. *Nature*, 485(7398), 298–300. https://doi.org/10.1038/485298a

Ziliak, S. T., & McCloskey, D. N. (2008). *The cult of statistical significance: How the standard error costs us jobs, justice, and lives*. University of Michigan Press.

Zingaro, D., Craig, M., Porter, L., Becker, B. A., Cao, Y., Conrad, P., . . . Thota, N. (2018). Achievement goals in CS1: Replication and extension. In *SIGCSE'18: Proceedings of the 49th ACM technical symposium on computing science education* (pp. 687–692). Association for Computing Machinery. https://doi.org/10.1145/3159450.3159452

Index

accuracy 42, 56, 104, 114, 159
action research 22, 65, 130
applicability *see* generalizability
application *see* generalizability
approximate replication 6, 16, 22–23, 26, 32, 73, 138, 158

bias 7, 13, 26, 28, 47, 74, 83, 104, 123
bootstrapping 94

case study 33, 60, 61, 64, 67
causality 22, 24, 37, 43, 44, 48–53, 57, 77–78, 80, 117–118, 121
certainty 5, 41, 90–93, 99, 101, 102, 112, 114, 123, 126, 127, 140, 148, 151, 156, 157, 159, 160
changes in replications 19, 20, 23, 24, 27, 34, 37, 38, 44–45, 53–55, 58, 65, 75, 76, 122, 126–127, 129, 131–132, 140, 148
choosing a replication 14, 42, 69–73, 144–147, 157
closeness 5, 65, 75–76, 79, 81–82, 92–93, 98–104, 114, 139, 143, 148, 149, 158, 159–160
close replication 5, 14, 19–22, 30, 31, 37, 39, 44, 47, 56–57, 65, 73, 75–76, 79, 81–82, 85, 91, 135, 157
comparison 22, 24, 28–31, 34, 45, 56, 59, 60–61, 63, 65, 70, 74–76, 86–87, 90–93, 95, 102–106, 108–118, 120, 124, 128–136, 141–142, 144, 149–153, 157, 160
concept 39–41, 44, 50–52, 56; *see also* conceptual replication
conceptual replication 6, 11, 16, 19–21, 23–24, 26–27, 29, 32, 36–58, 65, 75, 78, 92–93, 120, 122–123, 140, 158–159
conclusions 77, 91, 112, 113, 117, 128, 135, 137, 140, 141, 150–151, 156–161
conditions *see* contexts
confidence intervals 99–110

contexts 5, 6, 8, 9, 10, 21, 23, 25, 37, 38, 40, 47, 48–53, 55, 63, 77–78, 98, 116–117, 133, 135, 149; *see also* conceptual replication
controls 25, 28, 56, 109, 114, 130
correlation 78, 94, 95, 96
counterfactuals 28, 34, 44, 47, 48, 109, 114
cross validation 93

data analysis 20, 23, 29, 38, 64, 74, 82, 83, 86, 90–124, 131–133, 137, 140, 150
data collection 16, 19, 23, 28, 38, 74, 82, 83, 108, 111, 126, 131
data discussion 135
data interpretation 33, 62, 87, 118–123, 141, 150–151
design of replications *see* research design
difference testing 94, 96, 97–104, 109, 113
direct replication 5, 6, 20, 21–22, 26, 39, 73, 153, 154
distributions 56, 79, 94, 95–96, 100, 105–106, 113, 114

effect size 30, 54–55, 78, 79, 88, 95, 97–98, 106, 113, 114, 115, 134, 157
epistemology 32, 40, 41–42, 111
ethics 7, 28, 77, 84–88
evaluation 30, 65, 69–73, 108, 147–148, 153
exact replication 8, 10, 19–24, 30–31, 39, 42, 45, 91, 92, 93, 110, 124, 130, 133, 138, 150
experiment *see* randomised controlled trials

fairness 32, 54, 55, 56, 57, 84, 116, 149
fair replication 13, 34, 40, 42, 66, 72, 159
fair test *see* fairness
false negative 7, 13, 74, 78, 97, 114, 120, 121–122, 140

false positive 7, 13, 74, 78, 114, 120, 121–122, 140
falsifiability 4, 33, 41, 46, 56, 62
falsify *see* falsifiability
feasibility 147–148
'file drawer' 11, 141, 148

generalizability 5, 6, 7, 8, 12, 13, 19, 20, 21–24, 32, 33, 37, 38, 39, 45, 47, 51, 52, 53, 55, 62, 63, 64–65, 72, 92, 126, 127, 128, 132, 135, 156, 158
generalization *see* generalizability
grounded theory 107–108

hermeneutic 32, 42–43, 156
hypothesis 4, 7, 14, 19, 20, 24, 26, 27, 32, 37, 40, 41, 46, 49, 50, 51, 52, 56, 96–97, 116, 122, 124

indeterminate replication 5, 21, 37, 45, 47, 48, 52, 58, 66, 79, 91, 101, 108, 109, 112, 114, 115, 116, 117, 124, 137, 140
indicators 41, 42, 52, 57, 66, 77, 109, 112, 114, 147, 159
instrumentation 11, 13, 16, 19, 20, 21, 23, 25, 28, 31, 45, 51, 54, 55, 73, 74, 78, 82, 98, 109, 119, 127, 129, 137
interpretation *see* data interpretation
intervention 14, 15, 20, 23, 25, 27, 28–29, 31, 38, 43, 49, 50, 52, 55, 65, 71, 73, 74, 75, 77, 81, 82–83, 93, 98, 108, 126, 127, 129–131, 137, 149–150, 161

jackknife analysis 94
judgements 5, 25, 44, 57, 65, 67, 92, 105, 106, 114, 115, 117, 118, 124, 140, 144, 147, 151, 157

kurtosis 56, 94, 100, 105, 106, 113, 115, 134

limitations 30, 58, 70, 73, 98, 128, 130, 135, 137, 138, 156, 161–162

measures 19, 23, 28, 30, 42, 44, 68, 74, 75, 76, 78, 82, 83, 98, 104, 119, 124, 137
meta-analysis 9, 17, 72, 110
methodology 19, 20, 21, 22, 23, 27, 33, 34, 38, 40, 58, 60–61, 74, 81, 126, 127, 130–131, 137
methods 4, 5, 13, 19, 29, 31, 38, 54, 55, 60, 71, 73, 76, 79, 82, 92, 93–94, 104, 133, 136
metrics *see* measures
mixed methods 50, 108–109

National Academies of Sciences, Engineering and Medicine 5, 39, 94, 113, 119, 126, 144, 150, 152, 162
National Science Foundation and the Institute of Education Sciences 4, 6, 8, 20, 26, 31, 34, 44, 53
non-replication 5, 52, 79, 97, 114, 115, 116–117, 119, 122
null hypothesis 7, 96, 97, 113, 122
null hypothesis significance testing *see* statistical significance

ontology 32, 33, 34, 38, 40, 41–42, 111
operationalization 38, 68, 73, 76–80
over-determination 37, 50, 57, 122, 158

paradigm 33, 42, 59, 60, 61, 63, 67, 106
parametric data 78, 94, 95
partial replication 19, 20, 45
planning 68–89, 139–140, 144, 148, 154, 155
post-test 28, 71, 82, 97, 105, 109, 134
power *see* statistical power
precision 16, 18, 29, 31, 32, 38, 41, 42–45, 56, 62, 72, 90, 98, 99, 100–106, 113, 131, 132, 140, 151, 159
pre-registration 83, 84, 86, 113, 123, 124, 160
pre-test 28, 71, 82, 97, 105, 109, 134

qualitative data 64, 92, 93, 106–109, 111, 132, 140
qualitative research 21, 33, 34, 59–67, 87
quantitative data 92, 93–106, 108–109, 113–115
quantitative research 21, 34, 59–67, 93–106, 108–118

randomised controlled trials 10, 17, 33, 34, 46, 48, 50–52, 54, 77, 79, 130, 149
range 56, 65, 74, 76, 79, 96, 97, 99, 100–101, 102, 103–105, 106, 110, 115, 127, 134, 151, 159
regression 94, 96
reliability 8, 9, 28, 36, 45, 53, 72, 78, 82, 112, 113, 120, 140
replication: case against 10–12; case for 7–9, 14; definitions of 3–7; need for 13–14; purposes of 2, 8–10, 24, 62, 68, 73–75, 81, 91–92, 109, 111, 125–129, 137, 145, 148; *see also* accuracy; approximate replication; bias; causality; certainty; changes in replications; choosing a replication;

closeness; close replication; comparison; conceptual replication; conclusions; contexts; data analysis; data collection; data discussion; data interpretation; direct replication; ethics; exact replication; fairness; fair replication; falsifiability; feasibility; generalizability; hermeneutic; hypothesis; indeterminate replication; indicators; instrumentation; intervention; judgements; limitations; methods; operationalization; partial replication; planning; precision; pre-registration; qualitative research; quantitative research; reporting; reproducibility; research design; research questions; resources; sameness; similarity; statistics; successful replication; systematic replication; theory; training; transparency; types of replication; validity; variables
replication study *see* replication
reporting 121, 30, 44, 47, 77, 83, 123, 125–142, 143, 151–152
reproducibility 4, 5, 19, 24, 27, 39, 57, 77, 93, 110, 136, 144, 150, 158, 163
research design 28, 30, 80–88, 127–128, 130–131, 13, 19, 20, 21, 22, 23, 25, 38, 50, 55, 58, 98, 108, 127, 137, 153
research questions 5, 91, 111, 129, 135, 137, 140, 146, 163
resources 7, 14, 28, 71, 72, 82, 147, 157
risk 7, 11, 19, 20, 22, 26, 28, 45, 47, 61, 71, 78, 81, 83, 84, 97, 106, 110, 114, 119, 147, 157, 161, 162

sameness 18–35, 53, 58, 59–67, 68, 76, 132, 143, 154, 155, 158, 159
sampling 4, 6, 9, 15, 19, 20, 21, 22, 23, 28, 30, 38, 50, 53, 54, 55, 56, 64, 65, 71, 74, 75, 77, 78–81, 91, 94, 95, 96, 97, 98, 102, 106, 113, 115, 127, 130, 131, 134, 137
scalability *see* generalizability
selecting *see* choosing a replication
setting *see* contexts
similarity *see* closeness; sameness
skewness 56, 90, 94, 98, 102, 103–105, 113, 114, 115, 134
skills 143–155
standard deviation 94, 95, 97, 98, 102, 103, 104, 105, 106, 110, 112, 113, 115, 126, 134

standard error 79, 90, 94, 98, 102, 103–105, 113, 115, 159
standardisation 90, 94, 97, 98, 102–104, 106, 110, 113, 115, 159
statistical power 28, 56, 71, 78–79, 98, 105, 106, 110, 113, 115, 122, 124, 126, 134, 140, 153
statistical significance 7, 12, 13, 56, 83, 96–97, 99, 112, 132
statistics 86, 90–124, 132, 133, 137, 140, 150
successful replication 4, 20, 24, 30, 49, 54, 55–56, 57, 59, 66, 68, 77, 79–80, 83, 89, 90–91, 92, 94, 98, 99–101, 105, 108, 109, 110, 112, 116, 124, 140, 141, 148, 151, 155, 159
systematic replication 12, 19, 20, 23, 26, 73

teacher 10, 29, 43, 49, 50, 51, 52–53, 77, 88, 98, 122, 149, 150, 153
theory 7, 8, 9, 11, 13, 23, 32, 34, 38, 39–41, 45, 46, 52, 53, 56, 62, 64, 67, 90
training 29, 77, 81, 130, 131, 143–155, 160
transferability *see* generalizability
transparency 5, 7, 9, 14, 26, 31, 40, 42, 43, 47, 57, 72, 84, 86, 114, 129, 131, 136, 145, 146
Type I error 7, 9, 78, 88, 114
Type II error 7, 9, 15, 18, 88, 114
types of replication 3, 18–35, 36–37, 73

uncertainty *see* certainty
under-determination 37, 50, 51, 57

validation *see* validity
validity 8, 12, 16, 20, 21, 23, 28, 32, 39, 41, 45–46, 52, 53, 57, 70, 71, 85, 86, 104, 133, 156, 158
variables 5, 6, 9, 10, 16, 19, 20, 22, 23, 24, 25, 28, 29, 31, 32, 38, 44, 46, 47, 52, 53, 59, 67, 71, 73, 74, 75, 78, 96, 119, 126, 133
variance 29, 32, 43, 54, 94, 95, 98, 100–101, 106, 110, 151, 159

'what works' 10, 23, 37, 40, 41, 48, 78, 98, 149, 156, 162, 163
writing 137, 125–142, 148

z-scores 84, 102, 110

For Product Safety Concerns and Information please contact our EU
representative GPSR@taylorandfrancis.com
Taylor & Francis Verlag GmbH, Kaufingerstraße 24, 80331 München, Germany

www.ingramcontent.com/pod-product-compliance
Lightning Source LLC
Chambersburg PA
CBHW052023290426
44112CB00014B/2347